Time
Traveled

Krista Marson

TIME TRAVELED
Memory Road Trip Series Book Two
Copyright © 2023 by Memory Road Press

ISBN 978-1-7373284-2-1 (epub)
ISBN 978-1-7373284-3-8 (paperback)

website: https://kmarson.com
email: memoryroadtrips@gmail.com

book cover photo taken by kmarson in Payson, Arizona

CONTENTS:

CHAPTER ONE:
Environment, 1998-recent

Aldo

Imagine yourself standing – no – basking in glorious sunshine in the middle of a grassy field. A gentle breeze brushes tall blades of grass against your knees and causes a slight tickle. Imagine the humidity of a muggy Wisconsin summer day hitting the back of your neck as you look down to watch a butterfly sip nectar from a thistle. Picture yourself in this dream-like Wisconsin landscape that you thought only your mind's eye could conjure up, and then turn your head slightly to the right and take a hard look at the glorious shack looming in the distance. It is for this shack that you're standing in this field, yet part of you wonders why you're even here.

"So, is it everything that you imagined it would be?" I asked my new biology boyfriend, who more or less dragged me to this spot.

"Yes! Yes, it is!" he exclaimed as he, I think, wiped a tear from his eye.

"Are you crying?" I asked as I glanced at him and then over his shoulder to the shack.

"No," he assured me. "Okay, maybe a little bit. I mean, how can I not? Look at it! It's right *there!*"

And by "it," he meant the one tangible piece of evidence that practically determined the entire course of his life. For that shack was no ordinary shack – it was the Aldo Leopold chicken coop shack, and it symbolized everything he believed in.

I had met Eric only recently, but we ended up traveling to Wisconsin almost immediately after he learned that I hailed from America's Dairy State. I traveled back home quite regularly to visit my ailing parents, and he requested to tag along the next time I traveled there.

"So, you're saying you want to go to Wisconsin with me?" I clarified during one of our very first conversations together.

"Yes," he responded.

"To Wisconsin?" I wanted to make sure. "You do know where that is, right?"

"Yes!" Eric beamed.

I was suspicious. "Why do you look so happy whenever I say *Wisconsin*?"

"Because that's where the chicken coop is!" he replied.

A more cryptic response couldn't have been imagined.

"Say what now?" I replied.

"The chicken coop!" he repeated.

"I don't get it," I said.

"It's where Aldo Leopold wrote *A Sand County Almanac.*"

"I'm not familiar with it," I said.

"*A Sand County Almanac?*" he replied, almost disgusted. "You don't know it, and you're from Wisconsin?"

"Guilty on both charges," I admitted. "So, what's it about?"

"Agh," he started, "if you don't know it, it's going to be hard to explain it to you."

"Just try," I told him.

"Well, you *do* know who Aldo Leopold was, right?" he asked.

"Nope," I said.

"Agh," he said, thoroughly disappointed in me. "Well, Aldo Leopold is my hero. He bought some worn-out farmland in the 1930s, nursed it back to health, and proved that even the worst land could be redeemed. The book he wrote about his experiences became the gospel of land management and inspired me to become a biologist."

"That's pretty awesome," I replied.

"It has always been my dream to visit the site," he wistfully stated.

"Would you rank it as a top 10 must-see-before-I-die type of a place?" I asked.

"Absolutely," he said. "I'd rank it as number one."

"Seriously?" I asked. "Number one?"

"Numero uno. Yup. Without a doubt."

"And you haven't been there yet?"

"Nope. Never been."

"Well, then, we should go."

"I agree! But...I don't know where it is."

"What do you mean you don't know where it is?"

"I *kinda* know where it is, but I don't know where it is *exactly*."

"But you know that it's in Wisconsin?"

"Oh, it's definitely in Wisconsin," Eric assured me. "Somewhere north of Madison."

"Well, it can't be that hard to find," I declared. "I bet we could figure it out."

Everyone knows the phrase "famous last words," right? To be sure, saying "we could figure it out" in 1998 was truly going out on a limb since the internet wasn't an entirely dependable invention yet. Indeed, the internet did nothing to aid our search because we failed to pinpoint the shack's exact whereabouts before embarking on our trip. We naively

7

thought, "Well, that's okay. Someone in Madison will tell us where it is." Thus, I will reiterate the phrase "famous last words" and allow it to hang on this page.

The Elusive Chicken Coop

We were under no illusion that finding the chicken coop would be easy, but, my God, locating that shack proved to be way harder than it needed to be. Everyone needs to thank their lucky stars that the internet exists today because it was a little too easy to drive around in circles before its handy invention. As an experiment, I just now plugged in a search for Aldo Leopold's cabin and immediately got directed to the aldoleopold.org website. From there, I clicked on a link titled "visit the shack," which instantly led me to a page replete with tour times and directions. All this information would have been super helpful to us in 1998, not knowing where we were going other than "somewhere north of Madison-ish."

First, though, the trip officially began with the requisite visit to my parents. The excursion started with us bringing over some sloppy joes for my dad to make a mess with. A debilitating stroke landed him in a nursing home when I was only a teenager, which is a story that requires fleshing out some other time. After that, we went to my mom's and took her on a mini journey. My mom was an avid gardener who could recite the names of every plant she encountered, but I failed to inherit her scientific naming prowess. As a kid, I never appreciated her ability to speak in veritable tongues whenever we went to a garden store, but Eric quickly caught on to her botanical talents. Thus, I immediately regretted introducing them to each other when we all took a little stroll in a nearby forest.

"Oh, look at that *Latininus Wordis Floweris* over here," one of them would exclaim.

"I will, but you first have to come over here and check out this *Blueis Petalis Prettiness*, a rare specimen indeed," the other would counter.

I had absolutely nothing to contribute to their conversation because I had no idea what they were talking about for a solid hour. I more or less trailed behind them and said things like, "You guys just missed an *Australopithecus africanus* walk by because you were too busy looking at flowers." Of course, I now regret that I never asked my mom to let me in on her botanical secrets, for hers was the one botanical brain I now want to pick.

I, of course, learned nothing about gardening from my mom, but it wasn't from her lack of trying to teach me a thing or two about the secret world of nature. She was a great gardener, but I'm a mediocre one. I tend to ignore all the information printed on a specimen's label that explains what a gardener needs to do to make a plant happy. I know full well what "well-drained soil" is, and I know I don't have it. I've also developed the ridiculous habit of planting everything too close together, so everything eventually merges into an oversized clump. I will forever wonder if there is a difference between a bush and a shrub, and I will always confuse annuals with perennials. In short, I have to say that it really sucks that my mother is no longer around to guide me around my own garden.

After our little hike, we got on the road and gambled that the tourist office in Madison would be more than delighted to point the way to Leopold's old farm and maybe even be so kind as to provide us with a map and directions. Unfortunately, our hopes and dreams were immediately dashed when no one, and I mean no one, would reveal where the chicken coop resided. Furthermore, everyone quickly mentioned that the site was not open to the public. We explained that we didn't need it to be open per se because we just wanted to drive by and see it. Explaining ourselves didn't make a difference, though. Everyone's lips stayed resolutely sealed, and its location was to remain a mystery. No one was even willing to tell us which road it was on. It was as though everyone who worked at the visitor center was initiated in some Masonic rite that had them swear with their blood that they would never reveal where the Aldo Leopold farm was located. Seriously.

Eric was getting horribly discouraged, and I started feeling really bad for him. He must have given one of the ladies behind the desk some sad puppy dog eyes, though, because right as we were leaving, she sneaked up and whispered which road we needed to take. Of course, we only noticed later that she failed to tell us which direction to go in once we actually reached that sacred path.

All I really remember now was that we drove until we hit a "T" at the magic chicken coop road. We then took a 50/50 shot and turned to the right. It was a lovely forested area, straight out of a Wisconsin tourist brochure, and the scenery even included deer dashing through the trees. It was a perfect spring day with gorgeous sunlight and a gentle breeze. However, it seemed like we were driving for quite a long while without seeing anything that resembled the hallowed shack.

"Maybe we didn't turn the right way," Eric lamented.

Yet, the area looked correct, for it seemed like the perfect place for an old farm to be located. Old farms, in fact, were everywhere; we just weren't finding the correct one.

We turned around, but I was itching to get out before heading down the street again. I was desperate to pee, so I asked Eric to pull onto a dirt road. Thus, we pulled aside, and I took a moment to stretch out my legs. Once outside, I immediately started to admire the plethora of wildflowers surrounding me. I then had one of those strange moments you think only happens in dreams when life suddenly feels too perfect. Birds, bees, and butterflies proliferated. The sun was radiant, the breeze was divine, and we heard not a single noise from the cars that weren't coming. For a few minutes, life appeared utterly flawless. Butterflies were even landing on my shoulder. It was creepily perfect. It felt like I was standing inside a memory inside a dream. That was when I knew we were getting close to where we wanted to be.

We got back in the car and drove to where we initially made a right at the "T" and continued straight. Less than a mile later, we, lo and behold, had our hallowed shack sighting.

"There it is!" Eric exclaimed and almost drove the car into a ditch.

Of course, it was more than the shack that Eric wanted to see; it was the whole kit and caboodle he was seeking. He was on a personal quest to see, feel, and touch the thing that molded a big part of who he was. That farm, that shack, that man named Aldo Leopold burned inside Eric's mind and helped create the man he grew to become. Words are hard to find to describe what that genuinely means to someone.

"So, is it everything that you imagined it would be?"

"Yes! Yes, it is."

Where we were standing was, in Eric's eyes, holy ground. In 1935, Aldo Leopold bought an abandoned farm that resembled many of the abandoned farms that dotted this portion of Wisconsin. The land was worn-out from being overused, and weedy grasses invaded the once healthy soil. The previous owner left behind a burned-down farmhouse and a shack-like chicken coop filled knee-deep with manure. In most people's eyes, the land was "through," having been used up, done with, and tossed aside. Leopold, however, was appalled at how easy it was for people to declare land "finished." He was disgusted at how easy it was for people to ruin one farm and then move on to ruin another. He felt it in his marrow that land was not to be treated that way. He wasn't opposed to using land to reap its rewards, but he was wholly against using land so that it became exhausted. He knew there was a balance to be found somewhere in the soil, so he made it his life's goal to find and then present his methods of land ethics to the entire world.

Aldo Leopold successfully managed to nurse that worn-out farmland back to health, and his diary of how he did that became the book *A Sand County Almanac*, which he never saw published (his family published it after his death). The book was no-nonsense poetry to the land, even though the story itself made for some seriously dry reading. What stood out, though, was his heartfelt plea for everyone to understand that we all had the capacity to respect nature. And when Aldo Leopold said "nature," he meant soil, water, plants, animals, and people. All of it. We are all on this planet together. He never lets his readers forget that, and it's almost shocking how often we need reminding. Indeed, the world needs more Aldo

Leopolds to guide us into the future.

Nature

Eric found his hero in Aldo Leopold, and I found mine in the environmental activist and writer John Muir. I can sum him up in two quotes when he says: "In every walk with nature, one receives far more than he seeks," and "I went out for a walk, and concluded to stay out till sundown, for going out, I found, was really going in." I love what both of those sentences say, for he speaks of the riches to be found in the natural world.

Humans always seek wisdom and wealth, and John Muir knew that nature was the provider of both. Rare has there been a time when I went into the wilderness and didn't find something I didn't have before. John Muir's words will always be my mantra and the reason why I believe in the power of a muse.

I love nature, but not enough of it surrounds me. City life comes at a cost that is typically paid through the removal of trees. Yet, absence makes the heart grow fonder, and my admiration for the natural world grows the longer I'm away from it. I'm particularly drawn to old-growth forests, but they are sadly a rare commodity.

California serves as a prime example, for it exists as a shell of what it used to be. The California that prevails now is nowhere near the same as when the earliest pioneers first encountered it. The gargantuan forests that once blanketed the state in a seemingly endless sea of green no longer exist due to modern man's insatiable desires. All memories of those grand primordial forests have since been packed into neat little pockets in notoriously difficult-to-reach places.

Yet not all old-growth forests exist in remote locations. Muir Woods National Monument, for example, can be found 12 accessible miles north of San Francisco. This 554-acre park protects a small remnant of the estimated two million acres of ancient redwood trees that formally blanketed the state. To walk in that forest is to walk into Earth's memories. The average age of the redwood trees there is between 600 to 800 years old, and they silently watch the world drastically change around them while they willingly provide the lungs to support it. The Earth and trees are symbiotic; when one dies, the other gradually goes with it.

The fact that Muir Woods is so accessible means that it is often awash with visitors. Walking around that forest is incredible, but it's rarely completely silent. If a person wants to get truly intimate with an old-growth forest, it's best to go to one that's more difficult to obtain. I'd been wanting to visit the small pocket of redwood trees at Stout Grove in Jedediah Smith Redwoods State Park for a very long time, but getting there was never going to be cheap or convenient. Yet, its remote location and diminutive 44-acre size were the precise reasons why I harbored a burning desire to go there. I yearned to stand in the middle of that forest and quietly listen to the wisdom of trees.

I eventually seized upon my desire and made the journey to my fantasy forest sometime in the early 2000s. It took me two hours to drive to Stout Grove from Medford, Oregon, but it was a drive that I didn't mind doing because the landscape was entirely new to my eyes. There's something about unfamiliar scenery that keeps my interest piqued and makes me think that long drives go quicker than they actually do. I found myself standing at the entrance of Stout Grove in what was seemingly an instant, and my immediate reaction was somewhat unexpected. I was aghast that the forest was not tucked into some remote corner of the planet but stood at a cul-de-sac on the edge of a Crescent City neighborhood. Here was one of the world's last remaining old-growth forests, and someone who lived nearby could jog there before breakfast and still make it to work on time in the morning. I was stunned at the ease of accessibility and was half-tempted to go house hunting even before setting foot on the trail. I was dumbfounded and jealous simultaneously.

The woods invited me in by saying nothing. I approached the forest with a lot of noise inside my head, so it took a sudden blast of silence to make my inner thoughts cease. The trees in this forest were here before our nation was born. They were here when California belonged to Spain. They were here when Native Americans spoke their own languages. Their heights towered into the sky, which made me feel wildly insignificant. I felt too small and unworthy to be standing among them. These trees were significantly older and far wiser than I would ever be.

Forests allow people to put life into perspective. Sometimes it takes a walk in the woods to remind oneself that humans are not the only things that matter. As I walked the trail, I focused my thoughts outwards rather than inwards. I wanted to hear the forest and not listen to my own ideas. I intently focused on the sound of trees rubbing against each other in the wind. I looked up to see where the trees were touching but failed to see the tops of the rubbing behemoths. I tuned in and listened to a cacophony of eerie sounds coming from places beyond my vision. It felt like I was walking on the lowest layer of a universe that harbored multiple realms. Being inside that redwood forest was the closest I ever felt to being a character inside a fantasy book. Had I encountered a dragon sleeping beside a giant felled log, I wouldn't have been the least bit startled, mostly because I was actively looking for one.

It's incredible how the combination of sun and trees can inspire sublime introspections. There's something about how leaves filter the sunlight that makes it possible to recall memories buried deep inside the cerebral cortex. Going into a forest means remembering whatever it was that you didn't even know you forgot. There exists a philosophy of the woods and a primordial connection to the natural world. To go to the forest is to go back to the self. One's mind can stand naked in the wind. Unexposed, one's thoughts can then morph into an intangible collection of recollections, dreams, and ideas. Of course, all of this risks being blown by the breeze, and one's thoughts may zone into nothingness. I've often stood among trees and thought about nothing at all. My blank slate of mind then absorbs its surroundings as I look at the immediate world. In these moments, I find myself most vulnerable to the impressions of nature. It's during such times that I feel most one with the trees.

The forest itself had no interest in talking about massive floods, heatwaves, wildfires, droughts, melting glaciers, rising seawater, drowning polar bears, warming oceans, bleaching coral reefs, the depleting ozone layer, intense storms, shifting animal patterns, deforestation, earlier springs, drier winters, dying bees, or worldwide pandemics. The forest did not want to discuss my concerns about urban sprawl, expensive housing, gas-guzzling cars, useless wars, trillion-dollar debt, terrorism, immigration issues, health care woes, corrupt CEOs, oil spills, market crashes, drug wars, crack houses, substance abuse, homelessness, sex trafficking, guns in schools, elderly abuse, child abuse, stupid presidents, or the culture of fear. The forest harbored no desire to hear about anyone's problems about personal debts, bad relationships, horrific car accidents, traffic jams, long commutes, boring jobs, jackass bosses, incompetent coworkers, aging parents, wayward teenagers, cheating spouses, messy divorces, foreclosures, repossessions, getting sued, flat tires, broken roofs, leaky faucets, dirty dishes, or piling up laundry. Life itself can often feel daunting. Yet, despite all the world's woes, we all get up and somehow manage to go about our day. Every day. Day in and day out. We essentially become immune to the world, dare I say, even dead to it. We collectively feel that we don't essentially matter. And when I say "we," I mean the "I" in all of us. We all say that "I" can't make a difference, so why even bother trying? All those "I's" add up to becoming "we's," and that is why the planet is heading into the tailspin that it is. Yet, the forest wanted to hear nothing about these things. The forest simply wanted to share its small patch of peace and quiet. The forest only asked one thing from me, and that was stillness. Unmoving, I learned to stand with the forest. The forest revealed itself to me when I took the time to watch it do nothing and everything simultaneously.

The forest was truly enchanting, yet wayward thoughts still managed to infiltrate the minute crevices of my brain and disturb my reverie. The only way to exorcise the rude intrusion of ideas was to write them down in the notebook I was carrying. It was a guaranteed fact that my thoughts would get distracting, so I anticipated doing a mental purge of some sort.

As is often the case, the purging involved nothing more than documenting snippets of thoughts. "Strange that the color green is associated with both nature and greed," was the first entry. "It is as though we must use up all the space by sometime yesterday because we assume that there will never be a tomorrow," was the next. I penned a poem and titled it "Concrete Arteriosclerosis." I'm an avid poetry writer, and oftentimes poems serve as the only reminders that I experienced something while traveling. Allow me to share what I wrote while I sat under a 1,000-year-old tree:

Concrete Arteriosclerosis

Silence in my eyes
Wind in my step
I am the forest
the rain
the air
Nature
is
I
in the
city
we do not
need.

I adore poetry. Poems are snippets of thoughts, like pencil sketches done before a painting. Yet, I often think that paintings are nothing more than copies of original ideas initially set down on paper. As I see it, my poems are pencil sketches, and my books are paintings. I could have just as easily printed up all my poetry and delivered it to the public with a note saying, "Here you go. These are all my travel stories," but they would come across as gibberish. I may understand my words, but other people certainly would not. No one would necessarily know that I wrote that poem while I sat on a log in a giant redwood forest, but I remember exactly where I was. I remember that my eyes were full of nothing, *and it was sublime*. I could see the quiet. It felt like I was walking on air. I wanted the sunlight, the green, the forest; I wanted to stay sitting on that log forever. That is what I translate in my head when I read that poem, but not everyone else would know to do that. Hence the need to write everything out in long form. If ever my writing comes across as florid or poetic, it's usually because I'm copying sentences from a poem I wrote during one of my travels.

Olympic

I know that I have an idea in my head of what I would like my life to look like, and it looks completely different from the life that I'm currently living. I'm very much an active participant in the rat race, and I despise it. But like everyone else, I don't have much choice in the matter. I need to make money to pay for the roof over my head, the car I drive, the food I eat, and everything else that comes with the cost of modern living. It's all very unavoidable. But my ideal life would see me paying for none of these things. In my perfect world, I'd be living in a paid-off cabin situated far, far away from the bustle of the city. There, I would grow vegetables in a garden and collect an endless supply of eggs from chickens. I'd work on my hobbies during the day and gaze at the stars at night. My ideal life would be very uncomplicated. I'd go for a lot of walks and do a lot of reading. I wouldn't have any neighbors. My perfect life would be very tranquil. I would take up pottery. Or glass blowing. Something like that.

I don't like that I can't live amongst nature and still live a modern life. It's as though the two are not allowed to go hand in hand, which baffles me. Why did we not build our cities around nature rather than over it? Why did we not build up rather than out? Why the urban sprawl? Why the desire to possess both front and back lawns? Society does a superb job of teaching us to want and own things. Everything is never enough. There's always something more we think we need.

Well, there's one thing I always need, and that's getting the heck away, albeit preferably when it's not raining. I love immersing myself in nature and forgetting that urban life exists; however, I tend to obsess over comfortable couches and warm beds whenever I find myself hiking in miserable weather. The biggest problem with planning hiking trips in advance is not knowing what the weather will be like when you reach a destination. I'll be the first to admit that I suffer from the ailment of eternal optimism, which never does me any favors when I find myself in situations that I reluctantly have to admit are less than agreeable.

A case in point was when I planned a hiking trip to Olympic National Park in notoriously rainy Washington state. Naturally, I knew that precipitation would be in the forecast because rain in that part of the world always is, yet I don't know why I didn't think rain would be much of a problem. I guess I had never hiked in a perpetual rain shower before, so I might have approached the prospect of hiking in wet weather as a new adventure rather than a soul-crushing experience that should have been wisely avoided.

Even though I read that the Hoh Rainforest registered as one of the wettest places in America, I bizarrely convinced myself that it wouldn't rain much during a hiking trip there. Nevertheless, I should not have been surprised that it was drizzling when Eric and I picked up our rental car in Seattle, nor should I have been shocked that we were not out-driving the rainy weather as we edged ever closer to Olympic National Park. I had no reason to be disappointed that it was a torrential downpour by the time we arrived, nor should I have been dismayed that a park ranger greeted us in a parka. For whatever reason, I felt optimistic that the sun would start shining any minute.

Nevertheless, I asked the park ranger how long the rain would be around. He chuckled at my inquiry as if we pulled up in our rental car for the sole purpose to amuse him, and he didn't even bother to answer. I had to prove that I was asking him a genuine question.

"No, really," I had to say. "Is this rain going to stop either today or tomorrow?"

In his bemusement, he simply waved off my question with a flat-out "no," and put out his hand to collect the entrance fee.

I looked at Eric, who I dragged along on this hair-brained journey, and asked him if he was still interested in hiking despite the rainy weather. "Well, we came all this way now, didn't we? We may as well make the best of it," he said as he looked out the window while zipping up his jacket as far as it could go.

We only learned after the fact that we really shouldn't have bothered. The forest was insanely beautiful, but it wasn't easy to appreciate through a constant flow of water. The trails were muddy, and the slugs and snails were so numerous that we had to constantly keep an eye on where we placed our feet. The rain was making us wet, and it took only one day of hiking in the pouring rain before we both concluded that there was no joy in doing so. The rain was chilly, and the cold soaked right into our bones. We stayed out in the cruddy weather longer than either of us wanted to because neither wanted to admit that we were feeling miserable. We were making the best of it, goddammit! We were having fun! Wasn't this forest pretty?! We both secretly wondered how long we needed to pretend that this was where we wanted to be. Neither of us wanted to be the first to break out of character.

On day two of trudging in a rainy and muddy forest, we both started to sound a little too much like tuberculosis patients with our scratchy throats and hacking coughs. At one point in our hike, I finally reached my limit and blurted out that I had enough. There, I said it, and I didn't care that I said it first. I was done. I knew it was only day two of our four-day Olympic trip, but I couldn't take it anymore. I wasn't the least bit interested in seeing what day three would look like because I was completely over it. I was ready to move on and put Olympic National Park behind me.

"Is it okay to say that I want to go?" I asked.

"Sure, I'm okay with it," Eric said with a hint of relief.

So, move on, we did. We decided to drive four hours to Cascades National Park, thinking we'd be getting far enough away from the Olympic-sized rain shower. However, we discovered that four hours of driving in Washington state wasn't far enough to outrun rainy weather. I was pretty sure that the cloud parked over the Cascades was the same cloud parked over Olympic, which led me to believe that there was one massive cloud in the shape of Washington state directly over our heads.

"Do we make the best of it again?" I asked Eric in dire hope that he would say no.

He looked out the window and started to contemplate. The ball was in his court; he was going to have to be the one to make the call. What was he going to say? Did he think that maybe the Cascades' rain was more tolerable than the Olympic rain? He looked like he was considering it. Oh, crap, were we going to have to get back out there and be miserable again? I hoped that he would say to forget it. Maybe I needed to beat him to the punch. We had about six days left of our vacation. We could drive anywhere. Quick, I had to say something before he suggested we get out of the car and hike in the rain again.

"We could drive to Montana!" I spontaneously suggested, not even knowing how far a drive that would even be.

I'd been wanting to go to Montana ever since I saw the movie *A River Runs Through It.* There was something about that film that made Montana look like it was the kind of place that I wanted to come home to. I was under the impression that the landscape was filled to the brim with rivers and sunlight. The yearning for Montana was strong inside me. Part of me resisted the desire to visit the state in person for fear of disappointment. Yet, here we were, sitting in a rental car listening to the pitter-patter of a Washington rain shower, deciding what to do.

"Montana?" he inquired. "That sounds really far." He then started to poke around the seat cushions just as he said that. "Now, where did we stash that map?"

I gave a long glance out the window. "It's either Montana or more of this," I said. "I vote we leave this entire state."

He was still rummaging around for the map until he eventually said, "Voila! I found it. Let's see how far Montana is."

We opened the map and saw that Montana was still really far away, like, several hours' drive far away. Yet, in my eyes, it looked like the closest I had ever been to my fantasy state.

"You really want to drive that far?" he asked.

"Sure!" I said. "Doesn't it sound more fun to go there?"

He looked at the map. "Where in Montana do you want to go?"

I had no idea and said, "Anywhere there's a river."

He grimaced at the notion of doing more spontaneous driving and said, "No, you have to pick somewhere specific."

I looked for the closest national park in Montana and pointed to Glacier National Park. "There," I said. "We'll go to Glacier."

We calculated it to be a ten-hour drive away. To someone who didn't harbor a secret Montana obsession, a ten-hour drive sounded like a dreadfully long journey, but to someone who *did* harbor a secret Montana obsession, a ten-hour drive sounded reasonably close. I was ready to hit the road and make some good time, so I turned on the ignition.

"Oh my God, you're being serious," he said, sounding astonished.

I didn't realize that he wasn't taking me seriously.

"Yes, of course I'm being serious," I said. "I'm driving us to Montana. Right now. Here, watch me turn on the wipers so we can see where we're going." I don't know why I felt I needed to reiterate how rainy it was by turning the wipers on at full speed.

"It's not raining *that* hard," he told me.

"Yes, but it *is* raining. That's my point."

"What if it's raining in Montana?"

"Yuck! Don't say that."

"But what if it is?"

"Well, if it's raining there, at least we'll be able to say that we've been to Montana."

I wasn't going to let him talk me out of driving there. I was going to Montana, and since he was in the passenger seat, he was going with me.

I put him in charge of navigation. I told him to find places on the map that had even the slightest chance of sounding interesting along the way.

"There's a place called Ginkgo Petrified Forest State Park that we'll be driving near," he announced.

"Perfect!" I said. "You got me at *Petrified*. We'll check that place out!"

Ginkgo

Once we escaped the grip of the Cascades, the rain went away, and the sun decided to bestow us with its presence. I was so happy to see the sun that I reacted as if I just got released from solitary confinement. It was proof that our hiking trip could be redeemed after all.

My mind's eye was busy conjuring up visions of a lush, cool

forest as we headed our way to the Ginkgo Petrified Forest State Park. Words of John Muir were ringing in my ears, and he was saying, "Of all the paths you take in life, make sure a few of them are on dirt." However, most of the trails we'd been on so far were slathered in mud, so I was hoping that this forest we were heading to would be a great place to stretch out our legs and perhaps picnic by a stream. For some reason, my brain conveniently glossed over the "petrified" part of the title, and I failed to consider the possibility of walking around a "forest" made of nothing but stones.

We pulled up to the Ginkgo Park's headquarters and immediately noticed we were in a landscape completely denuded of trees. We got out of the car and were greeted by heat waves rising from the pavement. Fifteen million years ago (give or take a couple of million years), this place would have surely looked like what my mind's eye was envisioning, but since the planet was no longer in the Miocene epoch, the landscape now appeared decidedly barren. There were only a few trees around, which we assumed were planted to provide the only source of shade for the entire parking lot.

"Look at those leaves!" Eric exclaimed as he inspected one of the trees. "These are ginkgoes! Don't they have the neatest shape?"

I quickly realized that I had never seen a ginkgo tree before.

"Wait for the wind to blow and watch them dance in the breeze," Eric suggested.

I had gotten out of the car only two minutes ago and could already feel the sun beating down my neck.

"What is this thing called *wind* you're talking about?" I replied as I peeled off a layer of clothes. "How the heck is it so hot here? Are we even in Washington anymore?"

It was weird how different the weather was compared to where we had just come from. It obviously had something to do with the mountains and the fact that we were no longer around any.

"Well, at least you won't be complaining about the rain anymore," Eric quickly replied and glanced over the landscape. "Although, we should have brought some with us by the looks of it."

Indeed, whoever was in charge of Washington was really bad at drawing state lines. By all appearances, we had crossed at least three different borders.

"Well, shall we go have a look-see?" Eric asked as he tossed his jacket and sweatshirt back into the car.

"Most definitely," I replied. "Do you think I should bring along a jacket just in case?"

"In case of what?" Eric asked.

"In case I get cold," I said.

"Oh my God, no. I don't think that you'll need it," he said.

"I'll bring it anyway and leave it tied around my waist. We are in Washington state, after all," I said, and then never once put it on the whole time we were there.

Ginkgo forests once grew prolifically in North America and elsewhere in the world but were virtually wiped out during the ice ages. I learned from the visitor center's dioramas that the world's few surviving ginkgo forests retreated to safe enclaves deep in the crevices in China. The ancient Chinese valued the many health benefits the ginkgo tree provided, so they planted small ginkgo forests in many Buddhist monastery gardens. I learned that most, if not all, of the ginkgo trees worldwide today are descendants of those cultivated in sacred temple nurseries. I also learned that the trees themselves were tenacious survivors, for they were the only species of tree that managed to survive the Hiroshima nuclear blast. No other trees in Hiroshima went into leaf the next spring except for their ginkgoes. After reading that, I was hooked. I was in love with the ginkgo.

The visitor center whetted our appetite for ginkgoes and made us excited to see some petrified examples. With no shade to hide from the sun, we hiked uphill in a barren landscape littered with oodles of rocks. According to our handy dandy park map, we were apparently searching for ginkgo tree stumps that were supposedly tucked someplace amongst the many hills. Even though the park went by the name of Ginkgo Petrified Forest State Park, we were not finding any petrified ginkgo specimens. We had no problem stumbling across petrified stumps of maple, walnut, spruce, sycamore, chestnut, Douglas fir, and basically anything else that wasn't ginkgo. Nearly one hour into our hike under the blazing sun, we were unsuccessful in finding one single damn stump of ginkgo.

"Why isn't this map helping?" I inquired.

"Because it was made in crayon by the park ranger's five-year-old son, that's why," Eric explained. "This map is completely useless."

"I don't think they actually have any ginkgoes," I announced. "This is just a grand conspiracy to get fat Americans to walk around in circles."

We took a look around and noticed that not a single other person was out there. We were the only ones exercising.

The *Ginkgo biloba* tree coexisted with the dinosaurs.

Alongside the *Ginkgo biloba* tree stood other similar trees that were part of the overall ginkgo family; however, none of the other ginkgo-like trees are alive with us today. The *Ginkgo biloba* is the lone survivor of its kind and is described as being a living fossil. It's incredible to think that something, some catalyst, was able to wipe out entire species of living things, but that destruction was too weak to take out one particular headstrong species of ginkgo.

"How in the heck did anyone know that ginkgoes were buried here?" I wondered out loud, frustrated that we could still not locate a petrified one. "I think I'll elevate the guy who discovered the petrified ginkgo stumps to God status. There is no way a mere mortal could have found anything so unfathomably rare here."

Again, referring to what I learned at the visitor center, the discovery of the petrified ginkgo tree was not expected. In the early 1930s, a road was being built through the area, and construction workers were constantly pulling out chunks of petrified wood. By chance, a geologist from the Central Washington State area was driving by and saw someone walking down a hill with one of those chunks of a petrified tree. Now, imagine the sound of his car wheels screeching. He determined that since the mountain was belching out such an obscene variety of woods, he was hopeful that at least one of the petrified woods would be that of a ginkgo. Many academics scoffed at him because finding petrified ginkgo was akin to finding a unicorn. Ginkgoes left the fossil record in the Americas about 15 million years ago. However, many other types of trees remained, so chances were if anyone found any kind of petrified tree at all, it was certainly not going to be that

29

of a ginkgo. Nevertheless, this geologist named George F. Beck had a hunch, and as he dug his spade, he knew he was going to make a name for himself. He was the first to discover the petrified tree that no one believed anyone would ever find in America.

Right about when we were both ready to give up, we made the same discovery too. Our finding was, of course, only sensational amongst ourselves, but we felt duly rewarded. The elusive ginkgo tree was finally ours to admire. It was precisely there, on that remote hill in the middle of Washington state, that an incredible tree met its demise millions of years ago. Surprisingly, it was one of the smallest stumps we found that day. Most of the other tree stumps we had seen were much bigger, but no other stump got our admiration more. I can't say I've ever cried over a tree stump before, but, damn, that little bugger felt powerful right then and there.

Once, that petrified stump was alive. It was a seed that grew into a tree that bloomed and felt the warmth of the noonday sun. The time that separated us from when this tree was not a hardened lump of stone was vast. Fifteen million years was a stretch of time that I couldn't calculate inside my head. Fifteen million years ago, right where we were standing, there once was a bountiful, lush forest full of trees and creatures that were currently extinct. The once luxuriant landscape now looked like an abandoned rock quarry somewhere on Mars. A lot had changed in 15 million years, but not the *Ginkgo biloba*. It's the one thing that not even 15 million years had the power to alter.

Walking back to the car, I stopped to admire the planted ginkgo trees, and I thought to myself, "Sacred Chinese Garden, huh?" In 15 million years, when the parking lot would be long beyond gone, I wondered about an extensive ginkgo forest possibly being there instead. If so, it would undoubtedly cause a stir in the fossil record for future humanoids to figure out.

CHAPTER TWO:
The American West, 2001-recent

Purgatory

Getting back to the topic of poems, I, unfortunately, wrote a few of them as I watched the clock count down the time inside a family restaurant in Medford, Oregon, before heading back to the airport. I deliberately used the word "unfortunately" because that town rubbed me the wrong way. In my notebook, I called the place an "Elvis Purgatory" despite there not being a single Elvis impersonator in sight. I chose that phrase because it felt like I was stuck in a 1950s limbo. It was a conclusion I came to while I stared at a guy in a wife-beater t-shirt playing a video poker machine in the lounge section of the diner. It wasn't just him that gave off the Purgatory feeling; it was the whole eyeful of the place. He, with his feet propped on top of the poker machine, the faded orange 1950s *Cocktails* sign flashing above his head, and my waitress, who was old enough to have retired ten years ago, announcing to the entire restaurant that she was going outside for her cigarette break. All in all, the scene reminded me of a place I had never been to before but one I never needed to have gone to in the first place. Most of me wondered why I was even there.

For what it was worth, I have to say that Medford was not especially unique, for I have been to a few other places that were a lot like Medford in some way, shape, or form. What I have learned from all my travels is that a Medford-style "Purgatory" is a common enough place. I once was in a perfectly preserved turn-of-the-century Western bar in Virginia City, Nevada, replete with mahogany and mirrors, where I was shocked to hear a live band bust out with Jimmy Buffet songs. I left that bar and went next door to another authentically Western watering hole, where my ears immediately got assaulted by someone singing Roy Orbison over a karaoke machine. Personally, I would have preferred to have heard heavy metal at either of those locations because I imagined Jesse James listening to Megadeth rather than the Traveling Wilburys had he been sitting in my seat. In other words, those places were serious buzzkills, or as I like to call them, "Western Purgatories." I never know what sins I have committed to deserve a spot in these personal way stations, but I have found myself in Western Purgatory enough times that I've racked up quite an impressive collection of experiences, some of which I will proceed to relate.

Colorado

The Western United States is full of mini present-life way stations, and a good portion of them exist in the lovely state of Colorado. It is rather fitting that there is an actual city named Purgatory in Colorado, but it's my opinion that the whole state could easily sport that title. Most versions of a Coloradoan Purgatory involve quite a bit of driving, and the level of Purgatory one finds oneself in depends on what kind of rental car one gets stuck in and who one gets stuck driving behind. I was put into a Daewoo once, and it only took five minutes of coaching that vehicle into climbing over a small mountain by Coloradoan standards before I started to call the car the "Boo-hoo" due to its sluggish nature. What I remember most about the Boo-hoo was the way it smelled, for the scent of exhaust fumes will be permanently lodged deep inside my nostrils.

Driving the Boo-hoo in Colorado was a test of patience and nerves, and that vehicle enjoyed visiting Rocky Mountain National Park significantly less than I did.

A classic Coloradoan Purgatory is where you get stuck driving behind someone trailing a boat over a one-lane mountain pass that seemingly goes on forever. That version of Purgatory gets even better once a second lane finally emerges for going downhill, only to have your delight rewarded with a speeding ticket worth nearly two hundred dollars when you make it to the bottom. Naturally, the fact that you've spent the previous hour of your life going ten miles under the speed limit while staring at the butt of a boat is totally irrelevant, as no cop will ever be interested in hearing your side of the story.

Another one of my personal favorite Colorado-style Purgatories exists in the shape of an oversized plastic flappy thing whose only purpose in life is to slap people in the face like a giant wet noodle. The Glenwood Springs Adventure Park sits on top of a 7,100-foot mountain, and the views from that perch are insanely beautiful. My current husband, Ryan, and I discovered that the best way to "become one" with that mountain was to slide down it, and we did so on the attraction called the Alpine Slides.

There were massive signs near the bottom of the ride that warned riders to duck when they got to the end, and one needed to be absolutely blind not to notice the oversize warnings. Thus, I dutifully ducked when I got to the bottom of the hill, which meant that I successfully avoided getting smacked in the head with a device that would have slapped me silly. We had so much fun riding those slides that we went back up and slid down them again. When I got to the bottom the second time around, I knew full well what was coming, and I don't know why I chose to do nothing to stop the preventable from happening. BAM! I got smacked right between the eyes with a carwash-sized plastic flap so hard that it made me come to a complete stop quite abruptly. Ryan was riding behind me, and he darn near fell off his slide from laughing so hard. He said the scene looked straight out of a Monty Python skit that he wanted to hit rewind and watch it again. He was then kind enough to ask me if I was alright.

"Ya," I whimpered. "I feel wide awake now."

Before I continue with more Purgatory-like stories, I should say a little something about how I recall memories. Believe me when I say that I tried writing events in the order they occurred, but stories from the recent past infiltrated my brain and demanded to be purged. As a result, I kindly ask the reader to forgive me for presenting events wildly out of order. My intent is not to confuse the reader but merely to entertain. I want the reader to know that there are only three main characters to keep track of (me, Eric, and Ryan). Sometimes our timelines will intersect, and other times go their separate ways. Indeed, time matters not to memories, for everything is history to them.

So, continuing on, I have to say that nothing, and I mean nothing, defines a Coloradoan Purgatory more than getting stoned and then regretting that you did while finding yourself in a situation that you can't possibly undo, even though you want to. Colorado legalized recreational marijuana in 2012, and I don't know what possessed Ryan and me to want to try the most potent THC gummies we could get our hands on.

"It will be fun," we said. "We haven't been stoned in, like, forever," we said. Those would soon be some famous last words.

We bought the gummies earlier in the day but wisely saved them for later since we didn't want to be too incapacitated for the long hike we had planned. It was a beautiful August morning, so we were curious to see how much of the Colorado trail we could crush by afternoon. Neither of us would ever consider hiking the entire 486-mile trail through some of the state's most mountainous terrain, but halfway into our hike, we came across someone nearing the end of that incredible journey.

Most people who hike the Colorado trail start their trek near Denver and (hopefully, if they don't quit) emerge four to six weeks later on the same path we were hiking on outside Durango. It was obvious that this person had been on the trail for multiple days because she was much too haggard, windswept, and sunburned to assume that she was simply out for a morning jog. That, and her German shepherd looked like it was ready to jump off the cliff and die already. Merely looking at the two of them made us feel exhausted, and it got us talking about how we didn't have the stamina, desire, or guts to undertake such an arduous adventure.

We hiked for a good couple of hours, and when we were done, we saw that same girl and dog sprawled out in the shade on the edge of the parking lot. I couldn't resist asking her if she had just hiked the Colorado trail, to which she answered that she most certainly did.

"What day is it?" she asked us. "I think I know what day it is, but I want to make sure."

We told her what day it was, to which she said, "Wow! I was

out there for 35 days! That was right about what I was expecting."

I wanted to pick her brain, so I asked if she needed us to give her a ride anywhere.

"Sure!" she said. "There's a BBQ joint in Durango where I'm supposed to meet my friends. You can give me a ride there if you don't terribly mind. I'd really appreciate it."

"Not a problem!" we both said. "Hop on in!"

We helped her load her heavy backpack into the trunk and opened the door for her dog to jump in. It took the dog all of a second to get comfortable and fall asleep. The rest of us piled in, and the smell of unshowered guests was instantaneous.

"So, how does it feel to have accomplished that trail?" we asked her.

She quietly reflected on her emotions. "It feels bittersweet," she softly said while petting her trusty companion. "I couldn't have done it without her," she stated before giving her dog a gentle squeeze. "She did an awesome job at keeping the bears away."

We dropped her off and resisted the urge to join her because we were saving our appetite for a cowboy cookout that we had reservations for later that evening. I had read that the Bar D Chuckwagon was a "Durango institution that has served Western music, cowboy poetry, and rollicking Western humor at a chuckwagon-style restaurant since 1969." Indeed, it was an event we didn't want to miss, but it was apparently one we didn't want to experience sober, either.

We were excited to try the cannabis edibles we had bought earlier in the day, so we each ate one of the innocent-looking gummies as soon as we parked the car in the restaurant's massive dirt parking lot. I can't recall now what the gummies' potency was, but they were somewhere between the "Are you sure you wanna buy this?" and "I highly recommend that you start with something less lethal" range. The only thing I can say is that I'm glad we each only ate one because I can't even imagine what I would be saying next had we both eaten more.

The cowboy dinner was slated to be served at 6:30 p.m., but we got there two hours early, thinking there would be plenty of things to see and do on the site's extensive grounds. I saw on Google maps that the restaurant was nestled in a small patch of woods, so I was hoping there would be some trails for us to enjoy while we basked in our THC-induced buzz. Indeed, we did find some nature trails to meander on, but none of them went very far, and all of them were full of families with hyperactive kids that did nothing to enhance the spiritual quest we were seeking. We then saw a little choo-choo train that went in a large loop around the pretty patch of forest, so we bought a couple of tickets and went for a ride.

"Do you feel anything?" I asked Ryan.

"Nope. Do you?" he asked back.

"Nope," I replied. "Do you think we bought placebos?"

"Nah," Ryan said. "We just need to give it a few more minutes."

Well, that was how the conversation started, but it was definitely not how it ended. Somewhere near the third curve, the THC gummies kicked in.

"Oh my God, I so want off this ride," I said and started to grip the handrail that only went up to my knees.

"Why is this train so bumpy?" Ryan asked no one in particular.

Mind you; we were on a child-size train that went about as fast as a person could reasonably jog.

"It feels like we are speeding," I said, bracing for an inevitable crash.

"How far are we going?" Ryan wanted to know. "Do you think this train will go all the way to Denver?"

Man, we were so stoned, but not in a good way. We were stupid-stoned.

I don't even know how we got off the train when it finally stopped. All I remember is that we didn't want anyone to notice that we were ridiculously high. We were at a family destination, a place that prided itself in serving no alcohol, and we were walking around super lit. We had to do our best to blend in.

"Act natural," I said to Ryan while I bumbled around like a female version of Jack Sparrow. Ryan's legs, I noticed, weren't doing much better.

"Are you stoned?" Ryan asked me. "Because I'm *so* stoned right now."

"Yes," I assured him. "I didn't think those gummies would hit us this hard."

"I think everyone's staring at us," Ryan said.

I agreed and said that we needed to go shopping. We went into all the little stores that sold cowboy-themed trinkets and came out with several sticks of hard candy.

"Oh my God, these things must be fifty years old!" Ryan exclaimed as he took his first couple of licks.

"Ya, mine tastes stale, too," I said. "I think these are left over from when this place first opened."

Time went super slow, and we wandered around for what

seemed like forever. Eventually, we just picked a spot and sat down. Ryan pulled out his phone, and we started to watch an episode of *Ash vs. Evil Dead*. From our perspective, we were hiding deep in the woods where no one could see us, but in reality, we were sitting right in the middle of the woods where the train went around in circles. Everyone on the train could see us, and the conductor probably got on the speaker and narrated our antics to the passengers as they slowly rambled past us.

"And over to your right, you will see the highly stoned couple who thinks no one sees them. Be sure your kids get a good look at them so they learn not to do drugs."

It wasn't like we were doing anything too terribly weird, but we were definitely in a location where we were not expected to be. In Dante's *Inferno*, there were Nine Circles of Hell: limbo, lust, gluttony, greed, anger, heresy, violence, fraud, and treachery. We were in none of those circles, for we were hiding in the tenth circle: absurdity. Everything around us struck us as strange. We were laughing at everything. Having that little train going around us only made us laugh even more. We felt like giants sitting on lily pads. After an hour or so, there wasn't a single person there who didn't know who we were. Everyone saw us. We were definitely famous, and the cowboy show hadn't even begun.

Eating was the only thing that redeemed us. We couldn't wait for the food to coat our innards and soak up the gummies. I was initially disappointed that the cowboy show didn't start while the dinner was being served but eating in silence probably proved to be the better option. I have no idea how the cowboy show eventually panned out because we left as soon as our bellies were full. We decided to bow out the very second we were sober and quickly hurried to our hotel to sit in our Airbnb-provided hot tub.

"What is that bright red light next to the moon over there?" I said and pointed to what was definitely a foreign object in the sky.

"Oh, man," Ryan gasped. "That's gotta be a UFO!"

Yup. The gummies were not through with us yet.

"Wouldn't it be cool if they abducted us?" I asked. "Maybe we should wave to them."

And so we waved to the mystery light as only two potheads in a hot tub possibly could. We looked ridiculous, but unless there were any coyotes around, I guarantee that no one saw us — no one, except for the aliens that were watching us from binoculars, of course.

We had about twenty gummies left in the package, but we decided against lugging them around. We unceremoniously abandoned them in a Durango garbage can, which was akin to flushing $40 down the toilet. We both agreed it was the best $40 we had ever wasted.

It was good that we went to bed early because we had to get up bright-eyed and bushy-tailed the next day for a fun-filled morning of shallow river rafting. It was nearing the end of rafting season, and one look at the low-flowing Animas River assured us that our butts were going to get scraped. There was no way we could have done that rafting trip stoned because it ended up not being so much a rafting trip as it ended up being a walking one. Our guide was a jovial fellow; he could only laugh every time our raft got stuck on a rock every three minutes as we slowly made our way down the shallow river.

The rafting trip was a constant process of getting out of the raft and lifting it off boulders. It was a classic Colorado Purgatory-style trip, but I've learned to expect nothing less, and I always seem to enjoy it.

Montana

I've been to Montana multiple times now, but I have to say the most memorable trip was the one that I took with Ryan in the early 2000s. That trip sticks out in my mind simply because of the car, or I should say, simply because of the shell of a car we were given to drive.

Renting a car is a necessary evil in America. The United States is unlike Europe, for we don't have loads of trains to seamlessly glide us to our destinations. No, in America, you gotta drive yourself if you want to get anywhere, and I've learned the hard way that you have to stay on top of your car reservations. I now know how important it is to call a car rental company ahead of time and advise them if your flight has been delayed. This knowledge holds especially true if you're flying into a tourist destination at the peak of high season, particularly in remote locations where a person needs a car simply to get out of the airport.

We arrived at Missoula airport about two hours behind schedule, which meant that the compact car we reserved was given to someone else about an hour and 59 minutes before we arrived. We were admonished for not having called them to tell them we were running late, so we apologized and asked them to give us whatever size car they had available. Unbeknownst to us, this was not the car rental agent's first rodeo. He made such intense eye contact with us that it penetrated deep into our souls as he told us point-blank that they didn't have any cars available. He then made a huge sweep with his arms to encompass the entire row of car rental companies and told us that none of the companies would have any cars available. He then swept us aside, looked past our shoulders, and yelled, "Next!"

Of course, we didn't want to believe him. We split up, took our places in line, and went counter to counter asking for a car until we both ended up at the same car rental counter where we started.

"Look," I said to the guy. "I honestly didn't know we had to call to let you know we were running late. I simply assumed that your company kept track of delayed flights considering I had to provide my flight information when I booked the reservation." I begged and pleaded our case and told him that we were willing to stand there until they could give us something to drive. My gauntlet was thrown, and the standoff ensued for well over an hour until, lo and behold, a vehicle materialized out of thin air. I don't know where they found the car they scrounged up for us, but I suspect there must have been a vehicle assembly line nearby, and they stole an unfinished shell of a van just so that they could toss us something and get us out of their hair.

The van they gave us was totally gutted inside and looked as though it was ready to go to the moon. The van was devoid of seating aside from the driver's and passenger's seats, and the massive white monstrosity was nothing more than a hollow tube of unpadded metal. The whole thing was one roving echo chamber, and every pebble we drove over made an insane pinging noise as it ricocheted against its bare shell of existence.

Driving this thing, we both just knew, was going to be 100% pure, full-fledged fun-ness.

Aside from Glacier National Park, we harbored tentative plans to take the NASA vehicle (that's what we affectionately called it) all the way up to Canada, provided that our ears could tolerate all the obnoxious banging. Of course, we ended up driving that van to Canada and down more than a few nasty dirt roads. Yup, thinking about that trip now, I can recall exactly what rocks banging against an empty shell of a vehicle sounded like: Montana Purgatory. That van wasn't all that bad, though, because it saved us money in the long run. We canceled a few nights of hotel reservations, bought a couple of Wal-Mart sleeping bags and pillows, and slept inside that gutted-out van instead. All said and done, I now wish all my rental cars were NASA vehicles just like that one, although I would prefer not to go through all that hassle again to score such an unexpected prize.

The whole subversive reason why I even dragged my new boyfriend at the time to Montana was that I wanted him to take the huckleberry test. I had discovered the amazing flavor of huckleberries when I went to Montana with Eric a few years before, and their intoxicating taste was still very much on my brain. Ryan and I were still learning what made each other tick, and I was still in the grips of my personal Montana obsession. He had every right to wonder out loud why I was watering a withered bush on my patio that was more than obviously dead. I had to explain that the brown, sad-looking thing was supposed to be a huckleberry bush and that huckleberries were the most amazing things ever. I asked him if he had ever tasted huckleberries before.

"Are you saying that huckleberries are real?" he asked. "I thought the phrase, *I'll be your huckleberry* was only something Doc Holiday said."

The fact that he knew that quote revealed that our relationship was off to a stellar start.

"Whatever happened to Val Kilmer?" I wondered out loud. "He totally stole the movie *Tombstone* with that line."

"He sure did!" Ryan exclaimed. "It's the only line I remember."

"Hey," I wondered, "what does *I'll be your huckleberry* even mean?"

"Hum," Ryan pondered. "I have absolutely no idea."

Thank goodness the internet was finally useful. We looked up the phrase and learned that it was a Victorian idiom for *I'll be your man for the job*. In Doc Holiday's case, he was offering to be that person's pallbearer. Gosh, what a nice character he was.

"Have you ever been to Montana?" I quizzed Ryan.

"Nope, but does seeing the movie *A River Runs Through It* count as vicariously having been there?" he inquired.

Again, he name-dropped another excellent film. We were two for two now.

"No, that does not count," I had to break it to him, "but only because it's not possible to taste the flavor of huckleberries by licking a movie screen."

He paused for a moment and had to ask, "Okay, what's with your whole huckleberry thing?"

"Yummy!" I said and started my huckleberry spiel. "They are so good, but I can't get them here. They only grow in the wild where it's freezing fucking cold. I was in Montana a few years ago, and I had something huckleberry every day: huckleberry ice cream, huckleberry pie, huckleberry shake, huckleberry jam, huckleberry pancakes...and I absolutely hate pancakes, but those were amazing! Just thinking about them now makes me want to go back."

I don't know what it is about huckleberries, but they are my catnip. To me, one of the biggest tragedies in the world is that huckleberries don't grow anywhere near where I live. I already knew before I even tried to grow a huckleberry bush in the Arizona desert that doing so would be a complete waste of time. I thought if I babied it, I would somehow get lucky, but I knew deep down that I was just wasting precious water. Huckleberries don't even like to grow in any place that is not considered "wild," and they have a notorious reputation for balking at all attempts at cultivation. That's too bad because if I were going to be any kind of farmer at all, I would be a huckleberry one. Huckleberries are the most delicious flavor in the entire world, and even bears love snacking on those tasty little morsels. When huckleberries are in season, it's a race to see who gets to them first. Huckleberry hunters are the unsung heroes of the natural world, without which I would never have tasted huckleberry anything.

"Didn't watching *A River Runs Through It* make you want to drop everything and run away to Montana right after you saw it?" I asked Ryan.

"Heck, ya, it did," he said, "and I don't even know how to fly fish."

"I don't know how to fly fish, either," I said. "I tried once and immediately broke the tip off my friend's fishing pole," I divulged. "But, hey, do you want to go to Montana and do some hiking?"

Ryan didn't hesitate for a moment before he said, "I sure do! That would be awesome!"

"We can go to Glacier National Park," I told him. "It's not that hard to get to if we fly into Missoula. I drove there all the way from Seattle a few years ago, but that was a painfully long road trip. We'll fly into Montana and do it right."

Montana was to be our first real hiking trip together. I had to know who I was dating because if we went to Montana and he found the overwhelming beauty of that state to be incredibly dull, he would not be the right guy for me. Additionally, if it happened that Ryan took a bite of a huckleberry pie and spat it out in absolute disgust, I had already decided I would have to break up with him in the middle of our trip because I doubted that I could be with anyone who would scoff at the most delicious flavor in the entire world. Besides, I had already looked up all the places that sold huckleberry treats and designed a whole itinerary based around a daily dose of huckleberry-ness. If he wasn't going to partake in the most amazing huckleberry extravaganza the world has ever seen, well, then he would have to die of starvation at some point during the journey.

"But I'd offer to be your huckleberry," I told him if he died.

"Okay, thanks, I'll make a note of that," he said and pretended to jot the fact down. "Must love huckleberries while in Montana to stave off death."

By day two of our hiking trip, I was fairly confident I could identify a wild huckleberry if I saw one. I thoroughly studied the shape of the huckleberries in my pie the previous day, so I declared that I was officially on the prowl for fresh huckleberries in the wild. Under that premise, it should not have surprised Ryan when I disappeared on a trail knee-deep in bear country because he should have known that I was probably eating what I was pretty sure were huckleberries.

Ryan quickly caught me in the act purple berry-handed.

"What on God's green Earth are you doing?" Ryan said and slapped a scrumptious berry out of my hand.

My poor little huckleberry was now somewhere in the dirt, so I reached in for another one.

"I'm eating huckleberries!" I delightfully announced.

Okay, I know that we are city slickers. We city folks don't eat wild berries, for we think that we will automatically die if we do, for city folk believe that anything that grows in the wild is poisonous.

"How do you even know those are huckleberries?"

"Nom, nom, nom," I analyzed the flavor. "They taste like them!"

Ryan gave me a look, but I wasn't going to stop. He had a decision to make: either he could watch me eat all the huckleberries or he could join me and score a few for himself. Two seconds in, he saw that there weren't many berries left, so he reached in and nabbed a couple.

"Ah!" I said. "Now neither of us can be each other's huckleberry if we both die!"

"Oh, well," Ryan said as he cautiously popped the mystery berry into his mouth. "The bears will eat our bodies anyway if we drop dead under a berry bush."

"Well, at least we'll taste good," I added.

Who knew that eating huckleberries would be so morbid? We stood there for a few minutes to make sure that neither of us croaked before we moved on and jumped into a river. I have to say that life doesn't get much better than eating fresh huckleberries, hanging out by a river, and surrounding oneself with a 360-degree view of majestic nature. My Montana obsession will forever be well justified, for there is nowhere else in the world more alluring. Even Lewis and Clark couldn't resist the pull of Montana, for they spent more time there than anywhere else. Montana has a way of sucking people in and stealing their hearts as deposits to ensure eventual returns. It's a shame that winters there are as brutal as they are, else I would have moved there long ago. As it is, I have never even looked at real estate prices there for fear of actually buying something.

Ghost Towns

Speaking of real estate shopping, Ryan and I have a game that we play whenever we go to a ghost town. The game is called "pretend house shopping," and it requires us to each pick which derelict house we'd pretend-move into. So far, I have pretend-purchased a two-story house in Stumptown, Colorado that's infested with bees, an old dame of a property whose only redeeming feature is a big bay window that faces a mine in the nearly-impossible-to-get-to-unless-you-have-a-four-wheel-drive vehicle ghost town of Animas Forks, Colorado, an attractive commercial building that I hope to reopen as a store in Garnet, Montana, a fine specimen of a saloon with a decorative false front in Bannack, Montana, as well as a sizable collection of ramshackle cabins filled with drifted dirt and broken dreams scattered throughout a variety of forgotten towns in the Western United States. My pretend real estate portfolio is impressive. I have pretend-purchased many houses, none of which are even remotely inhabitable, so I will be moving into none of them anytime soon if anyone would care to join me for a cup of coffee at not a single one of them, ever.

Ghost towns appeal to my sensibilities because I like what they represent: they are visual reminders that man is fully capable of chasing his dreams. Although man may not always achieve his dreams, evidence of his indomitable spirit to try lies scattered as ruins in some of the most beautiful, remote, and rugged locations imaginable. The ashes of man's successes and failures stand as legacies that not even the greatest of heights, the coldest of climates, nor the driest of deserts are obstacles enough to suppress man's insatiable quest for riches. Indeed, no one ever walks to a ghost town. As a sort of unwritten rule, one must exert some measure of actual energy if one desires to stroll among the forgotten spirits of the past.

In modern cities, the air is something that one breathes, but in ghost towns, the air is something that one searches for. It is as though the air that hangs over a ghost town is the same air that was breathed by those who lived there long ago, and that air is incredibly spent. What little life is left in the atmosphere slowly decays along with the last breaths of all the rotting buildings. Air weighs heavy over ghost towns like a hangover unable to get out of bed. A feeling of lethargy exists when one walks down streets that lead to nothing in particular. I rather enjoy the laissez-faire attitude that ghost towns possess. They don't care where you are going, and they certainly don't give a damn where you have been. Indeed, whatever story you bring to them, they've already heard it before, for these towns were created by men that nurtured grander dreams than yours. All the former inhabitants reached bigger, worked bigger, and fell bigger as well. Ghost towns are the physical manifestations of what pies in the skies look like. They were never meant to be inhabited forever, for those towns were always meant to be eaten, preferably fresh out of the oven. What a person sees today when one walks around those vacant cities are the scattered remains of empty pie tins.

I have never photographed a ghost wandering the streets of its former stomping grounds. I have looked many a time for a ghost to share a drink with, but it's just as well that I have never found one because there has ever been an open saloon to drink in. Nevertheless, the walls always prove to be the best conversationalists anyway, and I learn more about abandoned cities simply by listening to the wind blow through the chinks of former abodes.

I don't necessarily have my own stories attached to any specific ghost town. I go to abandoned cities not to make my own stories but to hear the stories each town can tell me. It's always a gamble whether I'll be met with pursed lips or a wagging tongue, as not every ghost town has a penchant for revealing secrets. However, I have encountered a handful of talkative ones, a few of which I'll describe in further detail.

Lost Dutchman Gold Mine

It seems appropriate to start with the ghost town closest to where I live and the one that makes the news from time to time when another group of people goes missing somewhere in the desert. People come from all over the world to try their hand at finding The Lost Dutchman Gold Mine, which allegedly exists somewhere in the rugged Superstition Mountains outside of Phoenix. Unfortunately, most people don't even know what they are looking for when they wander around aimlessly in the desert because some insist that The Lost Dutchman Gold Mine isn't even a mine at all but rather a hidden cache of riches. Also, the "Lost Dutchman" wasn't even Dutch because he hailed from Germany. Alas, allow me to start this story at the beginning.

I learned about Jacob "Lost Dutchman" Waltz not at the Superstition Mountain Museum at the foot of its namesake mountain range but rather at The Vulture Gold Mine in Wickenburg, Arizona, a good 100 miles away. (A total side note that I want to throw out there is that I've learned that Elvis starred in a Western movie called *Charro!* and the chapel used in the film is, for some bizarre reason, now parked in front of the Superstition Mountain Museum. I've driven by that chapel many times before and never once considered associating that building with Elvis. I, for one, thought that he only did Hawaiian films. I guess I should now think of him as a Southern John Wayne to some degree, which strikes me as odd. Does that chapel bring a new meaning to the term "Elvis Purgatory," I wonder?)

At Vulture, I learned that Jacob Waltz was allegedly a run-of-the-mill miner who worked alongside hundreds of other miners in Arizona's most profitable hole in the ground. Pocketing gold nuggets for oneself (aka "high grading") was nearly impossible, as mining supervisors knew all the cubbyholes on people's bodies, and they never shied away from making examples of those who got caught stealing. The tour guide led me to believe that good 'ol Jacob Waltz somehow managed to circumnavigate the authorities and found a way to smuggle gold out of the mine by the fistfuls. Was he swallowing the stuff and pooping it out later? If he was, he must've had an iron gut or at least a golden stomach. Whatever tactic he used, his method apparently worked, for he went down in Phoenix history as "the reclusive German who paid for everything in gold." Not a single person knew where he got his continuous supply of gold nuggets from, for people generally assumed that his mining days were long over. He was living out his final years as a farmer on a sizable patch of irrigated dirt in the middle of nowhere near the base of the Superstition Mountains. Rumor was that he had a secret stash of gold tucked into a safe hiding spot somewhere in the rugged hills because he would disappear into that mountain range whenever he needed to line his pockets with some of the shiny stuff.

Before Jacob died in the early 1890s, he deathbed-confessed to a woman where he hid his golden stash. However, she failed to locate the loot despite being armed with a crudely drawn map. Since the gold didn't fall into her hands, the floodgates opened for anyone to find Jacob's booty. To add to the mystery, it's now generally believed that Jacob Waltz never even worked at Vulture Gold Mine, so that might mean a bona fide gold vein might actually be lurking in "the Sups" after all.

People like to tell themselves that there is a cache of gold waiting to be found somewhere in those mountains, and many people have convinced themselves that they will be the ones to find it. So far, no one has located it, and it's probably because those mountains are evil. They are called the Superstitions for a reason. If anyone desires to perish in some of the most jagged terrain imaginable, I know exactly which direction to point them in. I've slid down those mountains on my butt a few times before and busted the crap out of my tailbone, and I must say that it was a little too easy to do so. If Old Man Jacob tucked his gold in a secret spot, my hunch is that he kept it low, for I couldn't imagine an old fart climbing around those horrendous hills. Then again, what people would do for gold would probably surprise me, so no one really knows. He might have found a golden vein on the tippy top of some towering peak and conditioned himself to climb it even as a 70-year-old man, as all theories are possible.

Do I think there is gold in them thar hills? Sure, why not? Sometimes legends are born because there is an ounce of truth to them. Have I ever looked for the gold myself? Heck, ya, I have, for I always keep an eye out for gold when I go hiking out there. I'm constantly looking under rocks, which is probably a stupid thing to do because I'll surely startle a rattlesnake someday by doing that. I once found a Mormon Bible tucked under a small rock shelter on the top of Flat Iron's 5057-foot summit. It was probably put there to serve as an epiphany for whoever found it, but that sneaky trick didn't work on me. I put that bible right back where I found it and left it there for some other lost soul to discover. That bible will likely be the only thing I'll ever find in those mountains, though. I'm always searching for Gila monsters, too, for I have never seen one of those venomous creatures in the wild, either. Yes, I know they can be deadly, and I probably don't really want to come across one in nature because I have no idea what I'd do if one bit me. The most likely scenario is that I'll come across the Lost Dutchman gold only when it's the last thing my eyes will see before I drop dead right in front of it after I get bit by an elusive venomous lizard that I was always so desperate to find.

I am well aware that I will not be discovering the Lost

Dutchman gold anytime soon, but luckily there are other places to go in Arizona to scratch my itch for all things old-timey. Even though many of Arizona's original mines have long since played out along with their former cities, Arizona boasts two fine ghost towns that aren't technically ghost towns at all. Jerome and Bisbee both toyed with the idea of becoming ghost towns, but both ultimately decided against doing so. Walking around either of those towns feels relatively the same, though, since they are both slipping off the hills they're tenuously perched upon.

Both cities possess staircases that lead to nowhere, have foundations that lack houses, and contain empty buildings with peeling walls and overturned furniture. I'd be hard-pressed to pick which one I liked better because I don't prefer one's degree of decrepitness over the other. Both locations are falling apart, but that's precisely why many artist types choose to reside in those melting towns. The allure of decay provides an irresistible charm to a particular humanoid, such as myself. I don't know why I would consider moving into a house half teetering over an edge, has cracks running midway down its walls, and comes equipped with seriously questionable plumbing, but I have toyed with moving into such a dwelling on numerous occasions. Part of me wants to be brave enough to move to a town that fights to keep its head above the water. I find the tenacity of those cities tantalizing despite their inventory of despicable dwellings.

Jerome

Jerome is a strange place that many Arizona residents consider moving to but ultimately decide against actually doing. Those living there could all very well be ex-city slickers who have amazingly followed through on their personal threat; however, it's more probable that most residents originate from Clarkdale, the city that sits below Jerome's perch on Cleopatra Hill. Then again, the most likely answer is that everyone who lives there now originally came from California, but I'm only saying that because they are the usual suspects. The bottom line is that I genuinely don't know where any of Jerome's residents come from, but somehow, they are there; however, there used to be a lot more of them, as oodles of concrete foundations that no longer have homes on them attest. Jerome used to be more crowded, which is hard to imagine considering that there doesn't seem to be much space on the hill to live upon. I've often wondered what kind of people build a city on a 30-degree incline. I can only think of two types of people capable of doing such a thing: one being the Incas and two being men who desired the most convenient commute to work possible. Alas, the men who built Jerome labored in the largest copper mine Arizona had ever seen, and that mine was inconveniently located deep inside a very steep mountain.

Not only is Jerome strange, but it's also unique. No one builds cities like Jerome anymore simply because no one really needs to. The town was apparently named after some mining company chap, but the city could have just as easily been named "Vertigo," for one walks the streets of Jerome at an angle. I mean, my God, the Victorians must have had ankles of steel. Jerome today abounds in art galleries, restaurants, and saloons, but back in the day, I bet there had to have been a podiatrist office or two.

What makes Jerome so enduring is that it drips with charm

and is blessed with incredible views. It's impossible to get angry at that city even when it wickedly twists your ankle in directions that ankles were never meant to go in. Jerome is the city that hurts so good that it makes you not care. This would be a perfect town for zombies because if you injure yourself enough, you start to feel like one. A good pastime for any visitor is to watch people trip on sidewalks while eating ice cream cones. The entertainment serves as instant schadenfreude simply because you just did that exact same thing yourself two minutes ago. Yet, there is more to Jerome than just falling off curbs and trying not to get hit by cars. Indeed, one must take a gander around its massive copper mine that sits behind all the crumbling facades if one wants to get intimate with this fine specimen of a city.

Jerome's copper mine has been defunct since the 1950s, but its skeletal remains are a fantastic sight to behold. In its heyday, this mountain belched out riches beyond belief and made one man named William A. Clark one of the wealthiest people in the world. I recently fell down a rabbit hole of reading too many stories about Mr. Clark and his family, and it really surprised me that Hollywood hasn't banked on his convoluted tale, for Mr. Clark is the human personification of a gold mine waiting to be tapped. Indeed, the stories that would gush from the ghost of Mr. Clark would provide enough fodder to feed any pen pusher for years. I would think it would be impossible to starve if one had a plate full of railroads, mining, power, intrigue, art, wealth, bribery, thefts, mansions, deaths, heiresses, fires,and a bit of *Titanic* for dessert. Indeed, *The Clarks* is my favorite HBO series that hasn't been written yet. I need someone to hurry up and get that show onto the screen.

Bisbee

In comparison, if someone were to write a series about Bisbee, it wouldn't star any one man and his family but would instead star a whole lot of staircases and the strange motley of railings attached to them. Each episode would have the actors performing a scene on some random staircase, and the stairs would somehow play a pivotal role. Maybe a staircase would open up and swallow a character into another realm, or perhaps a staircase would have the hiccups and shoot someone into outer space. Maybe once in a while, a copper pipe railing would come to life and act as a jump rope before the entire staircase would turn into a river that the actor would have to bodysurf down. There are all sorts of possibilities, and all of them would be so completely stupid that they would almost be unwatchable. Bisbee's staircases are that ridiculous in real life, and they seem to lurk at every imaginable turn.

The landscape of Bisbee is hilly and looks as though it's been turned inside out. Half the town has been gutted like a fish, with its insides carted off to some processing plant. The big gaping hole on the edge of town is called "The Lavender Pit," but it doesn't mean that the festering pool of stagnant water sitting on the bottom of the crater fills the air with the fragrant scent of potpourri. Au contraire, the smell from that pit hits the nose more like the aroma of eggs rotting in the sun for the last 30 years. As to be expected, the scene looks just as dire as it smells. Indeed, this is what modern life appears like when we take a hard look at ourselves. We are essentially a disease eating the Earth like an ulcer, and our constant demand for minerals means that there will be no cure from us anytime soon.

Yet, Bisbee's mining ventures didn't always occur out in the open for the whole world to gawk at, for its humble beginnings started inside a mountain. Some 100 years and 2,000 miles of tunnels later, the Copper Queen Mine grew to become one of the largest underground mines in the world. The mine has since retired from spitting out copious amounts of copper, gold, silver, lead, and zinc and settled into being one of the world's greatest dark attractions. For a nominal fee, anyone can put on a hard hat, board a mining cart, and take a journey deep inside the Earth. I never knew that taking a mine tour was one of my favorite things in the world to do, but I discovered in Bisbee that it apparently is. I've been known to use The Copper Queen Mine tour as an excuse to drive 200 miles to a town with nothing else much to do besides taking the same mining tour that I've already done a few times before. Exploring the Earth's bowels via a little train tickles me pink and makes me very happy. Sure, I'm fully aware that the mine has caused more environmental damage than I could possibly shake a stick at, but I can somehow ignore that fact when I'm admiring the Earth from its insides.

The tour guides do nothing to romanticize the job of a miner, and I always leave the tour with the impression that mining is not for the faint of heart. Blasting the Earth from the inside while you're in it involves doing some terrifying things. The modern-day hero is the guy who is not afraid of a little bit of dynamite blasting near his face. Most of the raw materials for our cell phones come from I don't know where, and those retrieving those minerals from obscure locations probably do so at grave risk to themselves and get paid in mere peanuts. Maybe everyone should be required to work in a mine for a day and get paid a single almond to make us understand what it really takes to make the world go around. It's the people who we never see who are the ones actually steering the ship that we're all sailing on.

I don't know what it is about mining, but I could go on about it for hours even though I don't know anything about what it truly involves. What I can say, though, is that I'm a minor authority on what a place looks and feels like when mining is no longer an active contributor to a particular landscape. To be accurate, all mines remain active contributors to landscapes even when they are no longer being worked on because all mines leach, physically or metaphorically. Once a place has been torn apart, that land remains transformed forever. It will always hang on the horizon like a seared memory. In every defunct mine, it's always the land that remembers what it used to be. It's almost impossible for anyone to visit a ghost town and not get the sense that there's a feeling underfoot. It may be that a town is dead, but the ground gives off a sense of being very much alive. The soil is a part of this Earth, and no matter what form it takes, it will always remember the landscape from which it sprung.

Rhyolite

Ghost towns are curious places because they feel a bit off. Humans don't like to fail, so placing oneself inside a city that didn't quite make it jars the human psyche. Abandoned cities tend to make one feel a bit fritzy inside, and there is something about that strange feeling that I oddly relish.

If someone wants to bask in that particular fritzy feeling, it is overwhelmingly omnipresent at the Goldwell Open Air

Museum Sculpture Park on the windswept plains of Rhyolite, Nevada. There, one can stand before an eclectic collection of sculptures and wonder who placed them there and why. As visitors walk around a motley collection of lonely statues, they catch glimpses of the ruins of a three-story bank hovering over them like a shadow.

The most poignant group of sculptures there was created by an artist named Albert Szukalski. He titled his creation *The Last Supper*, yet his thirteen plaster-cast ghosts will forever wait for a meal to be served on a table that isn't there. It hardly matters that the place for a table sits vacant, as there's nothing inside those ghosts either. The whole sculpture is about the space that exists outside of us and how we all quietly internalize a feeling of emptiness. Those ghosts show us what we look like when we allow our true selves to be exposed. Stripped of our skin, we are no different than those hollow plaster-cast spirits. The wisdom of the ghosts instructs that there is nothing to hide from when we allow ourselves to be revealed.

The artist anticipated that the sculptures would survive maybe two years in the harsh desert environment, but 35-plus years later, the artwork is still there. Those sculptures stand quietly in the desert without any fanfare, without any roof, and without any walls. They are simply there. It is difficult to say whether they look lonely or not. My first impression was that they did look lonely out there in the middle of pure nothingness, but gradually the idea grew on me that the sculptures wouldn't look right anywhere that wasn't desolate. Our natural state of being is alone, and we often mistakenly surround ourselves with too many people, too many buildings, and too many thoughts. Those statues have it correct to remove themselves from the motley of everything. They are precisely where they need to be, and it's our human duty to come to them. I had to resist the feeling of wanting to get on that platform and live out the rest of my life right there next to them since they seemed to be the only ones who knew what it takes to survive.

Bodie

Keeping with the theme of imaginary possibilities, I've just now decided to hop into my handy-dandy time machine and beam myself back to Bodie, California, circa 1876, because, why the heck not? Actually, if I had a time machine, going to boomtown Bodie would probably not be the first place I'd travel to, for I've already reserved that destination as Ancient Egypt. Yet, I have to admit that Bodie would hover somewhere in the teens on my top twenty list of time travel destinations. That being said, had I been an adult in the 1870s, male or female, I likely would have found myself in Bodie because that was where everyone who wanted to get rich quickly went. I have this hunch that I harbor a latent personality trait of someone who would have been stupid enough to risk everything at trying my hand at the great outdoor gambling hall. I know this to be true because I tapped into that feeling when I visited Bodie in the early 2000s, and it certainly looked like a place that I would have been willing to take a chance on.

The city of Bodie was located above the treeline at 8,000 feet, smack dab in the middle of absolute nowhere, and my first impression was that it didn't seem like a place that should ever have existed. The landscape surrounding Bodie was a vast void filled with a seemingly endless supply of wind, dust, and grass.

Not a single tree broke up the monotony of pure nothingness. The utter treelessness of the place gave me the feeling that there must have always been something wrong with Bodie, and it was hardly a wonder why the city was abandoned. Indeed, Bodie wasn't built for generations to inhabit but was created because humans needed somewhere to stay for the time being. No one ever chose to live in Bodie because they wanted to; people moved to Bodie because they felt compelled to. Part of Bodie's allure was its austereness, for it presented itself as an empty slate for anyone to carve one's name across.

Although it was evident that no one lived in Bodie anymore, it appeared as though no one bothered to inform the buildings that they were standing empty. The city survives suspended in what the park service calls a state of "arrested decay," which is another way of saying that they are afraid to hurt the building's feelings by telling them they are abandoned. Bodie's sole purpose in life now is to stand there and look pretty, but I have to say that it was hard to resist the suspicion that there had to be a switch hiding somewhere that would turn the city back on. Basically, the place functioned as every photographer's wet dream come true, and the only regret I had when I ran around there was that I wasn't lugging around a daguerreotype camera. I had no idea what year it was supposed to be in Bodie, but I told myself that it was the 1890s, and there was very little to suggest that it wasn't true. Okay, maybe the old gas station hinted that it might have been at least the 1930s. Also, the leaning streetlamps and telephone poles did suggest that the turn of the century had already happened. Lastly, an old rusty car melting in the grass confirmed that 1890 had definitely come and gone, but it didn't matter; it all remained

1890 to me because that was where I wanted to be. Bodie stood as a testament that the past was once here. Time was nothing but a flash in the pan. Time sizzled once and then evaporated.

Bodie was built for one reason, and that reason was money. The bonanza that created Bodie was short-lived, and man was just as quick to leave the place as he was quick to build it. Although the town was still there, its inhabitants certainly were not, but they left evidence of their existence in their wake. They left the outline of their identities behind them, and walking around Bodie was akin to getting intimate with humanity's shadow.

Humans are strange creatures, and I sometimes struggle to understand who we are. I tried to grasp the purpose of creating something so completely, only to let it go in an instant. Those telephone poles that went over the hill and off to the distance, who in Bodie was using them now? No one, absolutely no one. Yet, there they were, standing exactly where they were initially placed. Those telephone lines stood there waiting to do their job for people that no longer existed. Their reason to be no longer mattered. That basically described Bodie. It had no *raison d'être* anymore, and that feeling was oddly identifiable. Humans harbor the capacity to make themselves obsolete whenever they invent new technologies. It's hard to shake the feeling that we are slowly creating a world that will have no reason for our being in it. The entire planet will become one big Bodie when it floats in space without humans inhabiting it.

Salton Sea

Photography is an art, and cities like Bodie beg to be photographed. Indeed, beauty is always in the eye of the beholder, but ruins aren't always beautiful. Something beyond beauty must draw so many people to places like Bodie. Everyone tries to photograph something that exists inside themselves when they see something that speaks to them. In essence, photography is a way for people to express how they see themselves in their environment without actually inserting themselves into an image. Taking pictures is a way to express one's mind's eye for all to see, although sometimes that vision gets lost in translation.

Sometimes it's impossible to express what a person sees when they snap a particular picture. This, I can speak with authority, as even I struggle to understand what I was trying to express when I took pictures of desiccated fish and rusted lawn chairs rotting on a beach in one of the bleakest locations on Earth. Alas, it's almost impossible for anyone to visit the Salton Sea and not come home with an assortment of unexplainable pictures.

I was obsessed with the idea of visiting the Salton Sea long before I journeyed there. Yet, I should have gone there sooner than I actually did because had I made it there years earlier, most of what I wanted to photograph would have still been rapidly decaying on the beach. As it was, I was too late, and everything I had come for was gone. In particular, I came for a trailer. One of the first photographs I ever saw online in the first throes of the internet age was an image of an Airstream trailer that was metamorphosing into a heap of nothingness on a patch of land that looked like it was once possibly a beach. The sheer oddness of the scene made me wonder where this whole spectacle was quietly happening, and I was taken aback when I learned that it was occurring at a location I could easily drive to in California.

Bombay Beach, where the aforementioned trailer was located, was a city born due to a mistake. Under normal circumstances, no one carves out a city 220 feet below sea level, but they do so when events accidentally create a lake in the middle of a normally parched stretch of barrenness. Civil engineers accidentally created the Salton Sea at the turn of the 20th century when they attempted to divert the Colorado River into agricultural canals. The engineers essentially missed their target, and for two years, the river flowed into an ancient seabed and thus created a lake in the middle of the desert. Cities sprung up around the lake but then shriveled in tandem with rising salinity. The lake had no outlet, so every day, the sun stuck a straw into it and greedily sucked out the moisture while deftly avoiding swallowing any salt.

The Armageddon-style destruction that defined the cities around the Salton Sea was something I wanted to see with my own eyes, except I wasn't in enough of a hurry to get there as I needed to be. I guess I just assumed that weird melting spectacles occurred at a rate way slower than they actually did, and I had a rude awakening when I went to visit the trailer, and it was nowhere to be found. Evidently, it did not wait for me to wave goodbye to it, and the only proof that it was ever there were some wood and metal shavings piled in a heap. The highly evocative and extremely photogenic trailer I saw parked in a strange salty abyss was completely gone. I was thoroughly bummed because there I was, holding a camera in a landscape that swallowed the one thing I had come to photograph.

The dry, salty seabed erased everything. The rotting smell of urban carcasses hovered in the spaces where objects used to be. I desperately wished that if I could take a picture of anything, I wished that I could take a photo of that smell – the smell of dead tilapia and abandoned 1950s. Both Ryan and I could only stand there while holding our breath for so long because of the aroma of dead fish and, I didn't know, sulfur, or, as Ryan assumed, cyanide, was making us nauseous. It was easy to wonder where the hell we were even though we physically drove ourselves to that very spot.

"Didn't you say there were other things to see around here?" Ryan said with his face muffled in his sleeve.

"Ya," I muffled back. "There's that Salvation Mountain place and that weird Slab City."

Ryan took his face away from his sleeve and defiantly said, "This place is atrocious. I say we ditch this hellscape and go somewhere else."

I took one last look at our personal patch of Armageddon, and said, "Sounds good to me. Besides, anywhere else can't be much worse."

Actually, Slab City could have been worse than Bombay Beach, but we were willing to take the gamble. We were quickly learning that nothing was a sure thing around the Salton Sea and that anything had the potential to disappoint.

We first spent some time pretend-real estate shopping at Salton City, "a large, planned resort community," and had the pick of the litter as to which abandoned unfinished tract home to pretend-purchase. We then made a little jaunt over to Salton Sea Beach Marina and debated which boat slip was the most desirable one to pretend-own. After that, we moseyed on over to Desert Shores, thinking that there had to be at least one decent-looking community surviving in this crappy landscape, but we were wrong, as everything was half-abandoned there too. I actually don't mind seeing an empty concrete swimming pool every now and again because the image of abandonment is kind of bittersweet when it's a pool. Still, there was just something about the Desert Shores' abandoned pool that made the whole town look especially dismal. In essence, that empty pool served as a reminder of just how utterly dreams failed there.

By the time we got to Slab City, we had zero expectations save for more despair. Even the palm trees we saw all over the place were folded over and missing their tops. Normally, palm trees invoke feelings of joy and happiness, but the palm trees fringing the Salton Sea invoked no such feelings. Salton Sea palm trees sucked their firewater straight from the pits of hell and stood as pathetic reminders that humans weren't all that fantastic. Alas, none of this would have made a news flash to those that lived in Slab City, though. Yet, it was questionable whether the people in Slab City even got the news, as that place was so far out there that it made me wonder if anyone there even cared about what was going on in the rest of the world.

Where to start with Slab City? The name alone made me want to drop everything and live out my remaining days in such a gloriously named town. Okay, I'm lying, but only because that has got to be hand's down one of the most unromantically named cities on the entire planet. Slab City. Is it even an official city? I don't think it is. It's more like a glorified refugee camp for the modern-day anarchist. Not that there's anything wrong with that because even those that drop out of society need a place to live. Slab City is there for them, like a catch-all net for those who try to leave but can't.

However, that being said, don't expect to be greeted by the welcome wagon when you first roll in, as someone yelling, "Get out of here, tourists!" from the passenger side of a pickup truck is a more likely scenario. This I can confirm as an unequivocal fact, but anyone is, of course, welcome to try to get an alternative greeting from a Slabber (a Slabbite? A Slabberdasher?) if they feel so inclined.

Slab City is there because the military no longer is. Concrete slabs exist where military buildings used to be. Certainly, the irony that Slab City used to be a military installation isn't lost on those that reside there today, for it takes a clever mind to eke out a day-to-day existence in such a forlorn location. The individuals who live in this anti-paradise do so without access to running water, electricity, trash collection, or any other modern services, often in 100-degree heat and often, surprisingly, on frigidly cold nights. The desert is not a kind place, but neither is society. If one gets pushed far enough, one could end up there, likely landing on one of the threadbare chairs facing the stage at their sole entertainment venue, "The Range." Indeed, just because someone gets pushed to the fringes of society, it doesn't mean they have given up their God-given right to be entertained.

If I had to summarize Slab City in one image, it would be of those cushionless lazy boy recliners and broken couches lined up all mishmash for the audience at their open-air theater. What incredible lives each chair and couch must have lived to end up there, all torn apart. It didn't take much imagination to see the seats as the personifications of the Slab City citizens. Each seat was uniquely battered in its own special way, but each harbored the potential to hold someone's weight. These seats were not about to give up, even though they were already thrown away once before. Someone picked each one of them out of the trash and carted them there, to that nowhere-of-a-place to most, to that somewhere-of-a-place to few. Slab City was sitting on the back burner of the world, slowly simmering in its little pot and piping its whistle to let those nearby know when the tea was ready. It was hardly possible to doubt the tenacity of human potential when I saw what the heck was going on in one of the world's most unlikely places. People were actually living there, like really being alive and not simply existing. I deduced that this had to be where most of the world's lemonade came from, for there existed nowhere else where people were more skilled at what to do with a whole lot of lemons.

I opted not to take a seat while we talked to a resident who made himself comfortable on a broken chair at The Range. He gave us a flier for an upcoming live music event on Saturday. I was instantly intrigued, not by the advertised music event itself, but by the fact that they had access to printers. It left me with so many questions. Namely, I wanted to know how it was that they didn't have a single chair that genuinely qualified as an actual seat, yet, they somehow had access to a xerox printer and nice sheets of pink paper. I was curious to know if some Slab City patron of the arts kindly dropped off freshly minted fliers in the middle of the night like an anarchist Santa Claus. Or was there some trailer chock-full of hodgepodge office gadgets hooked up to a solar panel that I wasn't seeing? Thus, I point-blank asked the guy how they printed the fliers. The answer was nowhere near as exciting as I was anticipating. He said they made the fliers at a print shop four miles away in Niland. In fact, he basically said that Slab City wouldn't survive at all if Niland wasn't right down the street. Thus, my image of an off-grid anarchy "Fuck You, society!" utopia was only half-realized. I didn't consider that these people needed somewhere to shop for toilet paper and jarred spaghetti sauce. I could say that the Salton Sea disappointed me again because I didn't discover a secret place to escape from the rest of the world but saying such a statement would be a misconception. What Slab City was, plain and simple, was reality. It wasn't trying to be anything or anywhere else, and that was the elemental beauty of the place. Slab City just was.

Salvation Mountain

Another place that just was but might not be anything in the very near future was the creation known as *Salvation Mountain*. This pyramid of painted dirt was constructed by a superhuman named Leonard Knight, and he created his melting masterpiece as his personal testament to his piety to God. To say that his mountain of painted words and fake rivers was folk art on steroids doesn't describe it enough. This monstrosity of devotional art was a creation that exists on a level all by itself and knows no peers, for there exists no parallel to his vision. Many people go to places in search of God, and those that find him don't usually feel compelled to carve their discovery in humongous letters across the face of a shifting landscape, but that describes exactly what Leonard did.

Leonard was a modern pilgrim in the desert searching for something beyond himself. It's possible that he didn't know what he was looking for, but he certainly found something when he found Jesus. It was evident that something about Jesus resonated deep inside Leonard's entire being, for he gave himself over to him completely. Everything that Leonard did, he did for a cause that became much greater than himself.

The mountain that he made was a steadfast meditation on his sincere allegiance to the God that redeemed him. He wasn't going to waiver if God wasn't going to. The two lived together in the desert for the rest of Leonard's life, which amounted to nearly 30 long years, and the mountain he left behind was a testament to their faith in each other. Unfortunately, Leonard was shuttled off to a hospital by the time we arrived, and I regret that we missed the opportunity to meet this amazing desert fellow.

In addition to creating a mountain, Leonard created a labyrinth. The maze of corridors served as the arteries that wound through the crevices of his own circuitous mind. Not a single visitor who walks the pathways of Leonard's hypothetical head will ever wonder what kind of thoughts entertained him, for it will forever remain obvious that he was taken with a singular reflection. This man thought of one thing and one thing only, and that was the meaning of love.

He simply wanted people to believe that love was possible, and, for him, there was no greater message than that. It is rather fitting that such a message was carved upon the surfaces of perhaps the most unlovable location on the planet. He knew that love doesn't always come easy, but he also knew that love was something worth fighting for. He was a warrior for love, and the mountain he made was his de facto battleground. *Salvation Mountain* stands today as a Gettysburg of peace, and all the words that Leonard wrote upon it are memorials of his message. His mountain can be interpreted as a religious site if one wants, but to do so, I think, misconstrues what he was trying to say. His message defies denomination and allows people of all faiths (or no faith at all) equal access to his heart. He opened himself to the world to share his joy for all things on this planet, and his passion was infectious.

Leonard Knight proved that love was indeed possible, even in the most unlikely places.

CHAPTER THREE:
Italy, Oct 2002

Where do I want to go before I die?

I've always loved history, and I can recall precisely how my interest started. I spent the greater part of my childhood cooped up indoors during some long Wisconsin winters, and I spent most of that time looking for creative things to do. I mostly did artsy-fartsy things, but I started to enjoy reading when I got a little bit older. I scoured the house a few times over for anything interesting to read, and it didn't take me long to discover that my choices were limited to either crime novels or art history books. I never once picked up a crime book other than to decide it was something that I didn't want to read, so ancient Chinese and Egyptian art it was, which ended up suiting me well.

When Eric and I had our "Where do you want to go before you die?" conversation, my answer was unequivocally Pompeii.

"You know, that ancient city buried by a volcano," I stated.

Eric, of course, had heard of it. "Oh, you don't have to explain it to me," he said.

I forgot to mention earlier that we made a deal when I agreed to go with him to visit his hallowed chicken coop. That deal was that if he got to check off his chicken coop, I would then get to check off Pompeii.

"A deal's a deal," I reminded him a few years later.

"What deal are you referring to?" Eric inquired.

"I'm ready to check off my bucket list's top item," I said.

"Oh? And which item is that?" he wanted to know.

"Pompeii!" I exclaimed, knowing full well that Eric wasn't

the world's biggest traveler.

"Well, have fun going!" Eric replied.

I was miffed that he didn't remember the deal we had.

"Don't you remember agreeing to go with me when the time came?" I asked him.

He had no memory of making such a deal.

"I agreed to go to Italy?" he questioned. "I don't know if I can get the time off to travel that far.

Seriously? I thought to myself. That was the oldest American excuse in the book. I have this theory that Americans are afraid to travel very far because they fear their small little world will somehow not be there for them when they return. Americans love making excuses, and I suspect our national ailment is separation anxiety. Even most of my co-workers at the travel agency preferred to stay home. Many didn't even touch their annual $1,500 company-provided travel bank funds except to buy tickets for other family members to fly in and visit them, thus alleviating them from having to go anywhere themselves. I, on the other hand, calculated my travel funds down to the last penny and mathematically figured out how many places in the world I could ship myself to for $1,500.

"I'm sure you could find time to travel to Italy for free," I said to him. "Remember, I have all that travel bank money to pay for airline tickets."

I had every intention of traveling to Italy for my next major excursion, and the only question now was whether or not Eric would go with me. It was surprisingly hard to convince him to let go of his American life for ten whole days to experience life on the other side of the planet; however, he eventually consented about one month before the selected travel date. He struggled to fight off his inner reservations, but the pull of Italy ultimately proved too hard to resist.

The Roman Forum

Rome is a place where the Western mind intuitively knows. A Westerner can't look at Roman ruins and not see reflections of themselves staring back at them. The Roman world was built of concrete and marble, and many of their public buildings looked a lot like how ours do today. Indeed, ancient Rome appears familiar to the Western eye because its ruins look eerily familiar. Hauntingly, deep down, the Western mind knows that the fallen columns and broken buildings are nothing more than windows into our very own future.

I went to Rome with preconceived notions. I thought I already knew what Rome would look like since I had seen it depicted in thousands of pictures. Rare is the person who can say that they don't know what the Coliseum looks like, for I suspect that Westerners are born with that image imprinted upon our brains. Rome is what we see when we close our eyes to sleep, for it is there where most of our memories discreetly reside.

Ancient Rome was the muse for generations of artists, and no art museum is complete without its painted collection of crumbling facades. It's easy to imagine what the Roman Forum looked like when it teemed with vendors, shoppers, Senators, politicians, priests, worshippers, and Vestal Virgins because it strikes the viewer as oddly familiar. The Forum was where all of Rome used to meet, and walking amidst its ruins didn't feel strange to me. It felt oddly normal to walk its processional way as if I had walked that road a hundred times before. There was something intuitive about the Forum that didn't need any explaining. All it took was one look at the pillars that seemingly held up nothing to know that they were holding up the Earth's ceiling. "When Rome falls, so will the world." Venerable Bede's words rang in my ears as an echo unsilenced by centuries.

Most trips to Italy start at the Forum because it's nearly impossible to know the rest of the country without first getting intimate with its foundation. It was here, in this former marshy lake, where Western civilization originally sprung. As I admired the ruins, I couldn't help but think I was looking at everything and nothing simultaneously. So many buildings were gone, yet nothing seemed missing. The entire place was empty yet crawling with people. Before me was time in an instant. Looking at all the damaged buildings, deserted temples, lonely arches, headless statues, and vast expanses of space was akin to witnessing the rise and fall of civilization in a single glance. Soon, too, modern society will meet its ultimate fate. Looking at those ruins was like seeing time march forward and backward with the same step. The Forum was where Rome began and ended and where much of humanity arrived and departed.

The Colosseum

The Forum is where Westerners go when they want to sow new ideas, but the Colosseum is where Westerners go when they want to take those ideas away. The Forum represents humankind's virtues, but the Colosseum represents our most hideous crimes. For every yin, there's a yang, and the Forum would hardly exist without the Colosseum standing in its shadow.

Just like the Forum, the Colosseum was also an oddly familiar place. Anyone who has been to a modern-day sports arena has vicariously stepped inside Rome's Colosseum, for the layout was practically the same. My feet instinctively knew how to navigate its entrances, hallways, staircases, and seats. It took no effort at all to find myself looking down at the Colosseum's missing floor to watch an event that wasn't going to happen, for this stadium's active days were long over. Yet, every generation becomes the inheritor of the Roman psyche so long as the Colosseum remains standing. We understand humankind best when we place ourselves in the very spot where we once enjoyed watching life suffer via the infliction of our very own hands.

It almost felt wrong to stand where the spectators once stood, for the Colosseum represents a time in history that showed humankind at its most heinous. Killing humans and beasts for the sake of entertainment defies comprehension, yet everyone can understand it. It wasn't hard for me to wrap my head around why the Colosseum existed. Death and gore sell; they always have. There wasn't much to it. Looking at where the Colosseum floor used to be, it wasn't hard to imagine the spectacles that used to unfold there. In an age before movies, this was where people went to forget their daily problems. It was here where people watched others suffer fates worse than their own.

The Colosseum may be in ruins, but the gladiator shows have never stopped. Modern man is the gladiator now, for we've inherited their Earth. We no longer fight lions but instead fight the entire world. Everything is game for the modern-day gladiator show, be it the atmosphere, water, minerals, animals, or people. The Colosseum is round, just like the planet, which makes them equivalent battlegrounds. It is us versus the entire globe now. Gladiators fought with swords, nets, tridents, and spears, whereas we today fight with money, lobbyists, AK-47s, and drones. The whole world is a stage, and everyone is in the audience. Modern society sits back and watches the world burn while cheering for the victor, who also happens to be the loser. What good is watching the world die when the winners will lose the only home they know?

Churches and Caravaggio

Moving away from the Colosseum, the Forum, and everything ancient, it was time to go inside and look at something dark. I don't mean dark, as in morbid (we had the Colosseum for that), but dark in the sense of lacking light. Rome was a city of churches, and most of them, we soon discovered, were not basking in glorious rays of sunshine emitted through a plethora of stained glass windows.

Linguistically speaking, the ancient Romans referred to their large public buildings as basilicas. These large, aisled structures served many purposes, such as holding court and other official functions. Gradually, Christian churches adopted the basilica's shape by embracing its central nave, longitudinal side aisles, clerestory windows, and semicircular apse as if they were their own inventions. Over time, the word's original meaning was forgotten and became synonymous with the term for religious structures.

Built in AD 324, The Basilica of Saint John Lateran is the oldest Christian basilica in Rome. Technically, it's wrong to call it a basilica, for it holds the title of "Archbasilica" due to its elevated importance. In case anyone needs a visual to demonstrate this church's place in the hierarchy of Roman basilicas, the world's tallest ancient Egyptian obelisk stands conveniently parked right in front of it as a beacon to guide the masses to this very spot. In fact, Rome is the proud looter of thirteen such ancient obelisks, and the stories of those obelisks are just as fascinating as any story of ancient Rome itself. Alas, there are not enough pages in this book to allow me to digress about obelisks; however, I do want to mention that the "Lateran" obelisk once stood in the center of the Circus Maximus (after having stood for roughly 1,750 years beside the great temple of Amun in Karnak). It was brought to Rome in the early 4th century on a specially designed "obelisk ship" that carried the heavy object underwater. That the ancient Romans were smitten with ancient Egypt makes them highly relatable to me since we have that fascination in common.

The Saint John Lateran Archbasilica underwent numerous interior redesigns, and its current form dripped in gold leaf and marble. Being inside there set the bar pretty high for all the basilicas that were due to follow, but this being Rome, we had no fear of being disappointed. I gained a lot of respect for Rome's religious buildings after I realized that most of them never sold off their original art. One can step inside a Roman church and witness an original creation. No disconnect existed between the artwork and the interiors because all was a symbiotic whole. Indeed, much of the artwork encountered in museums today have been unceremoniously peeled off of some church's walls. The worst thing about museums today is that they typically lack context. They have this habit of raping pieces from their places and taking shapes away to hang shapeless. People race around museums in a futile attempt to see everything in an hour. Masterpiece after masterpiece eventually becomes masterpieceless. Museums, I'm sorry to say, tend to be too rich for anyone's blood.

Roman churches were dark, and they made the paintings that hung in them appear even darker. Tucked in little alcoves, it was often difficult to see the faded artworks under such dismal lighting. To properly appreciate a painting, one needed to put a coin into a small metered machine that turned on a light for a paltry few minutes. It was always easy to know where the best art was in any Italian religious building simply by following the "ohs" and "ahs" that echoed down the corridors. The distinctive sound of someone dropping a coin into one of those machines was music to every visitor's ears, and just one flick of someone's wrist was all it took to gather a massive crowd. I can't remember now what art we saw inside The Archbasilica of Saint John Lateran, but I'm sure that whatever we saw was fabulous. All art in Rome had a way of blowing our minds; however, my eyes were seeking one specific artist, and his art wasn't hanging anywhere inside that building.

I came to Italy for Pompeii, but I came to Rome for Caravaggio. I encountered my first Caravaggio painting at the Louvre when I came across his convincing depiction of the "Death of the Virgin." There was something so three-dimensionally lifelike about the recumbent image of Mary that convinced me that this artist was someone to be reckoned with. I had to look at the date when the artist created this painting at least three times before I finally believed that the year 1606 was not a misprint. The image was so realistic, so emotional, and so haunting. There was nothing flat about it. The picture had everything to do with how the light emerged from the shadows. This was a masterpiece in the truest sense of the term, and I was instantly enamored with this man named Caravaggio.

I declared it my personal mission to spend all my loose change on illuminating every Caravaggio painting that was to be found within the vicinity of Rome. Many people come to Rome on pilgrimages, and our artistic voyage wouldn't be all that different from a religious one, for we would be visiting quite a few churches. Most of his paintings were spread out amongst nine separate locations, and we had two full days to hit each and every one. I didn't want to leave a single Caravaggio unturned, so I learned where all his paintings were ahead of time. I did some serious strategizing and planned to sneak one in wherever we could. The Colosseum was a fifteen-minute walk to The Doria Pamphilj Gallery, where his *Rest on the Flight into Egypt* was hanging. From there, the Pantheon was along the way to the church of Sant'Agostino, where we would see *The Madonna of Loreto*. It was a three-minute walk from the Pantheon to The Church of St. Louis of the French, where three of his paintings were hanging in their original positions. Caravaggio thus dictated the itinerary, and we weaved ourselves throughout Rome on a grandiose artistic journey.

We successfully managed to hit them all, and I didn't declare a single one my favorite. Each painting was individual, poignant, and illuminating in its own special way. There was never any gray in a Caravaggio painting; life, to him, was either black or it was white. His works were an expression of how he saw the world. Life was vulgar, or it was saintly – there was no in-between. On his part, he familiarized himself with the vulgar side quite intimately. He was only as religious as a man who was capable of killing another man in a brawl could possibly be. He painted religious scenes because he had to make a living, but he manipulated the subjects so that they would outwardly conform to his personal worldview. My impression was that he was not someone who looked at the world through rose-colored glasses. He always managed to find something of himself in the religious stories he was commissioned to paint. It was this darkness about everything that surrounded him in real life that greatly intrigued me. He was definitely the bad boy of Old Master artists.

People are attracted to a Caravaggio the same way a lanternfish draws in its prey. His works are easily recognizable as his subject moves out of the shadows and into a single blaring spark of illumination. By using his palette of contrasting darks and whites, he seized a pivotal moment in a subject's narrative and froze their transformation. He was insightful in a way that no other artist before or after him has ever been.

When he painted David presenting the severed head of Goliath, he used his own head to serve as Goliath's model. Most of the severed head is bathed in darkness, except for the portion that catches a bit of light bouncing off David's heroic body. As an earthly plea for divine intervention, he sent this painting as a gift to a cardinal who had the power to pardon him for murder. He was traveling back to Rome hoping for that pardon when he died en route, aged 38. Rumor was that quite a few people preferred him dead for a variety of reasons. Me – I wished he could've lived forever.

Ostia

We budgeted our time to allow for one day trip away from Rome's city center and ultimately chose to spend that precious day at Rome's ancient seaport, Ostia. Rome technically relied on two seaports to receive and store all the grain needed to keep the populace from rioting; however, Ostia offered more for a tourist than Portus (the large artificial harbor that we get the word "port" from) did when comparing the two destinations.

I had read that *Ostia Antica* ("ancient Ostia") was a large archaeological site filled with ancient buildings, frescoes, and mosaics. The city was quite possibly Rome's earliest founded colony, for the Romans knew early on that they needed access to the sea. In its original form, Ostia sat at the mouth of the Tiber River, but its current position placed it two miles away. The Tiber River silted up and incrementally moved further away from Ostia until it finally left it high and dry sometime in the 5th century. Until the inevitable occurred, Ostia peaked with 100,000 inhabitants at a time when Rome was home to one million. Being at the receiving end of all the goods that came to shore made Ostia a blue-collar city in the truest sense of the term, for this was where money was to be made. With wealth came marble to beautify well-to-do homes, so this was a city destined to look amazing in ruins.

I was prepared for the site to be large; however, I have no idea why I didn't think to pack a warm enough jacket to wear while walking around it. It was late October when we visited, but my brain told me I was going to a place where it never got cold. For some reason, I thought Italy was always balmy, so I packed nothing that would have staved off a chilly autumn breeze. Eric was naturally not impressed when I asked him if he was using his jacket.

"Of course, I'm using my jacket!" he said. "Don't you see that I'm wearing it?"

"Ya, well, if you ever get too hot, let me know, and I'll wear your jacket for you," I replied and walked headlong into a bracing wind.

"What's with you never dressing right?" Eric asked me. "You bring along a jacket when it's a million degrees outside, but only wear a flimsy pullover when it's ridiculously cold. You have the worst dressing sense of anyone I've ever met."

I didn't disagree with him and reiterated that I would take his jacket off his hands if he got tired of wearing it.

"Okay, I'll take it off when this blasted wind stops blowing," he said, which, of course, it never did. It wasn't his fault that I was foolish for not dressing appropriately, so I owned my mistake and told myself that I liked being cold. We were at Ostia, for goodness sake, and the ruins were astounding. This place was a precursor to Pompeii if there ever was one, and all that was missing was a looming volcano. All around us were the remnants of a formally great city, replete with crumbling apartment blocks, deserted mansions, ruined restaurants, empty bakeries, abandoned baths, a gutted necropolis, an idle theater, and a vacated Forum. Yet, there was something pastoral about the landscape that reminded me of old English paintings in the vein of Constable or Gainsborough. The rustic colors of brick ruins were tucked neatly below forests of umbrella pine trees, and being there made me feel like I had walked straight into a picture I had seen a hundred times before in countless museums. The scenery looked so familiar that I felt comfortable being there, yet the ruins were so alien that they seemed to have landed from outer space.

Looking back on it now, what I remember most about Ostia were the apartment blocks, the mosaics, the toilets, the cats, and the necropolis. I particularly recall the apartment blocks, mainly because they appeared so incredibly modern. The cramped apartment towers were very relatable, and it didn't take much imagination for me to believe that the ghost of one of my past lives resided inside one of those homes.

Ostia was a city of plebians, and they lived on top of each other in dense, unsanitary apartment buildings, so if the ghost of me was to be found anywhere, it would be found inside one of those buildings. Yup, that would be me, alright, just a nobody ghost living forever without indoor plumbing. If anyone were to follow my spirit, they would find me walking down the street whenever I needed to use the public toilet. If they followed my ghost there, they would notice that the public restrooms lacked any stalls, and they would see how all the ghosts would have to sit next to each other in one long row of stone-cold seats. They would also likely notice the charming mosaics decorating the bathroom floor, although they might comment how those mosaics were not as fancy as the ones they saw in other public spaces. Tourists might eventually grow to suspect that all the cats running around were the ancient souls of former Ostians, such as the one my ghost was no doubt inhabiting. It was through the cats that all the souls could continue going to plays, relax in the baths, ride on the chariots, buy bread from the shops, drink water from the aqueducts, and sleep on the mosaic floors without anyone paying them heed. Ostia was a Pompeii that never met its Vesuvius.

Speaking of buried cities, the rows of empty tombs outside of Ostia proper were a veritable city in and of itself. Eric and I lost each other quite a few times while we walked amongst the graves, and it got me thinking how strange it was to have a cemetery just beyond the city's wall. Life was typically short, and death resided just beyond a city's gate.

Many tombs were elaborate constructions, replete with dining sets for ritual banquets and stone seats for anyone to sit and contemplate the meaning of it all. "Why are we here?" one might have wondered. "Why am I born only to eventually die?" might have been another timeless conundrum. It was impossible to wander around Ostia's City of the Dead and not push aside countless morbid thoughts. This was where death was acknowledged as being an integral part of living. There's no life without death, and the ancient Romans were not afraid to embrace that knowledge and make it an essential part of their entire whole.

Alas, I should mention that I was insanely jealous of Eric's jacket the whole time we were there, but I was too cheap to do anything about it. There might have been a gift shop nearby where I could have bought a jacket, but I didn't bother to look for it. I instead chose to remain cold the entire day, and by doing so, I managed to catch a chill that would soon come back to haunt me.

On to Pompeii!

We took an early train to Naples, and I arrived there seriously dragging my feet. I felt a slight cold coming on, but I didn't think it was anything that a second cup of coffee couldn't resolve. I saw a coffee stand, but I was still somewhat new to Italy and had yet to understand how Italian coffee stands worked. I had yet to learn to order my coffee in thimbles and to refer to coffee as "espresso," but Naples was the perfect place to teach me how not to order coffee in Italy.

Of course, my first mistake was asking for "coffee." The two mid-20-year-old strapping Italians who looked like they lifted weights between making drinks did not hide their desire to punch me in the face for ordering anything that wasn't a tiny thimble of espresso. They immediately threw their arms in the air and acted like I tossed a cog into their machine. I don't understand Italian, but I was pretty sure they were saying, "Can you believe this fucking tourist ordering a stupid cup of coffee? Do we even know how to make regular coffee? Just pour her an espresso and fill the rest of the cup with spit. That should teach her to order a goddamn cup of coffee in Italy." I stood there regretfully as they took their sweet time making my special drink. I learned to only order espressos everywhere else after that.

With my prized, possibly spit-laced full-sized cup of coffee in hand, we proceeded to board the convenient "Circumvesuviana" train that literally ran in circles around Mount Vesuvius. The train allowed for a slightly elevated view of the sprawl that was Naples, and I found it fascinating that such a convoluted city existed under the shadow of a looming volcano famous for blowing its top and burying cities. I also found it more than curious how people seemed to completely disregard the fact that Vesuvius was not a dormant threat. Millions of people lived in the shadow of a ticking time bomb, and life seemed to go on like nothing was unusual. Yet, the whole place felt like it was living on borrowed time to me. That being said, all it took was one look at Naples to give me the impression that Naples didn't seem to care very much if its whole existence ended up being temporary. The town had a "run by the Mafia" feel about it, and I wouldn't necessarily call its vibe "organized chaos" but more like "pure chaos," and that, I admitted, was quite intoxicating. I decided that I could stare at Naples for hours, but it was out of my view almost as soon as I saw it. We arrived in Pompeii in less than 40 minutes.

Pompeii

I've always liked the idea of Pompeii. Just the thought that an ancient city could rise out of history's literal ash heap fascinates me to no end. I had devoured so many stories about Pompeii's resurrected existence that I felt like I knew the city before I even placed a foot there. I kept saying to myself, "We're going to Pompeii! We're going to Pompeii!" the whole ride over, which made me feel like Dorothy from the *Wizard of Oz* when she kept saying, "There's no place like home, there's no place like home." Indeed, there was no place like where we were going.

I didn't care that I felt a sickness coming on when I took my first steps through Pompeii's Marina Gate. I had seen images of that gate reproduced so many times before that it truly felt familiar. Indeed, I was ready to physically explore a place that I had up until then only mentally traveled to. Here was the city of my dreams, and I was going to experience it fully awake. No words were invented yet to describe how I felt when I crossed that gate's threshold. If I were to invent such a word now, it would have to encompass the feelings of elation, euphoria, exhilaration, and excitement, and it would apparently have to start with an e. Elpharment? No, that sounds too much like elephant. Epixment? Sure, that works. I was epixcited. Extremely so.

The first thing I did in Pompeii was stare at my feet. I couldn't get over the fact that I was walking on original Roman roads. The "cobblestones," if I could call them that, were gigantic! And they were set down like humongous Tetris blocks. I couldn't stop being amazed by them, and it was a fascination that continued throughout the entire day. It didn't matter where we were in Pompeii; I would occasionally blurt out, "My God, look at these roads!" over and over again, ad nauseam. At least when I would say, "and these ones have chariot ruts on them!" added some variation to the theme. More than anything, those ancient roads said to the world, "Rome was here," and they had no intention of going away.

Romans built their roads to remain, and they outlasted the Empire that created them. I liked toying with questions as to what that actually meant. What kind of Empire makes roads that last forever? Did they believe that their Empire would last that long? Forever? Did the Roman Empire believe in itself so thoroughly that it harbored no doubts about its eternity? Were we not doing the same today? How long will The United States last? Forever? We tend to think so. Looking at those ancient roads, I had to have my doubts. Forever, I had to admit, was not as long as I thought it was. Modern roads are not built even to survive a century.

Walking around Pompeii was an organic experience, for our feet went wherever the original streets led them to. At one point, Eric and I were walking along an old Pompeiian sidewalk, and we were so engaged in our conversation that we didn't notice how we ended up inside an ancient restaurant (or what the ancients called a "thermopolium," aka, a place that sold hot food). We looked back at where we had walked from and saw the worn-out foot treads that we followed without noticing that we did. We simply walked where hundreds of other people once walked to. In this neighborhood, all footsteps led to this particular restaurant. It was at that moment that Pompeii felt most real to us. We wanted to pull up some chairs and wait for yesterday to come again, considering that we missed it the first time it was here.

There was something irresistibly eerie about Pompeii. Its stone-laden streets retained the worn-out grooves made by the many chariots that rode throughout the city. The homes of the once well-to-do still had most of their walls plastered in colorful frescoes, and most of their floors were still paved with detailed mosaics. The ancient gardens still grew new flowers as each spring kissed its soil, although the ancient fountains no longer splashed any watery displays. The streets were walked by ghosts and tourists alike. One tried to remember while the other tried to imagine. Pompeii was a strange place. It was an ancient landscape locked forever in its last day of being alive. Visiting Pompeii was like visiting what a city looks like underneath its skin. Pompeii was a skeleton of itself. Pompeii had walls, streets, shops, homes, and public buildings, but it no longer had any citizens. No one lived in Pompeii besides the dusty plaster casts of people who *used* to be there. Twisted and contorted, those people felt their city die as it took them with it. Bent over, covering their hands over their faces, the people of Pompeii tried to fend off death, but death covered them in a pile of ashes. No one had a funeral for them, for no one knew

91

where anyone was buried. All anyone could do was venture to where Pompeii used to be and lay a laurel over its remains. Pompeii was over, swallowed by the jaws of Vesuvius. Time passed, new grass had grown, and all was eventually forgotten.

Well, that's not entirely true. It was impossible to forget Pompeii, for its legend lived on throughout the centuries. People always knew where Pompeii was – they just didn't know how to find it. Its location was officially confirmed in 1763 when an inscription that said *rei publicae Pompeianorum (The Republic of Pompeii)* was dug out of the rubble. Pompeii was buried for nearly 1,700 years, and the gods decided that the time had finally come for the city to see sunlight once again.

Pompeii will forever be a time portal. It had been 200 years since the city was rediscovered, and 1,900 years separated us now from when Pompeii took its last breath. Yet, so much within Pompeii was already incredibly old by the time the volcano took the city as a sacrifice. The House of Faun, for example, was built in 180 BC and buried in AD 79. That alone was a span of 260 years. People continuously lived in that house and never stopped remodeling it. The residence is most famous for housing the "Alexander mosaic," which depicted Alexander the Great in the heat of battle. The mosaic dated to 100 BC and was likely based on a Hellenistic wall painting from 315 BC. Furthermore, the imagery was a scene from the Battle of Issus, which was an event that happened in 333 BC. Time meant nothing in Pompeii – all was seamless. If ever there was a fold in the universe, the crease undoubtedly extended over that city.

Most houses in Pompeii were "atrium houses," and I declared that I wanted to live in one. I loved how the rooms encircled a central courtyard, and I adored how the sunlight filtered in from above. Unfortunately, windows weren't frequently utilized, so most rooms were shrouded in darkness. Thus, walls were vibrantly painted to remedy the poorly illuminated rooms. My favorite element about Pompeii was seeing what remained of its frescoes. I can best describe Pompeiian art as "Classical Impressionism." Only the barest uses of strokes were employed with the most minimal dabs of paint to create elaborate theatrical scenes. The artists embraced perspective and used it to their advantage, with the results being nothing short of astounding. Not only was their art impressionistic, but it was realistic and fantastic as well. Classical art was not static; it was convincingly alive. Yet, there was something quite distant and unfamiliar about all the frescoes clinging to the walls. It was as though the art did not belong to us – it belonged to them, to those who were no longer with us. The art in Pompeii was created by the hands of plaster cast beings who existed today as shells of the people they used to be.

Being there got me wondering when making that style of art was officially lost. I wanted to know who the last ancient artist was to have frescoed a wealthy Roman mansion. Unfortunately, when Rome fell, it took its artists along with it. No one was assigned to act as a receptacle for all the ancient artistic knowledge. How was it that hundreds of years' worth of acquired artistic achievement got unceremoniously thrown away? The preservation of creative skills would have spared the world from the medieval flat figures that slid off the canvas because the artists didn't utilize enough perspective to give them a convincing floor to stand on. Then again, the

Renaissance would never have happened had ancient artistic skills never been lost in the first place, so I suppose that was one silver lining. However, devil's advocate, Leonardo da Vinci might have invented spaceships in the year 1500 had he not squandered so much time dissecting humans so he could understand muscles better to create better paintings. In conclusion, I believe the world would have gotten smaller a hell of a lot sooner had ancient art not been forgotten about in the first place.

I remember a Pompeii exhibit I saw at The Los Angeles County Museum of Art in 2009. The show was called *Pompeii and the Roman Villa,* and I wanted to specifically see the fresco of a man and a woman holding writing utensils. I know it doesn't sound like much, but believe me, it was. Just like *The Mona Lisa* doesn't sound like much whenever someone tries to describe it, there was something about that fresco that made it worth so much more than words can express.

The Portrait of Terentius Neo and his Wife was a product of a very remote time, made by the hands of an ancient who we will never know. The past and the present collided in this painting, for the writing utensils they held looked wildly unfamiliar. Art, in general, typically does an excellent job at narrowing the gap between past and present, but this fresco failed to do that, for it made viewers feel that distance. Terentius Neo and his wife wanted the future to know that they were both literate, and modern viewers recognize that message even though we don't recognize the objects they used for writing. The shared humanity is there, and modern viewers can sense that, and that, to me, was what made that fresco unique. There was a vision behind it, and that vision endured throughout the centuries.

Walking around the exhibit got me thinking about how the ancient Pompeiians would never have imagined their hair combs or sundials being displayed in glass cases somewhere across the ocean in a land they never knew existed some two thousand from when they considered "now." But, alas, that was exactly what happened. I was certain that the ancients would have been somewhat amused at that knowledge, if not at least slightly baffled by it. I highly doubt that my hairbrush will someday be in a museum's display case some two thousand years from now on another planet in a different solar system, but one never knows. Always, anything can happen. In fact, I demand that it does.

On to Venice!

As at Ostia, I again failed to wear a warm enough jacket while I walked around Pompeii for six and a half hours. I woke up the following day with the chills and a desire for Vesuvius to erupt and bury me alive so I'd have an excuse not to crawl out of the covers. However, I woke up with the kind of sickness that even lying in bed required way too much energy. I had to give myself a pep talk to pull my body out of bed and make it to the train station. I couldn't decide if it was a good or a bad thing that today was a designated train riding day. Ahead of us was a six-hour journey that would take us from Naples all the way to Venice. The highlight of the trip was going to be looking out the window while buzzing through Florence and spying on Brunelleschi's famous dome. Of course, that was assuming that my entire being would somehow magically make it to the train station on time.

Make it to the train station, I somehow did, just barely. I arrived there hungry and craving something healthy. Since it took me so long to get my legs going that morning, we only had a smidgen of time left to grab something to eat. I bought a banana and slowly lagged behind Eric as we raced to the train. I peeled back my banana in a hurry and then helplessly watched the majority of it nosedive onto the dirty train station floor. I was left holding onto an empty banana peel with nary a bite remaining. I came to a complete stop and whimpered at my tragedy. Eric soon noticed that I was nowhere behind him, so he backtracked and found me blubbering over my loss.

"What are you doing?" Eric asked, all befuddled. "Why did you stop moving?"

I pointed to the tragedy that landed at my feet. "I dropped my banana," I muttered, "and I don't even have the energy to pick it up and throw it away." The banana was all I wanted in life at that moment, and it was gone. We had no time to get another. I had no choice but to board the train on an empty stomach. Surprisingly, I managed to make my stomach even emptier when I spent most of the trip in the lavatory. I didn't even see Brunelleschi's dome when the train stopped in Florence because there were no windows in the bathroom for me to see it. To Eric's credit, he assured me that the dome was quite lovely.

Venice

The six-hour rest and plenty of bathroom time did my body wonders. I arrived in Venice feeling good and more than ready to hit the canals.

Our first impression of Venice was that it looked like it was built for someone else. None of it looked real, for no modern city looks like it's floating on water. It takes an artistic culture to invent a place like Venice, and we are no longer a civilization of artisans. We are now much too practical to waste our time creating such beauty in this world. No, we today prefer to build our cities quickly to ensure they look sufficiently ugly.

The first thing we did in Venice was stare at it. Venice was an actual water world, a veritable floating dream. Architectural bits of Venice reflected on the water and made it impossible not to see the city wherever we tossed our gaze. When we walked over a bridge, the sight of an upside-down Venice made us feel sandwiched between reality and fantasy. It was easy to lose our place in the world when we explored nooks and crannies that seemingly didn't even exist.

Being in Venice was intoxicating, and it was easy to get drunk breathing its moldy air. Venice wasn't so much floating as it was sinking, and it was easy to see the damage that rising waters were causing. Venice was a city melting from within, and there weren't enough people living there to save it from itself. Venice is a city of tourists, and it functions more like a museum than a modern town. Like a museum that never has enough funds, the museum that is Venice struggles. It is unknown how Venice will manage to keep its head above the water that rises with each passing year, so if you want to see it, you have to see it now while it's still there.

We spent a total of four days in Venice and went into every museum that was humanly possible. We saw so many paintings and so many interiors that the pageantry, colors, and gaiety that Venice was famous for seeped from our pores. We became one with the city, and it was hard for us to separate the present from the past. It was a little too easy to believe that the past was no longer behind us when we looked at so many paintings depicting another age's reality. How did time pass Venice by when it seemed to be lurking just around the corner?

It's safe to say that we pretty much saw everything there was to see in Venice, including the rarely displayed drawing of Leonardo Da Vinci's *Vitruvian Man*. I'm not exactly sure just how lucky we were to see that original drawing in person, but it was an image that immediately stuck with me the very moment I saw it. There was something incredibly perfect about the way the figure was drawn that was immensely pleasing to the eyes and made me think that Leonardo was someone who knew the human figure better than anyone who had ever lived. Yet, there was something "off" about the drawing that I couldn't quite articulate, and it had something to do with the shapes surrounding the figure. This drawing was all about proportions, and yet there was something disproportionate about it. The message the *Vitruvian Man* implied was that a human body could fit into both a circle and a square in perfect geometric proportion. Yet, Leonardo succeeded in proving that it most certainly did not because he focused the center on two different planes. (The circle's center was on the navel, whereas the square's center was at the groin.) His drawing was directly inspired by the writings of the ancient Roman architect Vitruvius and his claim that architecture and the human body followed similar principles. Leonardo wanted to believe that was true, but he ultimately proved that it wasn't. Yet, Leonardo proved that the human body was proportional to its own imperfect laws. There was a secret beauty in the human shape that followed no architectural norms, and never will the human body fit into a circle and a square simultaneously despite how much anyone forces it to.

Now, before I go on, I want to tell a quick little story. So, I mentioned to Ryan that I was writing about *Vitruvian Man,* and he said that he always thought it was weird that the drawing was included with the *Voyager* space probe. He said that if aliens ever found it, they would think our species was endowed with four arms and legs. I laughed so hard when he said that because it sounded so utterly true. I, for some reason, also thought that image was engraved somewhere on the probe, and I said I couldn't believe how that thought never crossed my mind. Well, a quick Google search revealed that *Vitruvian Man* wasn't actually engraved upon it. There are two *Voyager* probes careening deep into outer space, and each one carries a golden record, but they don't depict any images of people. It was the *Pioneer* plaques that both of us were thinking of because one of them included an illustration of a naked man and woman, and each was drawn with the correct number of limbs. We were both sorely disappointed when we realized that the eight-limbed *Vitruvian Man* wasn't our inter-stellar ambassador because now we both want him to be.

There isn't much else I need to say about Venice aside from mentioning that it was impossible to do anything without constantly looking at Eric's watch. Thank God Eric was in the habit of wearing one, but it truthfully hardly mattered since places rarely opened according to the times they were supposed to be.

Most Venetian art resided inside churches, and each church possessed idiosyncratic opening hours. It was almost impossible to show up in front of a church and expect it to be open, so we learned to plan our meals whenever we found ourselves waiting. The one church I was most excited to see was the Church of San Pantalon because inside was the world's most incredible trompe-l'œil ceiling. We got there sometime around 12:30 p.m. The sign on the door said their viewing hours were 10:00 a.m. – noon and then again from 1:00 p.m. – 3:00 p.m., *maybe*. After being in Venice for four days, we learned to add the *maybe* part ourselves. The posted hours were mere suggestions, for one could never assume that the person holding the keys would actually show up on time, as that person could show up whenever. We always had a 50/50 chance of waltzing into a church whenever we happened to arrive, but San Pantalon threw us a curveball and left us waiting until well past their advertised closing time. For four long hours, we waited and did something else until the church finally opened at 4:30 p.m.

From the outside, the Church of San Pantalon looked like nothing. To say that it was plain doesn't even describe it, for the facade was entirely blank. Given how it looked on the outside, Eric had doubts that the inside would look any better.

"Are you *sure* this is the church with a spectacular ceiling?" he asked more than once during our four-hour wait.

"Yes," I kept reassuring him while secretly crossing my fingers. "I promise it will be worth it."

Holy crap, and worth the wait, it was. Neither of us had ever seen anything so incredible before. We looked up, and the ceiling wasn't even there, for above us was space that went on forever. An artist named Giovanni Antonio Fumiani painted the ceiling between 1680 and 1704, and to do so, he pulled out all the foreshortening tricks and then some. I'm at a loss on how to describe something that was so beyond what an average person could possibly create, for above us was a masterpiece in illusionistic art. The figures weren't falling, they were floating, and the pillars weren't standing, they were rising. An organized chaos danced above our heads, and the painting appeared so loud that I could practically hear it. It was a ceiling that I wanted to stare at forever, and if I ever become a ghost, I already know where my spirit will reside.

Torcello

For our last day in Venice, we took a quick boat ride to a nearby island called Torcello. The island was the first to be inhabited in the Venetian Lagoon, so it was rightly rich in history. Legend was that Attila the Hun's throne was there even though the same legend admitted that he never once sat in it. I was particularly excited to see their 11th-century Byzantine mosaics inside their 7th-century cathedral, and I was equally excited to climb their ancient bell tower for a nominal fee. These three reasons alone were enough to sell me on a trip to Torcello, and it didn't take any arm-twisting to get Eric excited about going there, too.

The first thing we did in Torcello was admire Attila's throne. The ancient stone seat looked like it was something straight out of *The Flintstones,* so it made perfect sense why Attila was rumored never to have sat on it. Attila wasn't a caveman, but he was known as "The Scourge of God" because he ransacked Europe something terrible, so I imagined he deserved a throne made of marble. The Roman Empire had already split into Western and Eastern parts by the time Attila rose to power, and he terrorized the east before setting his sights on the west. Word of his coming reached Northern Italy before he actually arrived, so would-be victims had enough time to retreat to the islands in the Venetian Lagoon. The 1,500-year-old "Attila's Throne" was not sitting in Torcello waiting for a barbarian butt to sit on it, for it harked to a time that came after those events. I guessed that Attila was credited with that chair simply because it was he who caused the people to retreat to Torcello in the first place.

Keeping in mind that Torcello was the first island to be inhabited in the Venetian Lagoon, it made sense why their cathedral was so incredibly old. When we stepped inside, it felt like we had crossed over a threshold separating the present from the past. Torcello Cathedral was where history clung to the walls and refused to let go. Before us were walls swathed in layers of gold with the classic images of Christianity decorated upon them. Mary held her infant in all her two-dimensional mosaic glory upon the central apse dome, and Christ was doing all his greatest hits across the flat western wall. I thought that maybe it was here where Christianity's iconography was initially created, and even if that wasn't true, it was still easy to believe. Being inside there felt special, as if we were witnessing the beginning of something very important. I knew that these weren't the earliest depictions of Christ to have ever been depicted upon a church's wall, but they were indeed the oldest ones we had ever seen. We had spent so much time on our trip looking at ancient Roman mosaics, and it was neat to see the continuation of the ancient tradition. As old as these mosaics were, they were not as old as all the other mosaics we had already seen, and knowing that really put Christianity into perspective. The classical world was long gone, and we are currently living in a wildly different age. Our modern origins couldn't be traced back to Pompeii, Rome, or Ostia, for they could be traced here, right where we were standing, beneath this golden dome.

When our eyes grew tired of looking at all the shimmering gold, we paid our fee and climbed up the tightly wound 11th-century bell tower. I had been up several bell towers before, but this one was narrow enough that I worried about my camera knocking against its walls. I find medieval engineering fascinating, and it will always be a mystery to me how stairwells like that were created, especially ones so incredibly slim.

We were both shocked when we emerged from the stairwell and spied a Japanese tourist taking pictures next to an oversized stuffed animal. We barely managed to get ourselves up the narrowest stairwell in the world, and here was someone who lugged a stuffed panda bigger than herself up it.

"How?" I wondered aloud. "Why?" I was filled with so many questions.

We couldn't stop staring at her and wondering if she had traveled with the panda from Japan. If so, did she have to buy a seat on the plane for it? Was she seriously taking her carnival-sized stuffed animal everywhere she went? I desperately wanted to see all the photos inside her camera, but I had to leave it as one of life's greatest mysteries.

We took our spot on the bell tower and threw our gaze over the expansive scenery that unfurled below us. The fall season was nearing its end, and everything was barren and crispy brown. Absolutely nothing was in foliage, so there was nothing to obscure the view that seemingly went on forever. I had never seen nature look so beautiful in all its decay. The views from there were so visceral that they made me want to cry.

"This," I said and swept my arms to encompass everything, including the girl with the oversized panda. "This is why I travel."

CHAPTER FOUR:
Spain, Jan 2003

The Rabbit Hole

Spain, for me, is a rabbit hole that I willingly fall into headfirst. I don't know what it is about Spain, but something about that country spurs me to overthink things. Maybe it's because of all the sunlight. The atmospheric refraction over Spain possibly hits my brain in such a way that causes my synapses to go haywire. Albeit, it was cloudy when I was there in January, so I don't believe the sunlight (or the lack thereof) adequately explains it. Maybe Spain mucks with my brain simply because it can.

I had wanted to visit Spain ever since I tried and utterly failed to learn Spanish in high school. Granted, the version of Spanish my school taught was of the Mexican variety, not the lispy Spanish one, but the mother country loomed enough in the background that it caught my attention. Thus, I attempted to learn about Spanish history but got instantly perplexed. There was just too much of it, and it zig-zagged all over the map as it followed the most non-linear path throughout time. I soon realized that Spanish history encompassed the history of the entire world. Everyone in every era seemed to have had a hand in shaping Spain's identity, and it wasn't long before I perceived Spain as being history's original melting pot. It would be a long 13 years before I found any answers to my long list of questions.

Museum of the Americas

The first museum I visited in Madrid when I went there on my own was not the Prado but the Museum of the Americas. I wanted to start my journey there because I was curious to see what was left of America's gold. I've always been morbidly fascinated with the conquistadors and their unabashed raping of America's riches. Gosh, maybe fascinated is not the right word to use in that sentence. I'm not so much fascinated as I'm bewildered at what they obtained. The conquistadors notoriously shipped boatloads of gold objects back to Spain, but it wasn't ever enough to satisfy their nation's insatiable quest for fortune.

Not much remains to be seen of those original gold objects, for most of those items were transformed into coins and used to purchase Spanish galleons. Strangely enough, some of those coins currently sit in treasure chests on the bottom of the sea in those same galleons bought with America's gold. Yet, some gold objects managed to remain intact and defied that most unfortunate fate by landing themselves inside a Spanish museum.

The smattering of gold objects displayed were the rare survivors of Spain's unquenchable thirst for riches. Inside the glass display cases were examples of what every conquistador destroyed cities to obtain. There were gold figurines, gold necklaces, gold earrings, gold nose pieces, gold masks, and gold anything. The pre-Columbian cultures understood the value of the metal that did not rust or tarnish, and the objects looked so fresh, so new, and yet so utterly foreign. As I studied the items, my mind puzzled over such questions as how exactly *did* someone wear a humongous flat sheet of gold as a nosepiece? Before me were the remnants of cultures that I didn't remotely relate to, and seeing their objects made me contemplate who those people once were. I wondered if the conquistadors found it easy to destroy them simply because they were so different. Or was it more the case that the conquistadors found it easy to eradicate them simply because the conquistadors were just that immoral?

As I stared at a gold cat with its tongue sticking out, I genuinely wondered how many beautiful, puzzling, and incomprehensibly bizarre objects we of the future were deprived of seeing. I was curious to know how much pre-Columbian culture was melted down and erased from this world forever. Undoubtedly, the aboriginal American world was not just made of gold, but gold was the only color the conquistadors chose to see. They consciously decided not to look at the natives as human beings and only saw them as extractors of the riches they wanted. They saw things no one else had ever seen, yet they remained emotionally unmoved. It made me wonder if the conquistadors were the most unsentimental human beings to have ever walked this planet.

In their mind, the conquistadors had plenty of excuses for their actions, and the main one was to rid the world of (what they interpreted as) heathens. "Why should a culture that murders its victims on top of pyramids be allowed to exist?" said men who hailed from the country that led the Spanish Inquisition. Would it have been suitable for some other culture to have descended upon Spain at the peak of the Inquisition and eradicate *them*? I often wonder what the pre-Columbian world would look like today had all the native cultures been allowed to continue at the pace that they were going. It was tantalizing to stare at the museum objects and ponder numerous thoughts.

The Temple of Debod

From the Museum of the Americas, I walked down a fairly major street while carefully dodging copious amounts of dog poo in my attempt to reach ancient Egypt. Smack dab in the middle of Madrid, there stood an authentic Egyptian temple called the Temple of Debod. Even after going there, I still have no idea what the word Debod means. I never figured out whether Debod was a city, a god, or something entirely else. I guess that it didn't matter, though, because not knowing what Debod meant did not take away from the experience of standing inside an ancient Egyptian structure.

The fact that the temple sat under a Spanish sky rather than the Egyptian sun was a testament to how time truly marches on. Had this temple remained in Egypt, fish would have been swimming through its doors because the Aswan dam would have placed this temple underwater. A handful of other temples, including the colossal one known as Abu Simbel, were facing similar fates and needed to be moved to higher ground. Moving Abu Simbel proved to be no small achievement, and it wasn't something that Egypt could have done all by itself. Spain was among the countries that assisted in that monumental endeavor, so the Temple of Debod was awarded to them as thanks for their participation.

The ancient Egyptians are gone now and will never return to reclaim anything they used to own. Proof that they ever existed at all resides in the buildings and objects they left behind. The closest anyone can get to a genuine ancient Egyptian experience is by stepping inside one of their authentic temples, where time and space hang suspended in rooms once inhabited by gods. The essence of the ancient mind remains infused inside temple walls, and it is there where modern man goes in search of ancient truths. It is my theory that all religions were born inside an Egyptian temple. Amun became Zeus to the Greeks, Amun became Jupiter to the Romans, and Amun became God to the Christians. All prayers end in praise of Amun (or Amen, or Amn – the Egyptians didn't utilize vowels in their hieroglyphics).

Ancient Egypt was a land of many temples because ancient Egypt was the land of many gods. Each temple was dedicated to a specific deity, and only priests were allowed inside the temple's heart. As an ordinary person, I would never expect to stand in a room that housed the statue of a sacred god, but I stood in such a space inside the Temple of Debod.

As I stood alone inside the sacred room originally dedicated to the God Amun, I took a moment to absorb my thoughts. It was here where either the lie began or where the truth was discovered. Either God was invented within those walls, or God revealed himself to humankind within this domain. Very likely, neither event occurred, and Amun just was. That's it, just was — kind of like how the notion of God is something that is simply felt. The Egyptians desired to build a house for that feeling. They took an abstract idea and gave it a tangible appearance. All the churches and mosques built today serve the same purpose. Religion is found within, and putting walls around a set of beliefs is something humans have always felt compelled to do. The ancient Egyptians codified the technique, and all we do today is follow their blueprint.

Born, raised, and died in Egypt, the Temple of Debod was resurrected in Madrid as a skeleton of itself. Its soul resided in its ancient land, but its body resided on Spanish soil. Yet, there was such a feeling of peace inside the Temple of Debod that I found it difficult to pull myself away. I didn't want to leave that domain knowing full well that the world was not a particularly peaceful place. Moreover, I knew what was coming next, and it was going to be nothing like an Egyptian temple. In Madrid, one could find God, or one could lose God. One could lose God by looking at a Picasso.

Guernica

I actually can't stand Picasso's style of art. I find his crazy shapes and stupid eyeballs annoying, and I would never normally go out of my way to see a Picasso painting. Still, everyone needs to see his *Guernica* painting in person if they genuinely want to know what human beings are capable of. We have the capacity to be cruel. We have the ability to inflict pain and suffering. We will use war as an excuse to do terrible things to each other.

Picasso's artistic style translated the feeling of war through a prism of disjointed shapes and dismembered bodies. The painting has a voice, and it screams via a menagerie of tangled throats. The horrified cries of horses, women, and children meld together in one ghastly crescendo. One does not look at this painting of *Guernica*; one listens to it. No other painting in the entire world is as loud as this one.

There's no God in *Guernica*, only man. It demonstrates the worst that humankind is capable of. We humans are the cause of the worst pain. I was going to say that it's a painting that demonstrates what happens when God fails humankind, but it's not that. It's a painting that shows what happens when humanity fails itself. The figures in *Guernica* are raising their hands to the sky in a desperate attempt of prayer, but their prayers are not being heard. It is man that is doing this terrible thing to himself, not God. As I said, there is no God in *Guernica*, so don't go looking for him there. Go to the Temple of Debod if you want to find God, but don't go there after looking at this painting, for it might make you think it's all bullshit. If there was a God, why did so many women and children of Guernica get slaughtered like cattle? It made no sense. If anyone approaches *Guernica* while wavering in their faith, one look at this picture may decide which direction the viewer will fall.

Segovia

The Roman aqueduct in Segovia looked like something that marched straight out of a Roman fantasy. The monstrosity of multi-tiered arches planted itself so firmly upon the landscape and rooted itself so well that it looked like it had always been there. Of all the photographs I've taken during my travels, the picture I took of Segovia's aqueduct ranks as one of my favorites. It looks as though nothing can stop it. Not time, not weather, not invaders, nothing. That aqueduct will outlast everything.

The Romans built the aqueduct in 50 BC to bring water to an outpost populated with soldiers and their families. In essence, those retired soldiers were colonists, and it got me wondering what life was like for those living in what could've easily been referred to as the frontier. Indeed, they were so far away from Rome that they created a version of Rome around them. Every colonial city followed a pattern that gave provincial towns a Roman appearance. The Roman policy of conquer, destroy, rebuild, and settle was so codified that it eventually became routine. I tend to think that the opening of the American plains was a land grab back in its day, and it most certainly was, but it pales in comparison to what the Romans did. The Romans grabbed land from Syria to Spain (east to west) and from England to Egypt (north to south). It was mind-blowing what they did, and God only knows how many cultures they bulldozed over in the process. They believed the whole world needed to be Romanized, and they made an impressively good dent at achieving that feat.

It always captures my imagination when I stumble upon a Roman ruin in the least likely place. To the Romans, everywhere was game, so I should never be surprised when I see a lone Roman pillar in the middle of a traffic circle in a provincial European town, but it does always manage to catch me off guard. "Dang, the Romans were here, too?" I often say to myself, "They sure got around." Alas, I digress.

Anyone who visits Segovia knows that the aqueduct is impossible to miss, for it marches across the city like an architectural army. I had read that water moved on top of it by the force of gravity alone, and I was curious to know whether or not there was any water still in it. The aqueduct supposedly still worked as a backup water source, but I honestly didn't know how that was possible. I was curious enough to investigate, so I walked the length of it to the point where it dropped to the level of the pavement. A little canal continued along the street, and I was impressed to see water riding inside it. However, the watercourse came to an abrupt halt at the end of a busy intersection, and I had no idea where the water disappeared to. I then walked to the other end of the structure and discovered that it, too, mysteriously vanished when it dead-ended against a tiled wall. Still, I had to believe that the aqueduct somehow worked, but it was a mystery to me how it did, considering that the water seemed to both begin and end nowhere.

The Romans had a knack for making civil engineering look easy. "Who built this thing?" I wondered. "Did they use slaves?" I tend to forget that they exploited slave labor. It is easy for me to romanticize the Romans, but I have no real idea what life was like under their rule. The Segovia aqueduct looked amazing, but what did it take to build it? Did it take lives? Most likely, yes. No doubt, there was also a team of true architects involved in building aqueducts, and when they were done building this one, they likely moved on to the next provincial town and built another. Regardless, whoever constructed the Segovia one did an excellent job, and they created a legacy. There exists no doubt in anyone's mind that the Romans were here. The Romans are gone, but they left this monument behind.

Seville

M.C. Escher himself couldn't have invented a more labyrinthine town, and he drew pictures of staircases that ignored the rules of gravity. I learned that Seville's tightly packed streets were built the way they were to weaken the effects of the sun. I supposed that the sun would have a more challenging time blazing upon a patio if it couldn't find a patio to blaze upon; however, that also meant that a human being couldn't find a patio to rest upon either. Or a hotel, for that matter. What I did manage to find, though, was two equally bewildered tourists. I kept running into them repeatedly when I was severely lost, and the three of us knew not to ask each other for directions. We silently acknowledged that we were wandering around a real-life Escher drawing, and there was no logical way to escape it.

When I finally, miraculously, found my hotel, I mentally hugged it. I unpacked my essentials and took a five-minute break. I plopped onto the bed, stared at the ceiling, and tried resetting my wits. I had to channel some energy before going back out there to find the cathedral. The map made it look like the cathedral was a hop, skip, and jump away from the hotel, but I wasn't fooled. I was upset with myself for not packing a shovel so I could dig my way through Seville's city streets. With their tall buildings and narrow roads, one step outside felt akin to being buried alive.

Of course, it took me eons to weave my way out of the Minoan maze and land at the foot of the architectural masterpiece. Yet, I was slightly disappointed when I successfully made it there because I had so much fun getting lost that I was tempted to run back into the snarl of streets and get lost all over again. It was at that moment that I decided Seville was for me. I can't help but appreciate a city that doesn't give a hoot if someone is trying to get somewhere. Seville is a city that tells people to slow down; life's not meant to be hurried. Seville knows that people will eventually reach their destination despite inadvertently visiting several side streets along the way. In Seville, there are no direct routes.

So, I'm debating right now what words I want to use to describe Seville Cathedral because marvelous and bewildering don't even come close. I'm thinking more along the lines of splendid, extraordinary, monumental, sumptuous, astonishing, breathtaking, and overwhelming. Even those words don't describe that cathedral enough. To say that it supplanted Hagia Sophia as the largest cathedral in the world when it was completed in the early 16th century might give a better idea of what I'm talking about. Seville Cathedral exists in a league of its own.

Interestingly, Seville Cathedral started its life as a mosque, making it Hagia Sophia's polar opposite. (Hagia Sophia began as a church.) When Seville was reclaimed from the Muslims, the former rulers handed over the keys to the city, and I viewed those keys inside the Seville Cathedral Treasury. For some reason, seeing those keys left me with more questions than answers, as I had no idea what those keys were supposed to open. Were those the keys that unlocked the city gates? I guessed that's what the "keys to the city" meant, but if that was the case, then those had to be some seriously wimpy doors. It then dawned on me that I had never seen keys to *any* city before, and I wasn't sure if they were simply ceremonial items or keys to actual locks. Again, I don't know why Spain makes me overthink the littlest things, but it does, and that happened a lot while I was there. Any time I'd look at anything, I'd ponder over the object, go down a rabbit hole, and emerge none the wiser. I never did find the answer to what those keys unlocked, and even an internet search right now didn't solve the mystery.

The inside of Seville Cathedral was too amazing to describe, so I'm just going to say the words "gold ceiling" and leave it at that. I could definitely say more, but I don't necessarily want to. However, I do want to say that I saw

Christopher Columbus' tomb there and wasn't expecting to. It caught me off guard running into him. "Hoo-hum, look at all this gold, holy crap, is that Christopher Columbus?" Straight away, I said to myself that Christopher Columbus was the reason for the ceiling, just like how the Earth's tilt was the reason for the season. Oh, Seville, why did you do this to my brain? You can't just plop Christopher Columbus' tomb someplace without providing a warning. But they did, and there he was. "Well, hello, you beautiful bastard," I said to him. I wanted to say more, but I found myself tongue-tied. I've always had mixed feelings about him, so I just stood there unprepared and stared at his elaborate tomb. I wanted to knock on it and ask him if he was really inside. (Turned out, only a tiny portion of him, like 4.4 ounces of him, actually was. The rest of him was buried in Cuba, in the "America" that he "discovered.")

I eventually pulled myself away from all the gold and wandered up a spiral ramp to the top of the cathedral's bell tower. I gained a bird's eye view of the city and observed the chaotic streets from an elevated perch. I immediately felt vindicated in my inability to know where the heck I was going once I saw how impossible the city was laid out. Seville was undoubtedly created by certifiably insane urban planners who were not the least bit claustrophobic.

Seville referred to their bell tower as *La Giralda,* and it originally functioned as a minaret. Its hulking presence loomed over the city like a landlocked lighthouse, and I couldn't help but think that it would have been helpful for that tower to have actually been a lighthouse, for its light could have guided me through the maze of city streets. As it was, the structure

116

held an impressive set of bells and an incredible perch from which to view the city below, and that, I had to admit, was satisfying enough.

Back in my hotel room, I unwound with the TV set on. I had ten channels to choose from, three of which showed live tarot card readings. It caused me to wonder if people were calling in to have their fortunes read live on air. I knew that Seville's streets looked medieval as hell, so I was curious if it caused Sevillians to think equally medieval thoughts.

I have since learned that two Roman emperors, Trajan and Hadrian, both hailed from a city near Seville known as Italica. I regret that I didn't travel the extra 9 km to visit the site and tour the ruins of its massive amphitheater. Italica was founded in 206 BC as the first Roman settlement outside of Italy, and it sat along the banks of the navigable Guadalquivir River. The Phoenicians had long before founded a city nearby, which the Romans called *Hispalis*, and that was the city that eventually became modern Seville.

Trajan and Hadrian were both the better sort of emperors that the Empire produced, so I wondered if it had something to do with where they were from. Trajan presided over the second-greatest military expansion in Rome's long and complicated history when he led the Empire to attain its maximum territorial extent. He was likely also Rome's most philanthropic ruler, for he oversaw extensive public building programs and social welfare policies. Hadrian, in comparison, passionately pursued his own stately goals and personal interests by visiting almost every province within the Empire's realm. Hadrian appeared to have been a shrewd and pragmatic politician and was known to demand military preparedness and discipline from his troops. He actively engaged in various civil and religious building projects and ultimately bestowed the Empire with the largest temple Romans had ever seen when he built The Temple of Venus and Roma, which looks like a bombed-out ruin today.

Both men were products of the provinces, and each possessed an itch to travel. Trajan managed to push the Roman Empire's borders to its furthest extent, whereas Hadrian visited nearly every district to determine if those far-flung locations were worth holding on to. Both men understood the innuendos of frontier life and fully grasped the concept of empire building and maintenance. These two men were not "Roman" Romans; they were "colony" Romans. By not confining their thoughts strictly to the city of Rome, they could grasp the bigger picture of the wider world around them.

Rome ruled Spain (aka *Hispania*) for a very long time, but Spain's history did not start with the Romans. Indeed, that honor goes to those who settled in Spain over 35,000 years ago, but who those people were, I'm not versed in explaining. I did want to visit Altamira cave and view the 14,000-year-old painted ceilings, but it was nowhere near where I was going. Instead, I was excited about the prospect of standing inside a 5,000-year-old Neolithic structure, for that was about as far back in history as I could realistically go.

The Dolmen of Menga

Spain has a deep historical well to draw from, and dipping a metaphorical bucket into that water will yield numerous discoveries. One of the more intriguing items I pulled up during my Spanish well-dipping adventures was something

118

called dolmens, and their heaviness weighed mightily on my mind. I couldn't read enough about these massive tombs of rocks, for their sizes struck me as incompressible. All over Europe, precariously balanced boulders were placed upon the landscape by Neolithic hands and stood unmoved for thousands of years.

Dolmens, I learned, dotted the European landscape like man-size molehills, yet were notoriously difficult to reach. Dolmens are appealing not only for their structures but also for their locations, for they typically reside in far-flung places where mass transit never journeys. However, "The Dolmen of Menga" was a pile of rocks that caught my attention simply because it resided within striking distance of my travels. This ancient tomb was a three-hour train ride from Seville, nestling outside a quaint little town called Antequera.

Antequera ended up being one of the most pleasant cities I've ever had the joy of strolling around. It was full of whitewashed houses, potted flowers, and commanding mountain views. Furthermore, it was far enough off the beaten path that I didn't encounter many other visitors. I thoroughly enjoyed eating in a restaurant where I was served bread with a decanter of olive oil. I instantly fell in love with their olives soaked in spices and ultimately decided I could survive on bread and olives alone if I lived the rest of my days in Antequera.

After my meal, I walked 20 minutes outside town to where the mysterious Dolmen of Menga sat perched upon a hill. I was the only tourist to show up for the 11:00 a.m. tour, and I feared that no one would let me inside. Thus, I was ecstatic when a tour guide eventually showed up holding the keys to the locked iron gate. However, I could see the look of disappointment on her face when she saw I was the only visitor there. I saw her quickly throw her gaze over my shoulder as she unabashedly plotted her escape route. I swiftly grabbed her attention and kindly asked her to show me the tomb. She immediately rebuffed my request as if she had one hundred other better things to do than conduct a tour for only one person, but I was determined not to take "no" for an answer. I stood there looking dejected and stared longingly at the massive heap of rocks that sheltered a 5,000-year-old enigma.

"Por faaavooor?" I pleaded.

A long silence passed as we each stood our ground in the world's quietest standoff.

I could tell she wasn't happy with me when she muttered something in Spanish and dropped her arms in disgust. She quickly scuttled up the hill and unlocked the iron gate of the enormous Stone Age burial chamber, and I stuck behind her like a shadow.

The interior of one of Europe's largest ancient megalithic structures was breathtaking, and I couldn't believe I was actually inside. I tried imagining what the air was like when the tomb was opened in the 19th century when they found hundreds of people buried. However, I found it difficult to concentrate on my musings because my tour guide's fast-talking spiel was ricocheting off all thirty-two megalithic walls in one resounding echo. She was, naturally, describing the tomb's fascinating details to me in Spanish, so I had absolutely no idea what she was saying. I tried asking her to slow down so I might catch a word or two, but she responded by talking even louder. It got to the point where I just wanted to enjoy the tomb in silence, but her bellowing voice ensured that wouldn't happen. I had to find that delicate balance of feigned interest in what she was incomprehensibly saying while simultaneously tuning her out so I could properly enjoy standing inside a human-made womb.

My mind was racing in a thousand different directions. I couldn't believe I was physically standing inside a megalithic tomb conceived by the Neolithic mind. The people of five thousand years ago assuredly thought differently. No one thinks in terms of large standing rocks anymore. "Why did the Neolithic people find it necessary to build with monumental boulders?" I wondered. I thought it was because we, as human beings, like to think big. Since concrete wasn't invented yet, the Neolithic builders went after nature's ready-made material. They would go long distances in search of the perfect boulder and then expend a significant amount of effort to lug that boulder clear across the land to its designated resting spot, usually installing it in some gravity-defying position. In other words, it was no small feat to create a megalithic structure.

The tombs were the final resting place for those that were, I assumed, important. "Who earned such a spot?" I wondered. "For how many years was a particular tomb used? A generation? Several generations? Hundreds of generations? Thousands? Who was the last person to have been laid to rest in the one I was currently standing inside? When did the culture that built this tomb finally decide it was time to walk away and forget that it ever existed?"

Neolithic tombs were built to last. "Was placing a body inside a tomb symbolically allowing them to live forever?" I wondered. "How integral were the dolmens to the Neolithic religion? What I wouldn't give to see what their rituals looked like or hear one of their songs. What musical instruments did they use? How did they illuminate their night to push aside the darkness? What kind of makeup did they paint on their faces? How long did their rituals last?" These were all questions that would never get answered.

The Dolmen of Menga was an organic structure strategically aligned with the summer solstice, allowing the morning sun to shine straight along the dolmen's entrance corridor. The space inside a dolmen was sacred and, in a sense, safer than anywhere else in the Neolithic world. There was a sense of protection when standing inside a room built of giant rocks. Many dolmens were built into hillsides and tunneled deep into the bowels of the Earth. This was the Neolithic spirit realm and where they went when it was time to return to their origins. They were indeed the children of the Earth, and we today have lost touch with our natural mother.

Standing inside that tomb was the only time I truly felt I knew where I was.

Cordoba

Religion and nature are symbiotic, and nowhere in the world is that relationship better displayed than inside the Mosque-Cathedral in Cordoba. A grove of slender Roman pillars locally harvested from the ancient forest of abandoned Roman buildings populated the structure's extensive interior. Repetitive red and white striped arches pirouetted like ballerinas across the room and acted as though they had all the space in the world to dance around. Indeed, the interior was incredibly spacious, and it all looked the same no matter where

I happened to throw my gaze. The Moors had an aesthetic eye for symmetry, and I enjoyed walking around all the pillars, knowing that I could either be going in circles or perfectly straight. There was security in the sameness, but that security was interrupted when I unexpectedly stumbled upon a cathedral.

The building began its life as a mosque in AD 785, and converted into a cathedral in 1236. However, the Christians couldn't accept the mosque for what it was; they had to do something to it to make it their very own. The Christians conquered the city of Cordoba, but to really own the place, they had to conquer the mosque as well.

Square in the center of the mosque, the Christians removed a small grove of columns and inserted a traditional buttressed cathedral as if it somehow needed to be there. The Christians have a long history of inserting churches into other cultures' religious buildings, so stumbling upon that shouldn't have surprised me. (There is a church on top of a Mexican pyramid (Cholula), a church inside a Roman temple (The Pantheon), and a church where a Greek temple (Syracuse) used to be.) It's mainly because of Christianity that the ancient world has come down to us in ruins, but it's also the very reason why so many ancient buildings have come down to us intact. Conversion into a church could be a blessing in disguise, but it was a mixed blessing at best in Cordoba's situation. The Christians ripped out the mosque's original heart and replaced it with an alternative one. I couldn't help but feel that it was unfortunate that the Christians deemed it necessary to alter the mosque's appearance in such a way. The original building was absolutely perfect, and they could've left it unchanged. The way I saw it, the Christians didn't desire perfection; they desired ownership. To the conqueror go the spoils, and this building screamed "victory" from the tippy top of its lungs.

I personally don't see why everyone can't simply worship inside a forest. The mosque, as it was originally built, was a forest recreated. To me, it felt as though the Christians cut down a swath of trees to construct a fancy cabin right in the middle of it. The inserted cathedral irritated me, so I went outside and walked around the structure. All along the exterior were many attractive Moorish doorways, so I surveyed the many choices before deciding which one I wanted to tackle with my pen.

I had been in Spain for a few days already, and I noticed that it was a challenge to sketch anything. Any details worth drawing were nearly always out of my viewpoint, for most buildings didn't get interesting until well above the doorways. Everything in Moorish Spain started above the door, so one needed to look up to see any detail, and even then, it was hard to make anything out. It was very unlike France, where everything happened on the sides of doorways (statues, ornaments, details, etc.). Not that there was anything wrong with that, it was just a different style that I wasn't used to. It posed a formidable challenge to sit down and sketch anything, and I didn't have a whole lot to show for my efforts thus far.

Nevertheless, I sat down with my sketchbook and attempted to draw. My actions caught the attention of every child within the immediate vicinity, and soon all my colored pencils were in the paws of very small children. Within seconds, I was surrounded by an entourage of pregnant mothers, each holding out their palms and asking for money. All I wanted to do was draw, but I started feeling too guilty to focus. One child designated himself as my assistant when he collected all my pencils and started to hand them to me as I needed them. So, I guessed that I would be stuck drawing despite being distracted by abject poverty. I never know what to do in these situations. I know I'm far more fortunate than anyone who has to live on the street, and I never think it's fair. It's *not* fair that I get to sit in front of a building and draw when someone else gets to sit in front of that same building and beg. How is that fair? It's not. It all boils down to luck. I'm simply luckier than them, and there's no reason why that is. Life is not equitable. It never was and never will be.

Mostly, I kept my head down and focused on drawing. The final result was nothing particularly fantastic, but it's infused with a lot of personal meaning. I can never look at the picture and not think of *them*. I'll most especially never forget the child I watched stick his entire mouth over a drinking fountain because I found his action so absolutely fantastic that I made a mental note never to use a public drinking fountain again.

The city of Cordoba was once a shining light in a significantly darkened world. When the rest of Europe was fretting about who among them were witches, the scholars in Cordoba were solving mathematical equations. The Moorish corner of Spain was one of the few places in the world where Christians, Jews, and Arabs knew how to respect each other and even (brace yourself) collaborate. Moorish Spain was unique in the medieval world. An insatiable quest for learning was nurtured like a well-tended garden. The Moorish court encouraged tolerance and actively sought the brightest minds to inhabit their realm. Yet, where was that same tolerance now?

Muslims aren't even allowed to pray in their former mosque anymore. I found it a shame that such a spiritual building could only be dedicated to a single religion. Cordoba was nothing like the city it used to be, and I got the impression that it lacked the energy to haunt its own corners. Cordoba used to be so much more. The Cordoba of today stands at the crossroads where no one anymore meets.

Medina Azahara

I relate well to Victorian passions and pursuits and their romantic desire to seek beauty in this world. I find it so agreeable when they lament over a fallen pillar lying in a field of flowers. I happened to think of the Victorians when I came across a large meadow of wild poppies, and I looked everywhere for some ruins to wax poems over. Alas, there were no ruins to be found, for the area was just a patch of respite in a sea of modernity. Bordering the field was a monotonous display of uninspiring modern buildings, stacked row upon row, end upon end, and they offered nothing for my imagination to play with. Seeing that field juxtaposed against the modern world made me look even more forward to my upcoming visit to Medina Azahara, an easy 8 km bus ride away from Cordoba.

All I knew about Medina Azahara was that it was a Moorish palace in ruins. I hoped that there would be fields of wildflowers growing around it, but I knew not to get my hopes up. Rare is the sight of ruins just like how the Victorians saw them. Indeed, there are so few ruins left in the world that are just that – ruins. Instead, we make them ruineds. Modern man does a fantastic job ruining ruins by piecing them back together and manicuring the landscape around them.

The fortified palace-city of Medina Azahara was built in the 10th century by an interesting ruler named Abd-ar-Rahman III, who believed he was powerful enough to declare himself Caliph of Cordoba. He moved his court to his newly built surroundings, which served as the center of government only for as long as he reigned. Almost as soon as he died, the city he created was abandoned, and what remains today only gives the slightest hint of what beauty it once beheld.

As I wandered around the scattered remains, my inner Victorian urged me to write a poem:

Azahara

Decorated archways,
fragmented pieces,
pillars holding up walls
to rooms no longer there.

Streets leading to dwellings
where no one sits and waits
to receive the delegates
that will never arrive
on pavements hardly worn.

Your arches crumbled,
your streets stolen,
your marble taken away.
An existence that lasted
the course of a dream
which now lies
awake.

Toledo

Sandwiched between the Romans and the Moors, Spain found itself ruled by a Germanic tribe known as the Visigoths. They were the same tribe that went down in history for famously sacking Rome, and after their little rampage on the most powerful empire the ancient world had ever seen, they decided to settle down and became rulers themselves. They essentially rebranded themselves as the world's new Roman overlords and ruled the area of Hispania from their designated capital, Toledo.

I went looking for Visigothic Toledo in forgotten nooks and crannies, but I wasn't entirely sure I would recognize what Visigothic anything would look like even if I saw it. I rambled down narrow passages and rubbed my shoulders against scruffy walls while exploring the parts of Toledo where only the alley cats went but emerged empty-handed. The streetlamps glowed weakly down the darkened alleyways, and the thought did cross my mind that if someone wanted to try out a new knife they bought at one of the many touristy blade shops, these alleys were the perfect place to give the weapon a stab. I quickly decided that it was probably a good idea to give up looking for Visigothic ghosts and reenter the modern age.

Toledo was once famous for its metalwork, and I learned I could buy a full suit of armor there if I wanted to. For a very brief moment, I contemplated becoming a Renaissance Festival nerd when I toyed with the idea of buying a suit of armor simply because the craftsmanship was so exquisite. I ultimately decided against doing so because I didn't want to attend more Renaissance Festivals than necessary to justify my purchase. That, and I wasn't a male. I then imagined a time when men actually required someone to be skilled in the art of armor-making. For a few hundred years, plenty of men pranced around in metal suits and chain mail, very likely on the very same streets I was currently walking upon. They had to get their outfits from somewhere, and chances were pretty good that somewhere was here. The Toledo craftsman would have also been happy to sell a knight a sword or a saber to match their armored attire. Toledo had a *raison d'être* and a reputation to uphold because its steel was so famous. As I walked past a plethora of metal shops, I couldn't help but wonder if the majority of artisans thought they were born in the wrong century. I was curious to know if any of them felt they would have had more buyers if they had lived 500 years before they were actually born. I got the feeling that Toledo already had its golden age, and everyone, tourists and artisans alike, was basking in its afterglow. We were all deep down pretending that Toledo was still medieval. All of this crossed my mind as I considered purchasing an expensive set of pewter chess pieces that I knew I would rarely use.

I'm not exactly sure how to segue into my next train of thought, so I'm just going to say one word and let it hover on the page: blue. More specifically, El Greco's version of the color.

Every artist has their own palette: Rembrandt had his browns, Van Gogh had his primary colors, and Pollock had every color imaginable, but no one used blue the way El Greco did. However, one must see his paintings in person, for reprints do nothing for him. No other painter makes me believe in myself as El Greco does when I see his creations in real life. So many artists are either too intimidating or too uninspiring, but El Greco is approachable. As an artist, he stretched life out and made it look abnormal. He then threw blue over everything and made the weirdness look surprisingly okay. I often find myself surprised whenever I read that one of his paintings previously hung above an altar in some church because it makes me wonder if the congregation dabbled in psychedelic drugs. I waver between the opinion that El Greco was a good artist and a terrible one, sometimes while staring at the same picture. Yet, his blue always convinces me that he was one cool dude, and all that medieval hullabaloo didn't fool him. He could have lived in any age.

If the artisans at the tourist shops thought they were born five hundred years too late, then El Greco must have thought he was born five hundred years too early. How it was that anyone in the 1500s embraced his art really baffles me. I would have thought that the artistic patrons in El Greco's time would have had certain rigid expectations of what art needed to look like, and El Greco was by no means a traditional artist. His figures always look like they could have been Gumby's parents, for they are all absurdly stretched and elongated. Nothing about his paintings convinces the viewer that he painted scenes straight from reality. What the viewer does get a sense of, however, is that he painted scenes straight from feeling. El Greco was an emotional painter and aimed his brush to strike right for the gut. His art is very intuitive, and the stomach understands his art before the brain does.

The whole reason why I was in Toledo was to stand before the few El Greco paintings that were not in museums. I wanted to visit his art in situ and hopefully gain a smidgen of insight into the world he once inhabited.

I started my journey at the El Greco Museum, but I don't

feel too compelled to discuss any paintings I saw there. No, I'd rather discuss the monumental painting called *The Burial of the Count of Orgaz* that hung in its original location inside the Iglesia de Santo Tome, for it was impossible to walk into that church and not be struck by the utter weirdness of that picture. It was almost as though a hundred floating heads stared at me the moment I entered the confines of their intimate space, and I found it difficult to discern who was looking at who. Was I looking at the painting, or was the painting looking at me? And did anyone know what was going on above and below the row of floating heads? This was a painting that had a lot to take in, and everything seemed to be happening all at once. I was having a difficult time deciding where to focus my gaze. Do I watch the lowering of Count of Orgaz into his tomb, do I try to figure out who's populating the earthly realm, or do I try to dissect the events happening in the heaven above? Never mind that the figures all looked extremely elongated – I wanted to know what everyone was doing because they all seemed engaged in doing *something*. This painting was telling a million different stories, and looking at it made me feel like I was watching an entire movie all in one scene.

The other painting I want to discuss is El Greco's *The Disrobing of Christ,* which hung inside the Cathedral of Toledo. This was the rare El Greco picture where the dominant color was red, and very few paintings in the world bleed quite like this one does. The use of red was meant to be felt, and looking at it made me want to put a band-aid over my eyes. Here was El Greco at his most visceral, and nothing else mattered in the painting except that one single color. His red had a voice that screamed 360 years before *Guernica* did. Here was humankind at its worst as they stripped off the clothes of a man they would soon murder. The use of red symbolized that blood was on our hands, and the repercussions of our cruel actions would be handed down for generations.

Toledo was El Greco's stomping grounds, and they saw something in him that no other city did. "Why here?" I wondered. Was there something about Toledo, or was there something about El Greco himself that led to his success? El Greco's paintings were never exactly "normal," but the people of Toledo were the first to "get" him. El Greco had patrons who embraced his art and proudly encouraged him to decorate Toledo with his religious pictures. I highly encourage anyone to go to Toledo and admire El Greco the way he was meant to be seen: in situ.

CHAPTER FIVE:
Belgium, Oct 2003

Tapestries

Northern Europe has never been known for its balmy climate, so it is slightly odd that some of the world's draftiest buildings sprouted there. Castles and cathedrals were built to be imposing; they were never built to be comfortable. So, it's hardly a mystery why so many medieval paintings depicted people wearing piles of clothes. Nor is it a wonder why so many European museums own extensive collections of faded tapestries either, for large swaths of cloth hung on cold stone walls and acted as clothes for buildings. The medieval tapestries kept the cold from leaching into the bones and allowed European culture to flourish, for one needed to be warm in order to think.

Given the wealth of beautiful tapestries in museum collections, I assume that no self-respecting castle owner ever hung boring pieces of cloth on his walls. In the medieval world, art imitated life, and beautiful tapestries were expensive luxuries. A well-created tapestry came at a cost, so if a wealthy lord was going to spend his money on carpeting for his walls, his discerning tastes demanded the finest productions imaginable. Tapestries functioned as paintings on cloth, albeit they were never a substitute for painted canvases. Indeed, any cultured castle owner hung up plenty of fine paintings as well; thus, castles were essentially the precursors to art museums.

There was a region within Europe endowed with talented artists and crafty merchants who learned how to follow the money backward. These enterprising creators became the designers and suppliers of the fine works of art that wealthy people paid good money for. This was also where many artists lived and created beautiful oil paintings. Today, it is rare to visit a castle or church that still displays all its original art in situ, for much of what was sent to wealthy purchasers no longer remains in private hands but now resides inside public museums. All this explains why much of the best art displayed in European museums all hail from a single region known as Flanders.

Flanders

For the longest time, I had no idea what the words "Flanders" or "Flemish" meant. I'd go to a museum and see those two words together, and I'd always be like, "Oh, ya, I have to look those words up," and then I never would. It wasn't until I started visiting European museums more regularly that I realized it was high time I figured out what the Flanders-Flemish thing was all about since they described nearly everything that appealed to my sensibilities.

I can narrow it down to one specific work of art that officially sparked my investigation into all things Flemish. At the Cluny Museum in Paris, I saw a series of six tapestries titled *The Lady and the Unicorn*. Each piece owned some serious real estate upon the wall, for all were incredibly massive. The dominant color of all of them was red, and they each sported a motley of intricate flowers. The tapestries were all very playful, and the best part was they all featured a unicorn. I mean, honestly, who can resist an adorable unicorn? The tapestries hung in a darkened room illuminated by spotlights which greatly enhanced their emotional impact. Yet, I didn't care as much to know where the tapestries originally hung as I was curious to learn where they were made because those hanging pieces of cloth were by no means the usual run-of-the-mill works of art.

Alas, who the original creators were was not explicitly known, but it was known to have been produced in a weaving workshop somewhere in Flanders. I had just about enough of not knowing anything about this Flanders place, so I finally decided to do some research. I was thrilled that the internet was available when I was ready to investigate because it was way easier to research via the computer than it would have been to scour through boring encyclopedias at the library like I almost did back in 1991. Reading about Flanders online was fun because most of the write-ups included hyperlinks to a plethora of pictures that elevated my study to the level of art porn. In the end, what I ultimately learned was that Flanders could be summed up in two simple words: art and money.

To clarify the terms, I learned that Flanders was a region in Belgium, and Flemish was used to describe someone who hailed from there. Without getting too involved in Belgium's history, it's enough to say that an independent Flanders existed well before a unified Belgium did. The Golden Age of Flanders occurred in the 1500s, but the entire region was a cultural beacon long before and after that time.

Flanders was an influential region within Europe, for it was the wealthiest and most urbanized. I happily learned that Flanders was not confined to one specific location, for it used its Midas touch to create several beautiful cities for people to live, work, and grow rich in. I also learned that a city's specialty determined the extent of its wealth. For example, the wealth of

Bruges depended upon its markets, Antwerp thrived on its location as a port while simultaneously discovering its niche in the jewelry business, Ghent was the center of the textile industry, and Brussels acted as everyone's middleman. Flanders produced all the paraphernalia that rich people desired; thus, Flanders determined what rich people wanted. The whole of Europe willingly paid copious amounts of cash to allow Flanders to decorate Europe entirely.

It was interesting to follow where all that money went, and many Flemish cities proudly displayed their wealth upon their buildings. It was hardly an argument to say that some of the world's most beautiful cities were located there, and I'd go a step further and say that the most beautiful city in the entire world was located in the shape of the city known as Bruges.

Introduction to Bruges

Thus, to Belgium I went with my trusty travel companion, Eric, on what we knew would be our final trip together. He would graduate with his Ph.D. in Biology in a few months and then move across the country for the next phase of his career. We were in a relationship that we knew would be temporary, so we always made the best of our time together and went with the flow. It was never implied that I was to join him on the next phase of his journey, for my future plans were destined to keep me in Arizona. I was nearing the end of a two-year-long waitlist to get into x-ray school. By the time I'd start my program, Eric would already be gone. Ours was a good relationship while it lasted, for we went into it knowing not to get too invested, but it wasn't without its complications. It suffices to say that temporary relationships are good to experience only once, for it definitely wasn't something I desired to make a habit of.

Our first impressions of Bruges were perfection and bicycles, but not in that order. When Eric and I exited the Bruges train station, the first sight we came upon was the biggest pile of bicycles our eyes had ever seen. I'm not kidding when I say that the bicycle pile was truly a sight to behold and that it practically struck us as a religious experience because it was so breathtaking. We were so in awe of how many bicycles could be chained to rows of metal poles that we almost didn't care what the rest of Bruges had to offer when we had this amazing sight before us to admire in all its astonishing glory.

Alas, as impressive as it was, we couldn't stare at the bicycle pile forever. We gradually peeled our eyes away and successfully moved on. Only then did we finally notice how perfectly delectable the air was. There was a slight haze hanging in the atmosphere that caused the sunlight to diffuse in such a way that it made it unnecessary to put on a pair of rose-colored glasses. The light was naturally perfect, which made it easy to fall in love with every brick building that bathed in its glow. And then we saw swans. SWANS! How perfect are swans? I'll tell you how perfect they are: they are absolutely perfect. No other bird could bathe in that glow as splendidly as the swans did. The colors of the trees along the canals in October made it look like Bruges was always lit in gold. All it took was the 10-minute walk to our hotel to make us decide that we already wanted to come back to this city that we hadn't even begun to explore. We were exactly where we wanted to be.

We arrived at our hotel too early for a proper check-in, so we waited until the gentleman behind the counter was done checking out the other guests before we could ask him if we could drop off our bags. What transpired was easily one of the most impressive 15-minute waits of our lives when we listened to the polyglot hold conversations in English, French, Dutch, and German. When the phone rang, he answered and switched to what sounded like Swahili. And he spoke *fast* in all the languages as if they were all perfectly natural to him. To say I was jealous didn't even describe it; I was in awe of his abilities. And there I stood as someone who struggled to dream in my native language. In short, it was the perfect introduction to Flanders.

The Gruuthuse Museum

Bruges offered a bottomless supply of museums, and if I remember correctly, I think I threw a dart onto a map and let wherever it landed determine where our journey would begin. Thus, the first museum we visited was The Gruuthuse Museum, dedicated to applied arts (i.e., arts that apply design and decoration to everyday objects). The museum was housed in a medieval mansion formerly owned by a certain someone named Louis de Gruuthuse, and it was full of all the wealthy objects that would have made medieval life quite comfortable. Just like a book, it's easy to judge a museum by its exterior, and one look at The Gruuthuse Museum's facade was all it took to know that this museum would not disappoint us.

Disappoint, the museum did not. In fact, the museum looked just as good on the inside as it did on the outside, for the gothic elements were not restricted to just the facade, as many interiors revealed. Moreover, the mansion included an architectural addition that linked the house to a 15th-century gothic church which provided the Gruuthuse residents a birds-eye view of the sermons. As museum-goers, that same perch allowed us to observe all the unsuspecting church visitors from the comfort of a pew, where we contemplated throwing objects at people's vulnerable heads. Alas, as tempted as we were, we proudly refrained from giving in to our impish desires, and thus we allowed the church visitors to be blissfully unaware of our looming presence.

There was one object in that museum that I want to focus on now simply because I didn't know how important it was when I saw it. The museum's most famous object was a painted terracotta bust of Charles V, and I didn't know how to appreciate it because it didn't strike me as being all that significant. The portrait was of a young man with longish brown hair cropped in such a way that it made him look like a character from *Huckleberry Finn*. However, his wide-brimmed hat and fancy clothes indicated that this was not a man who ran around barefoot, yet I still didn't give the figure much of a second glance. "Another portrait of someone I know nothing about" was what I might have said to myself as I walked right past the 16th-century portrait of a man who tried to rule the entire world.

To say that he was Charles V doesn't imply very much, for it's more accurate to call him Charles V, *Holy Roman Emperor*. That "Holy Roman Emperor" part is extremely important and should never be left out when discussing him. Yet, even tacking on that title doesn't cover everything, for his full titulature was impressively extensive: Charles, by the grace of God, Emperor of the Romans, forever August, King of Germany, King of Italy, King of all Spains, of Castile, Aragon, León, of Hungary, of Dalmatia, of Croatia, Navarra, Grenada, Toledo, Valencia,

Galicia, Majorca, Sevilla, Cordova, Murcia, Jaén, Algarves, Algeciras, Gibraltar, the Canary Islands, King of both Hither and Ultra Sicily, of Sardinia, Corsica, King of Jerusalem, King of the Indies, of the Islands and Mainland of the Ocean Sea, Archduke of Austria, Duke of Burgundy, Brabant, Lorraine, Styria, Carinthia, Carniola, Limburg, Luxembourg, Gelderland, Neopatria, Württemberg, Landgrave of Alsace, Prince of Swabia, Asturia and Catalonia, Count of Flanders, Habsburg, Tyrol, Gorizia, Barcelona, Artois, Burgundy Palatine, Hainaut, Holland, Seeland, Ferrette, Kyburg, Namur, Roussillon, Cerdagne, Drenthe, Zutphen, Margrave of the Holy Roman Empire, Burgau, Oristano and Gociano, Lord of Frisia, the Wendish March, Pordenone, Biscay, Molin, Salins, Tripoli and Mechelen.

Charles V believed in "universal monarchy," and he desired to be the King of the World, and I dare say that he almost achieved that. *Almost,* but not quite.

I wouldn't have known that the terracotta bust of Holy Roman Emperor Charles V was the museum's most famous object had I not read about it during my "refreshing" stages of research for writing this chapter. The bust itself looked interesting enough, but it wasn't something that I recall lingering over. It's funny how perspectives change once one learns more about something. Had I known that I was staring at the likeness of a man who attempted to be the world's first "universal ruler," I might have studied his expression a little bit more and tried to figure out what he was thinking.

Charles V reigned from 1519 to 1556 over an empire where "the sun never set." The lands he reigned over were so extensive that it seemed as though it was always daytime somewhere.

Charles V spent much of his life on the road, either visiting or expanding his vast territories, and if anyone was going to be *Dominus Mundi* (Lord of the World), it was going to be him. Just as there was only one God, so could there be only one emperor, and I can't help but think it's not an entirely bad concept.

I don't know if anyone has noticed, but nationalism isn't working. Globalization has shrunk the planet, and borders should no longer matter. We need to start thinking in worldly terms if civilization wants to continue. It doesn't make sense to fight over resources when we can all work as a team and share them. So, why not have one world leader at the top of the helm to organize an equitable distribution? Oh, wait, I know why not. It's because we're goddamn human beings and prone to greed, malice, and corruption. We are our own worst enemies and have no qualms about taking the planet down with us. I can't help but think that we don't deserve to be here anymore. We've taken humanity to its farthest reaches as far as individualism is concerned, so now the only way forward is together. Unfortunately, no one knows how to get along, so the only direction left for us to go in is backward.

The Groeninge Museum

I would never claim there was such a thing as "art overload," but I dare say that visiting the Gruuthuse Museum and the Groeninge Museum back-to-back might have qualified as such. "Might" is the operative word in that sentence, though. As I said a second ago, I would never claim there was such a thing as art overload but seeing those two excellent museums on the same day did admittedly blur things and cause me to forget what we saw where. It's not a stretch to say that we saw more incredible art in the space of several hours than we normally see on entire trips elsewhere. If anyone wanted a crash course in Flemish Art, I can genuinely say I know what two museums to send people to.

The range of art in the Groeninge Museum spanned six centuries, from the 1400s to the 2000s, or as I would describe it, from neck ruffles to pointillism. Somewhere near the neck ruffles end of that range, visitors encounter Hieronymus Bosch, and I always find it weird to find him there because I always think that I would discover him closer to the pointillism end of that spectrum.

Hieronymus Bosch wasn't the world's most prolific artist, as only about 25 known paintings have been attributed to him, and the Groeninge Museum happened to own one of the strangest ones (and that's saying something as far as the Bosch department is concerned). God only knows what was going through Bosch's bizarre brain in 1482(ish) when he painted *The Last Judgment.* He certainly left it to the viewers to ponder the meaning of such things as fish demons, a hooded man walking around without a torso, a woman with bird legs frying a human on a skillet, and an unidentifiable creature-thing wielding a very large knife. And all that I just described was simply the tip of the iceberg. I don't have enough words in my vocabulary to even try to describe the rest. If Hieronymus Bosch wasn't on drugs, then I don't know what his excuse was. What I do know, though, is that the world needs more people like him to throw some wooden clogs into wheels, for we have become way too boring in our sedate way of looking at ourselves.

Lace and Beer

About just as baffling as a Bosch painting was the secret art of lace making; yet, unlike a Bosch picture, the mystery of lacemaking was revealed to us when we watched women hand-make lace at the historic Lace Center. Hand-making lace involved the use of wooden bobbin pins, and the noise of the pins rubbing together filled the room with a constant "tappety-tap-tap-tap-tap-tap-tap-tap-tap" sound. The noise was almost deafening with the way it echoed against the walls, and my biggest takeaway was that I never knew that lacemaking was so loud. Yet, I still have no idea how anyone succeeded in making lace simply because the skill looked so complicated. Everyone there had lightning-quick fingers that allowed them to whip up lace doilies like it wasn't a big deal. They evidently had an incentive to work quickly, though, because they were doing a brisk business as far as the lace trade was concerned. They were definitely not giving their doilies away cheaply, for they charged big bucks for their finished products. I've never had a use for a lace doily before, so I resisted purchasing one even though I desperately wanted to after I saw how lace was actually made.

Eric and I discovered Belgium beer on our first evening in Bruges. In no time at all, I quickly learned that one of my favorite things to do was drink Tongerlo brand beer poured straight from a tap and have it served on a patio that overlooked a canal that had SWANS! swimming in it. Someone is undoubtedly living my perfect Belgium life right now, drinking that beer while looking at those SWANS! I'm totally envious of my doppelganger, for I know she is enjoying herself immensely. By the second day, we were already asking each other if 10 a.m. was too early to start drinking beer, and we quickly discovered it most definitely was. Holy crap, was Belgium beer strong – it made us want to go to sleep by noon.

Bruges was a Gothic wonderland, and every turn revealed an arch or a turret. The whole place was pure eye candy, and we loved every minute of it. There's a movie called *In Bruges* that tickles the funny bone because the main character hates how pretty Bruges is, so he just wants to leave. In real life, no one wants to leave Bruges because it's near impossible to tear oneself away from a place that is so utterly ideal.

Ghent

It was hard to go from Bruges to basically anywhere else, so we unsurprisingly found the following location not nearly as beautiful. Ghent was one of Belgium's oldest towns, and the wealth of historic buildings lining its canals was an impressive testament to its prosperity and power. Yet, the Ghent of the modern era consisted of traffic, tram wires, and modern buildings. It felt like the city was playing a trick on us by being something we thought it was not. I believe that we both wanted Belgium to be like one giant time capsule, and it took a city like Ghent to remind us that time did indeed march on and didn't feel guilty about leaving history behind.

Thus, we deemed it necessary to be adequately lubricated before tackling Ghent, so we beelined it to the first attractive pub that caught our wandering eyes. Disregarding what we had just learned the day before, we ponied up to the bar and ordered ourselves some delicious Belgium beers for breakfast.

We both looked a little too happy to be enjoying beer so early in the morning that the bartender couldn't resist asking us what the hell our deal was.

"We're on vacation!" we told the bartender as if that wasn't completely obvious.

"Where are you guys from?" the bartender asked.

"America," we said.

"New York?" he inquired.

"Nah," we said. "We're from Arizona. But that's not important, 'cuz we're in Belgium now, and we love it here!"

"So, what other countries will you be visiting?" the bartender wanted to know.

"None. Just Belgium. Belgium is awesome!" we said and toasted our drinks.

The bartender was dumbfounded.

"You mean to say that you flew all the way from Arizona just to visit Belgium? No one does that. All Americans come to Belgium only as a side trip from somewhere else."

"Not us," we explained. "Your country offers a lot for a tourist. We're gonna do it up!"

At that point, our presence was announced to the entire staff of three to come over and meet the anomalies. We impressed everyone with our appreciation for all things Belgium. Our enthusiasm for their country evidently made an impression on them, which indicated that they didn't hear enough good things about their country. They seemed totally resigned to the notion of being perceived as an afterthought. We had to practically convince them that Belgium was worth visiting in its own right, and we described all the sights their country had to offer. At the end of the conversation, I think everyone there was ready to book their own Belgium holiday and visit all the interesting places within a 100-mile radius.

Anyone visiting Ghent does so with the intent of seeing the

one piece of art that puts Ghent on the tourist map. *The Ghent Altarpiece* by the van Eyck brothers is rightfully famous for many reasons, including that it's simply an impressive sight to behold. The artwork was created in the 15th century, but it looked as though the Victorians painted it sometime in the 1800s. The only giveaway that it wasn't a Victorian creation was the pair of nude figures flanking its sides. (The Victorians were too prude to paint nudes sans fig leaves.) That this altarpiece was created in the 15th century was almost impossible to believe because every figure (and there were many of them) looked so convincingly modern.

The van Eycks painted two different worlds when they created the altarpiece: the world they wanted to live in and the world they actually inhabited. They blended the two worlds together and formulated a symbiotic whole. As I admired the grandiose work of art, I couldn't help but feel a sense of familiarity with it. The worlds they painted were the worlds we inherently recognized inside our very own beings. The painting depicted the human desire for joy coupled with the all too human feeling of shame. It also illustrated how humans achieved their collective sense of place through routine rites of passage. Life on Earth is reduced to a series of rituals until we graduate to a realm that exists far beyond the familiar terrain.

Even if one failed to feel an intimate connection toward the painting, the artwork was so easy on the eyes that it took no effort at all to lose oneself while staring at it. There was always a sizable crowd standing before the gigantic folding contraption, and half the people standing there probably didn't even realize that they hadn't moved for quite a long while. It was a work of art that was almost impossible to walk away from, and it was worth traveling to Ghent to see the masterpiece in person.

Even if *The Ghent Altarpiece* wasn't there, I still would have insisted on traveling to Ghent anyway because I desired to see a notorious building. The Gravensteen castle was infamous for reasons it probably didn't want to be, but I'm saying that from a modern perspective because in its heyday, I'm pretty sure the Gravensteen castle was exactly what it wanted to be known for. Every castle has a unique reputation, and this particular castle had a sinister one, for it was known as being a house of torture.

The castle was constructed in 1180, and its reputation quickly preceded it, for no one truly wanted to be "invited" there. The Counts of Flanders had a reputation for abusing their power, and that abuse extended into various forms of torture. To say that Gravensteen castle had a torture chamber doesn't quite describe the private hell on Earth it truly possessed. There were no medieval torture instruments unknown to The Counts of Flanders: the iron maiden, the rack, the thumbscrew, the breaking wheel, you name it – they were familiar with it, and they weren't afraid to use the devices to their fullest extent. It felt kind of macabre to admit that I wanted to visit a torture museum at a location where gruesome acts of torture actually occurred, but there are some things in life that I need to see with my very own eyes to gain a fuller understanding. The iron maiden was the one item I wanted to see the most, and I think that was because I'm a huge Iron Maiden fan. I can't express how many times I have sung the lyrics to *Run to the Hills* in my head over the years. Every time the world goes to shit (and it seems to go to shit a lot), I sing that song to myself as a sort of anthem. One of these days, I'm going to run to those damn hills and escape all the craziness, but I fear that's a whole 'nother story.

Antwerp

My first memory of Antwerp hangs in the warm glow of a cozy coffee shop. We had just gotten off a train early on a dark morning, just as the sky unleashed a faint, almost imperceptible drizzle. We instantly dipped into the first coffee shop we saw, cozied up to a window, and watched a gray light diffuse through the slow pitter-patter of raindrops. Outside was damp and dreary, but inside was cheerful and comfy. The overall atmosphere felt strangely nordic, and I thought this must be what living in Scandinavia felt like. The coffee shop was playing the best European chill music my ears had ever heard, and to this day, whenever I hear anything remotely similar, my mind automatically interprets the vibe as "Antwerp morning."

I've always been jealous of the European lifestyle, and experiencing that coffee shop intensified my jealousy even more. There was something so cool about how people weaved in and out of that coffee shop freshly armed with a croissant and espresso that caused me to despise American-style drive-throughs. I don't know. Maybe it was the music. Perhaps it was the atmosphere. Possibly it was the location. I didn't know *specifically* what it was, but my God, *something* about that place made me insanely jealous. It just felt *better* inside there, as if everyone had figured out how to live more naturally. There was no hustle, no bustle. Everything was seamless. Being there was the perfect way to start our day, and I was envious of those who lived in Antwerp, for they could always start their day like that. I instantly wanted to move there, and we hadn't even seen anything beyond the coffee shop yet.

I forget where we went right after that, but if I had to say, I believe that we went to the Museum Mayer van den Berg first. I recall the museum housing an impressive collection of Gothic and Renaissance art, but the painting that stands out most in my mind was the one titled *Dulle Griet* by Pieter Bruegel the Elder. I just now became curious to find out whether or not Pieter Bruegel the Elder was contemporaneous with Hieronymus Bosch because their artistic styles were so similar; however, I learned they lived nearly 75 years apart (Bruegel came later). Again, I don't know what Pieter Bruegel the Elder's excuse was, but he was another weird one. I don't even know how to describe *Dulle Griet* other than to say that it used a lot of red. On top of all the red, there was a variety of birdmen, fish creatures, demon frogs, and a man with a butt for a mouth (or was that a mouth for a butt?). The painting depicted "Mad Meg" from Flemish folklore, but I had no idea what I was looking at without knowing the story. To me, the picture was nothing but crazy, but I guessed that was the point, for something had to put the "Mad" in "Mad Meg," so I have to say that he did his job well.

I often forget how spoiled we are to be living in the current age that we do, for life in the Middle Ages couldn't have been easy. I take it for granted that I can just pop into any 'ol museum and admire hundreds of years' worth of great works of art. Most people who lived at the time when *Dulle Griet* was brand new had a snowball's chance in hell to know it even existed. So, thinking about that got me wondering who that painting was created for. It was most likely intended for someone's private collection, and that someone was presumably wealthy. Regular people back then didn't get to enjoy great works of art, for they were lucky if they saw much of anything beyond their own short and brutal lives. I love art and greatly appreciate it, but I often forget how highfalutin that admiration is. I often wonder what kind of person I would be if I were born in any other era, for I don't know how I could be the person I currently am without an artistic foundation. It's a thought that I often revisit because I seriously wonder who we are at the core. Do I truly know myself, or do I just *think* that I do?

We walked down some cobblestone streets from the museum and reached what was affectionately called "The Bacon Building." It was built at the turn of the 16th century as the guildhall for butchers, and its official name was "The Vleeshuis" (translated as "The Meat House"). It was a building worth seeing in person because it was the rare chance to see a structure with "bacon layer" strips of red brick and white sandstone. Inside, there was a museum dedicated to music, but we opted not to visit it because unless they were serving bacon, we preferred to spend our time elsewhere, such as the Antwerp Cathedral.

I had read ahead of time that most people visit Antwerp Cathedral because they want to see the four enormous Rubens paintings displayed there. When I think of Peter Paul Rubens, I think of museums, for there seems to be hardly any museum in the world that doesn't have one of his 1,400 paintings. In my mind, Rubens must have lived to be 300 years old, for his output was so prolific that no mortal lifespan could have possibly achieved what he did. I would soon learn that his output was not the result of one single man, for he had a large team of artists working for him at his workshop down the street. Everything would soon make perfect sense, for we planned on visiting his studio next, but until then, we had some large Rubens to admire inside a building that was definitely not a museum.

Rubens always strikes me as someone who was born to be an artist. He applied brushstrokes so freely as if it was synonymous with breathing. His paintings were never stagnant, for he depicted lives that were always moving. It's almost too easy to get lost in a Rubens' painting, for the viewer effortlessly steps inside most of his pictures. Additionally, his use of vibrant colors always succeeded in making life look better than it actually was, so being inside one of his paintings is where most viewers would rather be. It's easy to understand why the nobility adored him so much – he painted the lives they wanted to live.

The four paintings hanging inside Antwerp Cathedral were classic Rubens, through and through. All four pictures focused on well-known Christian events and were displayed most appropriately inside a sacred space. The sense of movement lent an intimacy to the events, as if the viewer was right there watching the religious scenes unfold. Rubens was a master of his craft, and it helped me understand him better to see his paintings hanging somewhere that wasn't a sterile environment.

We concluded our Antwerp journey at the place where we should have begun, that being, of course, at the Rubens House. Walking inside that time capsule of a museum was like walking into one of his paintings for realsies. We both had a difficult time distinguishing reality from pictures, and it was evident that Rubens was paid handsomely for his craft, given how incredibly posh the interior was. There were more than a few moments when I pointed to something luxurious and said something like, "Do you think that's real leather pasted on those walls or fake?" (Leather wallpaper? Yup, it was real.)

By all appearances, Rubens must have lived quite comfortably, albeit I don't know how comfortable he could have possibly been wearing one of those obnoxious ruffled collars around his neck. (Did he paint while wearing one? Gosh, I hope not. How annoying that would have been!) Thankfully that's one fashion trend that has not, and probably never will, make a comeback. I supposed they had to find a good use for all that lace Flanders kept churning out, so the fashionistas of the time decided to flaunt them around their throats. I was super glad that the only thing people bought nowadays were doilies.

Tongeren

The oldest city in Belgium is Tongeren, and it was essential for us to differentiate it from a place called Tongerlo. Distance-wise, the two cities were only 45 minutes apart, but time-wise, Tongeren was roughly 1,200 years older than Tongerlo. It took some effort to grasp that there was a difference between the two locations, and the most confusing element of our trip was when we sipped Tongerlo brand beer somewhere knee-deep in the city of Tongeren. It was a pleasant confusion we most happily dealt with, though, and one we were willing to experience again and again.

We went to Tongeren because I wanted to see what remained of the Romans. The Romans called the city

Aduatuca Tungrorum, and it functioned as the base for the largest contingent of Romans in the entire region. Before the Romans arrived, the area was inhabited by a Belgic tribe known as the Tungri. This tribe faced the difficult choice of displacement or integration and ultimately chose to go to war. Caesar wrote a commentary about the Gallic Wars, and in it, he described the Belgae as being the bravest. He went on to describe a chief named Ambiorix, and I envision him looking exactly like Jean-Claude Van Damme. I could just imagine the surprise on Caesar's face when Ambiorix entered a battle doing a series of splits and spinning kicks. We have the "Muscles from Brussels," but Caesar must have had the "Tiger from Tungrorum."

It turned out that there wasn't a lot to see Roman-wise in Tongeren, aside from the occasional low wall and small bits of pavement. The city more than made up for the lack of ruins, though, with the displays they had inside their Gallo-Roman museum. Truthfully, I don't remember much of what we saw there besides one single object. I had never seen or heard of a "dodecahedron" before, but that museum had one, and they dedicated an entire floor to displaying a single bronze object.

I would like to go on and say that I know exactly what a dodecahedron is, but the whole point of the exhibit was to ask visitors if they knew what it was because no one at the museum did. The dodecahedron was a small hollow object consisting of twelve flat pentagonal sides. Each side had a circular hole pierced in its center that varied in diameter. The object's exterior was studded with knobs, allowing it to sit upright no matter how it was set down. This particular object was found outside the city walls in 1939 and ranked as one of 116 such

Roman objects discovered mainly north of the Alps.

Ancient Roman literature made no mention of dodecahedrons, nor did they ever depict them in any works of art. What they were used for is not remotely obvious to modern viewers, so the Gallo-Roman museum genuinely entertained all possibilities. "Was it a candlestick holder?" one of the displays wondered. "Was it a measuring device?" another one asked. "Was it a toy? Was it a mitten-making tool? Was it anything that you, the public, can think of because, seriously, folks, we need you to toss out some ideas and see what potentially sticks." Eric and I had so much fun trying to figure it out, and we kept running back to it in earnest attempts to be the ones to solve the dodecahedron mystery. Alas, we didn't come up with any new ideas, as the entire floor was dedicated to potentially cracking its code, so there was nothing we could come up with that the museum didn't already think of. Overall, we found the exhibit incredibly unique, for we had never seen a museum display quite like it. It's not often that museums admit that they don't know what an object is, and I was recently disappointed to learn that the exhibit has since been discontinued. The dodecahedron is still there, but it now sits in a lonely glass display case with very little fanfare to capture anyone's imagination.

It's been 20 years since I went to that museum, and I still occasionally muse over what the dodecahedron was. It's still fun to think about, and it reminds me that there is so much about the past that the current era will never know. History is full of wonderful unknowns, and I like that we got to see one of its more baffling mysteries. The dodecahedron was innocently complex, and I liked how it symbolized how much humans have changed. Before us was a tangible object straight from the past, yet it left its purpose in the time from whence it came.

After the museum, we wandered around quaint city streets and ended up in a particularly adorable section. We apparently found ourselves in a UNESCO World Heritage site known as "the Béguinage." It was the first and only time I wandered into a UNESCO World Heritage site without knowing I did. I didn't fault us for not knowing the area's specific history; however, we were observant enough to notice that the buildings suddenly appeared much cuter than everything else we had been seeing.

Béguinages were a common phenomenon in the Middle Ages, for they gave women who didn't want to get married or join a nunnery a secure and comfortable place to reside. I tend to regard them as precursors to hippy communes, so long as I take the sex, drugs, men, and fun out of the equation. When I think about what my life would have been like had I been born in the 1600s, I think the odds would've been pretty high that I would've found myself living in a Béguinage. If I were the same person then as I am now, I would have been absolutely terrified about giving birth at a time when many women died from doing so. I also don't think that a nunnery would have suited my sensibilities either, for I wouldn't have been confident enough in my faith to give my life over entirely to something so intangible. No, my personality would have craved a quiet and simple life, and I might have founded my own Béguinage if I couldn't have joined an existing one.

The Tongeren Béguinage confirmed that my hunches were correct, for I sensed a peaceful aura hanging over the place.

This was definitely where I could have seen myself living out my life as a fiercely independent female. I would've been perfectly content living inside a walled neighborhood where my biggest concern would be whether or not I'd get a good crop of turnips any particular year. In a world that predated women's rights, holing up in a community with a bunch of like-minded females would have seemed the safest option compared to all the other alternatives.

We, of course, couldn't resist stopping inside the cutest little pub and having ourselves some Tongerlo beer along with some overpriced sandwiches. We stumbled out of there with what was now a familiar buzz and proceeded to aimlessly wander around, seeing where our footsteps would take us. The city center wasn't very large, and we soon found ourselves outside the city walls and in an extensive patch of trees. I still don't know where we were or how we got there, but it was there where I snapped my favorite picture that I ever took in Europe. I can honestly say that I've never taken a better photograph before or since, for not only did I capture the scene exactly as I saw it, I fully immortalized how I felt. I was feeling so calm, so restful, and oh so very pleased. The photograph genuinely portrays that. One cannot look at the picture of those trees and not know that I felt completely one with my surroundings.

From the forest, we walked back a different way from how we came, and again, I don't know where we were, but I do believe that we emerged from a time portal and found ourselves in AD 117. I don't know how we managed it, but we somehow found ourselves at the foot of a muddy racetrack where men were riding horse-drawn chariots à la Roman

Empire style. The scene was straight out of a *Ben-Hur* movie, and it was a memory I thought I might have imagined until Eric confirmed that he had the same memory of seeing those chariot riders, too. Neither of us remembered how we got there nor if we saw the race until it ended, but we both agreed that the chariot race existed and was one of the stranger sights we saw.

We came to Tongeren to see what remained of the Romans and left believing that the Romans were still there.

CHAPTER SIX:
France, Aug 2005
Winter in Summer and the Train to Rodez

I had never traveled to Europe in the summer before, so I blamed my naivety for packing only one pair of jeans. Actually, I just told a lie. I didn't pack any jeans. Nor did I pack any regular pants, either. As it was, I was wearing the only pair of jeans I had brought, and they were already getting stinky. I could tell by the collective groans at the sight of the miserable weather outside the windows that I wasn't the only one who failed to pack appropriately. The lady on my left grumbled about how she only brought sandals, and the guy on my right complained that he didn't pack a jacket, whereas I, in the middle, chimed in that I only packed shorts, three pairs of them. By all appearances, it looked like absolute winter out there.

"Welcome to Paris?" the pilot questioned over the loudspeakers, to which everyone sighed.

I had just graduated from x-ray school earlier that month, and this vacation was my reward for getting the job well done. Well, at least I assumed I got the job well done, for I had just taken my x-ray boards the day before, and I had no idea what my final score was. These were still the days before instant gratification, and I wouldn't know whether I passed the test or not until I returned. The last thing I wanted to do was sit around at home and wonder if I had failed, so I figured a trip to France would be the perfect distraction. I wouldn't normally ever splurge on an expensive plane ticket at the peak of high season, but these weren't normal circumstances, so I made an exception and packed for what I thought would be a warm summer vacation.

The sky above Charles de Gaulle airport was steely gray, and the clouds were hanging so low that I could practically touch them. A bracing wind leaked through a crack between the aircraft and the jet bridge, which gave me a teaser of the future I was walking into. I honestly don't know how the weather caught me off guard, but I likely didn't bother to look up the weather report ahead of time and just assumed the temperature would be comfortable. "Weren't summers in France notoriously hot?" I wondered to myself. Yet, one step outside placed me right back to the only version of Paris I was familiar with – the Paris where I'd never run around in shorts and a t-shirt.

"Paris in August, huh?" I said to myself as I zipped my jacket up as far as it could go. "Sure does feel a lot like October to me."

I took the unseasonably cold weather in stride only because I left Paris as soon as I landed. I figured the odds were in my favor that the weather would be warmer at my final destination, which was a good seven-and-a-half-hour train ride away. Alas, I would eventually discover that I was sorely mistaken. Until then, I had seven and a half hours to enjoy the toasty warm comforts of the train while being entertained by the antics of a one-man traveling show. I had brought along a book to read, but I kept putting it down to watch the production of "Rat Man" instead. The performance was riveting and included such unforgettable scenes as "Man Showering Rat with Kisses" and "Watch Rat Scurry Down Man's Shirt and Emerge Out of His Sleeve." I tried not to watch him, but I found it difficult to be entertained by *The Letters of Vincent Van Gogh* when I had a guy with a very large rodent to observe instead. A big part of me kept an eye on him to ensure the creature didn't escape, for that animal scurried pretty quickly, and I didn't want it to inadvertently land on me.

Conques

I was heading to Rodez because it was the closest major city to the UNESCO World Heritage Site of Conques, where I was ultimately aiming. Unfortunately, Conques' remote hillside location meant that no trains or buses traveled there, so I had yet to figure out how I was going to reach it. The best plan I could come up with was to take a small commuter train to a halfway point and hoof it the rest of the way à la ancient pilgrimage style. I don't know how I thought this idea looked good on paper because the walk I was planning to do would have taken me nearly four hours to complete one way. Yet, I was stupid enough to believe that I could get to Conques by sheer perseverance, and it was at that halfway point where my plans started to unravel.

I arrived at the St-Christophe-Vallon train station well-rested because I had gone to bed early the night before. I spent the night dreaming about Conques' narrow medieval streets and half-timbered buildings. The Abbey Church of Sainte-Foy figured predominately in my dreams, and I imagined myself walking under its soaring ceilings. I woke up full of energy and took the earliest train to St-Christophe-Vallon, and it was there where my journey to Conques both began and ended.

I stepped out of the train station and couldn't believe I was in a location where trains actually dropped passengers off.

160

Across the street was a horse enclosure surrounded by a sea of grass filled with the sound of cows mooing. I was quite literally in the middle of nowhere, and my backup plan of taking a taxi to Conques was immediately dashed when I realized there were no taxis to be found. I walked up the road and searched for a sign that would point the way, but I got to an intersection and didn't see a single sign with the word "Conques" written on it.

"No worries," I said to myself. "I'll just go back to the train station and ask the attendant which way to go."

So, back to the train station I went. I optimistically opened the door, waltzed up to the attendant, and showed him a piece of paper with the word "Conques" written on it.

"*Où est?* (where is?)" I asked.

The attendant looked up and promptly gave me no answer.

Undeterred, I tried again with a slightly fuller sentence.

"*S'il vous plaît, où est Conques?*" I pleaded.

Again, no reply. Not even a grunt. Not even the acknowledgment that I was so much as talking.

"Conques?" I asked. "Taxi?" I tried really hard to get my point across.

"Ah! Taxi!" the attendant perked up. He marched me straight to a pay phone and promptly left me alone with it.

Leaving me alone with a payphone wasn't going to help my situation because the phone wasn't going to call a taxi all by itself. I tried to make the best of my predicament, but that was hard to do when there wasn't even a phone book to look any numbers up.

Honestly, all I really needed to know at that point was which road would lead me to Conques. So, I went back to the attendant and made that little walking motion that people do with their fingers and asked, *"Où est Conques?"* one final time. I could tell that the attendant was getting irritated with me. He basically threw up his arms and told me he didn't know. If I wanted to go to Conques, I would have to find my way there myself.

I went back outside and consulted with the horses about what I needed to do. I knew there was no way I'd figure out how to get to Conques on my own, considering there wasn't a single sign anywhere that acknowledged it even existed. It would be a long five hours before the next train to Rodez would arrive, so I could either twiddle my thumbs or find something interesting to do. I could always go back inside and propose a marathon staring contest with the world's least cheerful train attendant, or I could stay outside and see what the farm animals were doing. It was a tough decision, but I opted to see what French farm animals did with their time.

It started off looking like it would be a long five hours of just me and the cows. The scenery was as pastoral as it came, but it was idyllic to the point of being boring. What in the world was I supposed to do with myself until the return train whisked me away? My only option was to go for a walk, so off I went in search of a road sign. I was still hoping to find a sign pointing the way to Conques, but I was starting to realize that even if I found one, I didn't have enough time to walk 11 miles one way. I eventually saw signs pointing to all sorts of places, but not a single one suggested the way to Conques. It slowly became apparent that I was definitely not where I thought I was supposed to be.

I don't know where I thought I was going when I just picked a direction and went with it. It was a nice enough day outside, so I decided to enjoy the ramble. The air was pleasantly cool, so I took my hypothetical lemons and made make-believe lemonade. I figured I had plenty of days left of my vacation to figure out the Conques situation later. I gave up hope for an actual destination and tried to enjoy my impromptu vagabondness. Yet, I genuinely wanted to aim for somewhere. I woke up that morning with a purpose, so I had an internal hole that was yearning to be filled.

I naturally read every sign I came across, hoping that one of them would point to somewhere I had read about when I researched the area. I eventually came across a sign pointing the way to "Belcastel." I got giddy because it was a name I was familiar with. I had read that Belcastel (translated as "beautiful castle") was one of the most picturesque villages in France, so I decided to aim for that, even though it was an unrealistic nine miles away. I almost didn't care that I knew I wouldn't be walking all nine of those miles because I knew deep down that I would eventually stick out my thumb and hitch for a ride.

I was surprised at how many cars passed me by for such a rural area and somewhat unimpressed at how nearly everyone felt the need to blare their horn at me. At some point, I knew I would allow one of the cars to pick me up and take me to where I needed to go, but I tried to stave off the inevitable for as long as I could. One mile in, it started to drizzle, so the rain decided for me that the time had suddenly arrived. I flagged down the next car that honked at me, and an elderly farmer in a barely sputtering Peugeot pulled over and asked me if I needed a lift.

"Oui! Belcastel?" I sheepishly inquired.

"Ah! Belcastel! Oui!" he replied and waved for me to get in,

which I unhesitatingly did.

The gentleman was super nice, so I feel guilty describing the inside of his car as looking as though it hadn't been washed since 1982. I had no idea what time it was because his clock was stuck at 1:15 a.m. Nevertheless, my personal savior was beaming with energy and drove on the slick rural streets like a youthful race car driver.

"Belcastel!" he assured me as he zoomed right past a sign that pointed to it while failing to steer toward its direction.

"Seriously?" I wondered. "Was this how I was going to die? Murdered in a barn way out in the French countryside?"

I pointed to the sign behind us and uttered the only common word established between us, *"Belcastel?"*

The kindly gentleman nodded, *"Oui! Belcastel, plus ou moins"* (more or less).

"Plus ou moins?" I thought to myself. What the heck was that supposed to mean?

His picking me up apparently inconvenienced him, so he compromised and dropped me off at the nearest reasonable location. I was more than happy that he took me as far as he did and doubly pleased that he didn't chop me up into little bitty pieces.

He pointed to a downhill road and said, *"Belcastel. Six kilometers."*

I thanked him profusely and exited the retro mobile.

Belcastel and the Return From There

Six kilometers was about four miles, and I crushed that walk quickly. I spent as much time in Belcastel as my heart desired, which turned out to be a little under two hours.

Belcastel was a perfectly quaint medieval village tucked away from modern civilization, but there wasn't much to it. There was a river, a stone bridge, a ruined castle, a church, and a handful of charming houses. The place dripped with charm, and I just wanted to reach out and hug it.

One could look at Belcastel and see it all in a single glance. It made me think that perhaps most medieval towns once looked like this – so small that one could fit the entire village into the palm of one's hand. I sometimes despise big cities. Why do big cities offer more than what anyone ever needs? Perhaps the answer to an easy life was to be found somewhere around a Belcastel corner. If I had more time at my disposal, I would have lingered and searched for the meaning of life there. I sensed there were answers to be found, but I didn't come prepared with the right questions. I didn't know what living a small life meant, so I didn't know how to approach a village as small as Belcastel properly. I was generally so used to always going that I didn't know how to stop. I could have slowed down in Belcastel, but I didn't. Time wasn't on my side, but when was it ever? Time always feels so fleeting. Life is made of moments, and rarely does anyone recognize when the moments are happening. Routine events tend to clump into one giant heap and reduce life into one conveniently-sized ball. It's too easy to forget that every minute that one is alive has value solely because each of us are allotted only so many of them. Once all our minutes are spent, they are gone. Time is well-spent, or it is wasted, but it all gets used up either way.

I eventually hiked back up the hill to whatever village the farmer dropped me off at (Rignac) and concocted a plan to hail a taxi back to St-Christophe station. Unsurprisingly, I counted a total of zero taxis hanging around the village square. I had a sneaking suspicion that hailing a cab back to the train station would prove to be somewhat difficult. Demand for a taxi in that neck of the woods was apparently nonexistent, so it would be up to me to magically conjure one up somehow. Great.

I didn't have the patience to mess around this time, so I resorted to making a nuisance of myself. I needed someone to call me a taxi, so I chose to irritate the unlucky saps that happened to be working at the local post office. I basically refused to leave until someone was kind enough to call for my ride. It definitely was not one of my finer moments in life, and at one point, I thought they were going to call the cops instead of a cab. It was a fifty-fifty shot which vehicle would ultimately pull up to whisk me away, and my internal dialogue was betting that it would most likely be a police car. I almost didn't think the taxi was for me when it pulled into the parking lot, but the postal employees shoving me out the door convinced me that it was. Yea! I didn't have to risk getting murdered this time! I was pleased as punch with myself even though I knew I could never show my face in that post office town ever again. Staging a sit-in at a rural post office right at closing time was not an endearing way to make an impression of myself, so I have learned.

Rodez

I returned to Rodez at a reasonable hour, which allowed me to get a head start on what would soon become my jean-washing ritual. I was keeping my fingers crossed that the weather would eventually warm up enough for me to wear a pair of shorts, but I doubted it would ever get pleasant enough for that miracle to happen. One would assume that my Belcastel day occurred under a lovely, cheerful sky because I didn't hint at anything otherwise, but in truth, I did all that walking around in a steady drizzle. The sky never did clear up into a bright, sunshiny day. Like I said earlier, the weather started off nice enough, and for one solid mile, the sky showed me what skills it possessed if it wanted to be benevolent. However, I must have done something to piss the sky off because the weather instead chose to settle into that familiar crud that hangs over me nearly every time I visit anywhere in the lovely country of France.

As it happened, I chose to make my base in a city where I could not find a public laundromat for the life of me. I was on day three wearing the same pair of jeans, and they were getting rather smelly. I washed them in the sink and tried to air dry them overnight through a slight crack in the window. However, I had to wake up at 5:00 a.m. to blow dry the crap out of them because they were still soaking wet, and I needed to wear them that day. Despite how much fun doing laundry in the sink was, I had to rank drying the jeans with a blow dryer as not nearly as much fun as watching the guy with a rat for seven hours was.

Rodez was a rather petite city whose primary point of attraction was its fortified cathedral. I found an affinity for the massive edifice, so I figured it behooved me to look at it as much as possible while there. One of the reasons why I liked the cathedral so much was because it looked like it was built as an afterthought. The cathedral was built on top of a wall, and from all appearances, it looked as though the wall was the more important of the two constructions. I don't even remember how I entered the cathedral because there were no doors anywhere on the building that I can recall. My impression was that Rodez cathedral was not built to be entered – it was built to be stormed. This building was a divine fortress that protected its pious citizens.

I bookended each of my days at Rodez cathedral. I caught the organ playing a few times while there, and there's something about an organ playing inside a stone building that makes me not want to leave. If it were up to me, I would have stayed inside that cathedral forever, but then I would have missed all the excitement of getting almost stabbed by a flying patio umbrella while touring one of the most crowded tourist attractions in the entire country.

Carcassonne, Revisited

Seven years had gone by since I last went to Carcassonne, and the place had always haunted me in a good way. I had fond memories of running around and exploring its nooks and crannies, and I never forgot my vow to return someday. Well, someday had arrived, and it brought with it gray clouds and rain. Of course.

It was a windy and wet day, but the weather wasn't reason enough to prevent the place from being swarmed with people. Judging by the plethora of tourists, it was evident that many French citizens had planned their holiday around a designated Carcassonne day, and there was nothing the weather could do to dissuade anyone from deviating from their itinerary. The city could have been sitting smack dab under a funnel cloud, and I doubted anyone would have cared because Carcassonne had a knack for looking incredibly good even under the crappiest of skies.

Everyone has their fantasy of what a walled-in medieval village should look like. Carcassonne, with its collection of turrets, curtain walls, pointy roofs, and cobblestone streets, fulfills everyone's requirements and then some.

What makes this city so special is that it's easy to identify as one's own, for Carcassonne is everyone's imagination realized in stone. I had fun exploring the city's hiding spots because it was like exploring the crevices inside my mind. Yet, the place was overrun with way too many people, so it felt like everyone was running around my brain and causing me a headache.

In short, the place was so crowded that it was impossible to get a good picture without some random person loitering about. I was desperate to recreate the same photo of the castle I took years before, but the only way to get a decent shot of it was to wait for that one magical moment when the building was briefly devoid of tourists. "Magical" proved to be the operative word, for I needed to conjure up some medieval wizardry to sweep the cobblestones of the touristic hoard.

Apparently, my thinking about magicians duly summoned the French version of Merlin to rally to my cause. An evil wind materialized from the nether regions of the atmosphere and rather benevolently took people out like bowling pins. For a brief moment, perfection was achieved, and not a single person was standing in front of the castle. Unfortunately, I wasn't able to capture the fine moment, for I was not even aiming my camera in the castle's direction when the pristine moment was occurring. No, I was instead running around in circles and tripping over picnic tables while simultaneously trying to determine where a massive flying patio umbrella dagger would potentially land.

The oversized acrobatic weapon was rather beautiful to behold as it initially danced in the air, but it quickly turned into a horror scene once it decided to hurl itself back to Earth with its spiky end first. There were three of us on the ground and each thought that one of us was in for it as we exchanged horrified glances at each other. Very soon, all eyes turned toward me when the dagger landed just inches from where I stood. Yup, I almost died. That was a mini-war zone; thank you for that, you vicious umbrella torpedo. I suspected that the ghosts of Carcassonne were itching to play a round of joust with someone, yet they apparently forgot to supply me with a horse and a weapon. Had I a horse at that moment, I would have left the scene as fast as the horse could run, although I probably wouldn't have ridden all the way to Conques because I never did figure out how to get there. Instead, I probably would have ridden the steed to Narbonne, considering that was where I went next after my lovely visit to Carcassonne. Oh, and I never did get that picture, in case anyone was wondering.

Narbonne

I wanted to go to Narbonne because I've developed a thing for unfinished cathedrals. I don't know why I'm so drawn to things that have been left undone, but I get easily enchanted by incompleteness.

Narbonne's unfinished sanctuary stood as a stubby grand testament to the meaning of being born at the wrong place at the wrong time. This building had every intention of becoming the most magnificent edifice in all of southern France, but fate, unfortunately, decided otherwise. The Black Plague, several wars, and years of bickering among the clergy caused cathedral building to remain low on the priority list. For over 700 years, this cathedral has patiently waited for someone to complete it, but no one ever will. This building stood as a demonstration of what people were capable of imagining but not always capable of achieving.

I spent a lot of time exploring the unfinished cathedral and found something sublime about its incompleteness. Pillars raised long ago spent their entire existence holding up nothing. Tall stone walls enclosed massive rooms filled with emptiness. The idea for a building was there, but the final construction of a building was not. It was the Gothic age's unfinished passion standing on a precipice. It was a death-defying balancing act that the building performed every day just to keep itself from falling into the abyss. I thought it was commendable that humankind managed to refrain from tearing the half-finished cathedral down. Humans do not prefer to be reminded of what we're unable to do, so the fact that the building still stood at all deserved a lot of respect. It represented the side of ourselves that we generally don't like others to see. We may be strong, but we are also weak. We'd rather hide our weakness than show it off for others to point at and ridicule. I appreciated knowing that people throughout the ages have accepted Narbonne cathedral for what it was. This building was, without a doubt, one of us in the truest sense of the term.

Humankind tends to cover up their weaknesses with any device possible, and the method of disguise employed at Narbonne cathedral was the manipulative placement of a massively oversized organ. Where the church's nave was supposed to be, an enormous closing wall was there instead, and on it was an equally gigantic organ. Certainly, putting a large organ on the wall was a manipulative way of distracting people from noticing that there wasn't much of a church erected around them. I spent more time wondering how anyone got that organ to hang on the wall than I did wondering where the rest of the cathedral was. Besides, who really needed a completed church when one had an organ nearly the size of a building? They apparently stuck that organ on the wall and declared the structure complete. There, that was their cathedral. There was nothing that I didn't love about that.

After Narbonne, I began my slow crawl back to Paris via Lyon and Dijon. I wasn't exactly in a rush to get back to Paris, but then again, I didn't especially want to be so far south in France in the event of yet another train strike either. Taking a bus ride with a drunk bus driver was something I had already checked off the bucket list, so I thought it wise to make my way north while the trains were still operating.

Lyon

I sometimes wonder why France is my favorite country to visit because it tends to be a pain in the ass with all the strikes that spring up whenever it's most inconvenient. Oh, wait, I know why I love France. France is fantastic because it forces me to exercise whenever it's impossible to find a metro. Apparently, there was a metro somewhere in Lyon, but it was so elusive that I never did locate it. Supposedly, there was also some old-timey funicular hiding in plain view as well, but I failed in finding that too. What I can tell anyone with certainty, though, is that Lyon has some of the longest staircases in the world, and they are a beast to climb, but they do give the legs a good workout.

Well, there existed a good reason to climb Lyon's ungodly staircases, and that was to get to the ancient ruins scattered on top of Fourviere hill. The ancient Romans ruled much of Gaul from the top of this perch, so I desired to see the view they once saw while imagining an empire sprawling under my feet.

The Romans called this city *Lugdunum*, and its importance in history cannot be underestimated. No doubt, Lugdunum was in the provinces, but it was no backwater, for it ruled as the capital of Romanized Gaul. This city had some serious clout, and it proved itself by giving birth to two Roman emperors, Claudius and Caracalla. The fact that these emperors were born 200 years apart attests to Lugdunum's longevity.

From this vantage point, it was easy to see how empire building took its familiar shape. Lugdunum modeled itself after Rome and became a miniature Rome of the North. All that the leaders had to do was conquer and copy. Rome was no longer just an idea once it settled on this hill; it became an entrenched reality.

Lugdunum essentially became the world's first model home community, replete with public baths and outdoor theaters. Lugdunum's promise to the rest of Gaul was that other cities could look as they did and reap the same benefits of Roman rule so long as they submitted. Within time, there was little reason for anyone to recall their Celtic roots anymore when their whole world became Romanized. The idea of Rome bled the people red, and their blood soaked into the soil where I presently stood.

Ruins are the only voices that can speak through the

vacuum of time. Ruins don't say much, but they speak volumes. "How many deaths did you inadvertently cause?" I wanted to ask Lugdunum's ancient theater, but I knew that it wouldn't be able to provide a straight answer. The ruins would tell me to do the math: divide the number of conquered by those who did the conquering, and the value would give a rough estimate of how many had to die so this theater could exist. There would have been no point in asking the theater who those people were that were vanquished in the name of Rome because the theater didn't concern itself with anyone who was not a Roman citizen. Members of Celtic tribes had no reason to be inside any theater unless they were Roman citizens themselves, so the theater had no concept of who anyone was outside of its domain. Conquering cared little for getting intimate with the conquered.

In my eyes, the ruins of Lugdunum were the tombstones for everything that was buried when Celtic France was laid to waste. Rome came, saw, and conquered, and all of Gaul became theirs for the taking. Indeed, native warfare was no match for the Roman machine, yet something outwitted Rome eventually. I have always wondered what the one thing was that ultimately caused the Roman Empire to stop. Everything they did proved to be all for naught in the end. Perhaps they simply overreached and stuck their hands into the void. Evidently, it proved too hard to hold on to something when there was nothing left to hold on to anymore.

The distance between Roman Lugdunum and medieval Lyon was physically only the length of one exceedingly long staircase, but mentally, the distance was not something I could easily comprehend. I needed the hill to be exposed like the

Grand Canyon, where the passage of time was revealed in easy-to-read layers. It was difficult for my brain to jump from an ancient mindset to a medieval one when there was no helpful transition in between. My mind was stuck wondering what happened to all the time that happened in the middle. What was life like during all the years that occurred between those two vastly different eras? It was almost as though all that time had just slipped away like sand in a bottomless hourglass. Time essentially emptied into an abyss, and nothing remained to show for all the time that got away. The story of those who lived amongst the gradually decaying Roman buildings for nearly 700 years was apparently not one for the history books. The unwritten tome titled *Transitional Folk Tales* will most likely remain unwritten forever.

Time sloughed itself down the hill and was greeted at the bottom by a vibrant culture that expressed itself through an astounding ability to make a complete maze out of life. After getting lost a thousand times in Lyon, I think I now fully grasp the thought processes of a Renaissance mind. These people obviously did not think in linear terms, for their streets would have been straight if they did. As it was, *Vieux Lyon* (Old Lyon) was a warren of windy streets, tall pink buildings, spiraling staircases, and ingenious courtyards. Walking around Vieux Lyon was like exploring the inner workings of Da Vinci's mind as he calculated yet another invention of primitive machinery. Of course, Da Vinci probably never needed a map to navigate the twists and turns of his own head, but I'm sure that he would have appreciated having one handy for the few occasions when he got lost in his thoughts.

I certainly could have used a decent map because it

gradually became apparent that the tourist map I picked up at the train station wasn't something I could depend on for accuracy. Frustratingly, the map only vaguely suggested where certain monuments were located and only slightly indicated routes to reach them successfully. Following that map allowed me to experience several inadvertent excursions, and unintentionally walking down a freeway ramp was only one of the map's more precious diversions. Also included was a detour to the part of Lyon where all the delinquent kids drank liquor and sprayed graffiti, as well as a tour of the part of Lyon where all the street names were in the process of being changed. It was a good thing that Lyon looked as good as it did because I could hardly get mad at it when I ended up at another dead end because some gorgeous old stone building stood in the way. Oh, and before I forget to mention it, I have to say that the Gallo-Roman Museum of Lyon-Fourvière had two dodecahedrons, and they didn't make a big deal out of them. They certainly didn't dedicate a whole museum to those objects, but they did admit that they didn't know what they were either. Thus, I made absolutely no progress in solving the dodecahedron mystery, much to my chagrin.

I enjoyed Lyon mainly because the place let me get my mind off anything personal. I was feeling a tad sorry for myself after my visit to Carcassonne because it reminded me that I was relationshipless once again. Eric had already embarked on his next phase in life, and there was no one at home waiting for me. Thus, Roman ruins and medieval courtyards were the perfect diversions to derail any thoughts about heartache, but there were no such ruins to distract me when I walked the lonely streets of Dijon.

Dijon

Seeing the historic buildings of Dijon through hazy rain reminded me that I was feeling depressed. It had rained in every city I had visited thus far, and I decided early on that I wasn't going to let the rain bother me. However, there was something about how the buildings of Dijon held themselves in the miserable weather that triggered a sadness inside me. The buildings knew they were gray, they knew they were old, and they knew that their era had left them behind. The vintage buildings were still beautiful, but they looked as though they didn't want to put forth effort anymore. They looked like they were done with it already and tired of the game. I related to that. Relationships were games that people played, and I was tired of losing. Love was about as inanimate as the buildings were to me. Thus, my mood was hardly lifted when I watched an impossibly handsome couple kiss passionately in front of a historic structure. I wanted to punch them and then let myself morph into one of the tall gray buildings, allowing the rain to soak me to the core.

Being alone doesn't depress me, but loneliness does. I don't often feel alone when I'm by myself, for I think and function quite well without someone else around to distract me. Yet, I sometimes need another person to egg me along and act as my partner in crime. I've noticed that I reach a creative standstill when I obsess over finding someone to love. Yet, once I secure that love, I tend not to nurture that love very well. I know I am a passionate person, but I perhaps throw my passion into things that don't matter very much. I need to learn how to prioritize my desires appropriately. People should matter more than art, more than hiking, more than traveling, more than anything in the world, but I sometimes don't think of people that way. People sometimes don't matter that much to me because I often find people unkind. I know that I need to be more open and receptive, but I tend to hold back because I hate feeling vulnerable. Yet, is it not human to want to protect one's own feelings? I want to become someone who cares for my own feelings as much for another's, but that sounds impossibly lofty. Humans are selfish creatures. That might just be our nature, but even nature can be trained to grow into unusual shapes.

However, life is not always about the self. I was thinking about that while I admired the many artistic objects housed at the Dijon Musée des Beaux-Arts. Much of the art housed there was created not in the name of humankind but in the name of something entirely else, be it God, king, or glory. Humans have the capacity to be more than they are, and they go to great creative lengths to reach beyond the earthly realm. If there is more to life beyond the horizon, humans will gladly fall off the map in search of it. We are insatiably curious creatures, and I admire our ability to be inquisitive almost to a fault.

I adore humankind's curiosity, but I also respect our surprising ability to remain perfectly still. Being a monk and not thinking of anything beyond codified concepts is not something that would ever appeal to me; however, I'm fascinated by the communities that groups of like-minded people created in the Middle Ages. In particular, I find the Cistercian order to be appealing because of its straightforward simplicity. Something about their clean lines and unadorned walls appeals to my sensibilities. I've long desired to experience one of their abbeys in person, and my top pick has always been

Fontenay Abbey. With my mind being as muddled as it was, I was looking forward to my upcoming visit there, for I hoped it would cure me of my psychological afflictions.

Fontenay Abbey

The Cistercian Abbey of Fontenay was founded in AD 1118 by Bernard of Clairvaux because he felt that Cîteaux Abbey (which he also founded) was not austere enough. He envisioned the monks at Fontenay Abbey strictly observing the Rules of Saint Benedict, which meant they would live poor and simply. He didn't want the Fontenay monks to be distracted from living ascetic lives, so he built this monastery in an isolated area where they had no choice but to depend on themselves.

I took a 45-minute train from Dijon to Montbard and immediately started my 6 km trek to Fontenay Abbey under cloudy skies. Thankfully, unlike my failed walk to Conques, the area helpfully provided me with signage, so nowhere along the way did I have to doubt where I was going. It was amazing how not worrying about directions freed up my mind to think about other things and appreciate the scenery. I was delighted that it wasn't raining for a change, so I could truly admire all the natural beauty that surrounded me.

The closer I got to Fontenay Abbey, the more beautiful the landscape became, and walking there allowed me to clear out my head. When I reached Fontenay, I was ready to accept an austere environment. My mind was utterly blank, so I was prepared to receive the lessons the abbey was willing to teach. However, I got there too early and had to wait for the site to open.

"No worries," I thought. "I'll just bask in the glow of quiet contemplation."

I was right at my most calm when I heard them. The cacophony of every cyclist from the town of Verona came pedaling down the hill, chatting very loudly in their native Italian. Their voices reached a crescendo, and their words bounced off the ancient stones and straight into my ears. My reverie was broken, so I had to find an escape route to avoid their sounds for the next 20 minutes. I found my reprieve on a trail in a nearby forest and discovered what I was unknowingly looking for. I ended up staying out there until well after the time the abbey opened because it was hard to walk away from pure, unadulterated peace.

The groves around the abbey were historical, for they harked back to the building's founding. The forest was perceived as an extension of the contemplative space, and many monks once walked on the same trail I was currently on. It was also very likely that many monks had the same thoughts as I did (and did not have) as well. I felt a connection to history and a sense that I was getting an insight into a mysterious lifestyle that no longer existed. I respected the desire to live a simple life, including essential strolls through nature. The Cistercians believed in the value of working the land by hand, and they depended on the charity of others for that which they could not provide for themselves. I desired to emulate their simplicity but disagreed with the need for alms. I'm not opposed to a bit of paid work in return for self-sufficiency, but such an act would have belied their purpose. Their existence was contemplative and plain. They lived far removed from urban temptations, and their daily thoughts focused on the small things that made them human. They lived life at its elemental core, and I found their lifestyle alluring.

"Vines and trees will teach you that which you will never learn from masters," Bernard of Clairvaux was quoted to say, but those words could have just as easily been uttered by either John Muir or Henry David Thoreau. Every era seems to have its own naturalist that beckons their contemporaries to find themselves in the natural world. The fact that Bernard of Clairvaux recognized nature's value as a place where someone could find themselves is impressive, for he lived at a time when people mostly avoided forests out of fear. To envision monks strolling through nature in the 1100s was difficult to conceptualize. However, it felt insanely special to walk on the paths outside Fontenay Abbey, for they were the precursors to almost every nature path created ever since. I'm exaggerating, of course, but it was a thought that struck me when I was there, and I found the potential of that concept tantalizing.

I went inside Fontenay Abbey and happily discovered that I had the entire place to myself. The interior was just as I expected, for it was as plain as plain could possibly be. The only thing that filled the abbey was light that entered through a wall pierced nearly entirely with windows. Standing inside the sanctuary helped me understand the true meaning of quiet. To be quiet was to stand still in a space filled with nothing. There existed no chaos in a room filled with a pure glow. I felt my mind go numb, and I contemplated absolutely nothing at all. Not thinking about anything made me feel good. It felt good not to feel restless inside and not feel a sense of emotional dissatisfaction. I felt at peace with myself for the first time on my journey. I was happy to be in the moment, in the moment of pure bliss.

As much as I desired to imitate a Cistercian mode of existence, I knew that I harbored too many superfluous things that would render me unable to strip my life to the barest of bones. I knew deep down that I would never be worthy of calling myself a Cistercian monk. I was exactly what they were telling people not to be. I felt that inside. I felt that I could do better with a lot less. It got me thinking about what I was willing to give up. "How much of my life was pure excess?" I wondered. "Would having a car be considered too rich for a medieval monk's blood? Would living a non-communal lifestyle be considered too wasteful of resources?" Going to Fontenay Abbey inspired me to clean out my apartment when I returned home. I did a massive Goodwill run with all the unused items and hoped my things would have more value for someone else. I figured that it couldn't hurt to start small. It has been forever since I visited Fontenay Abbey, and I'm still purging little by little. I'm always trying to chip away at myself to see how close I can get to a semi-Cistercian level. I estimate that it will take my entire lifetime to get anywhere near.

Travel is indeed life transforming, so long as one is receptive to the lessons a given place imparts. Yet, having just said that, I have yet to learn what lesson the Dijon train station was trying to teach me when I looked out the window longingly at the Van Gogh book I left sitting on the bench. I watched my literary travel companion disappear from view as I contemplated jumping off of a moving train to reunite with what I regarded as my best friend on that entire trip. Even though I have since bought another copy of *The Letters of Vincent Van Gogh*, it's simply not the same. The one I left sitting on the Dijon train station's bench resonated with me more. Hopefully, whoever picked up that book understood English well enough to be inspired by all the conveniently underlined passages. Perhaps the lesson was one of detachment. I needed to let that book go to its new owner?

The Louvre

It was a perfect day not to be outside like all of us tourists were. It was still early in the morning, and the Louvre wasn't due to open for another 30 minutes. We all staked our claim in line under a gray sky sticky wet with rain. There existed no sun, so, therefore, no shadows. The statues that decorated the facade appeared unphotogenic under such dismal lighting, and everyone looked forlorn in their various positions of crouching. I couldn't help but think how ridiculous we all looked standing around former palace grounds in such casual clothing, and the thought crossed my mind that we'd all look a heck of a lot better wearing corsets and tuxedos. None of us looked contemporaneous with the historical structure surrounding us, and if any French king returned from the dead, I was certain we'd all be deservedly shot.

Raindrops continuously pittered and pattered in the flat fountains surrounding the glass pyramid that served as the Louvre's entrance. All was water from above and below, which was a sight my eyes were too familiar with. Everyone desired to just get inside and away from all this wetness. Yet, I could tell that little note was being taken that we were about to enter a building that had been embellished upon since the 12th century. I also knew that many visitors would depart the Louvre unaware that they missed visiting the excavated basement that revealed the foundation stones of the original Louvre castle. Indeed, it had taken nearly 900 years to fine-tune this impressive structure and many generations of monarchs' exploits to fill it. It was unreasonable to think that one could experience its entirety in one measly day.

Entering the Louvre was a thoroughly modern experience. If there were any whimsical notions that one was entering an ancient castle, that dreamy thought was instantly dispelled when one passed through a glass pyramid and onto an escalator, for there was nothing medieval about either of those things. Here was a building with perhaps fifty doors, yet people gained access through a hole carved into the ground.

Once past the entrance stalls, visitors get immediately confronted with colossal statuary. The Louvre does not build the visitor up gradually; it just smacks people between the eyes straight away with incredible sculptures.

"Welcome to the Louvre, dear visitor, and prepare to be overwhelmed," was what those statues said. Yet, those figures also said something else, something way more unsettling. They were the voices of long-dead people who spoke in unison as the ambassadors of the past. Yet, for many visitors, the only sound they heard from those statues was silence – for rare was the visitor that took the time to stop and listen to what those statues had to say.

I'd been to the Louvre a few times before; however, I never once stopped to learn anything about those massive figures that greeted visitors at the entrance. I don't know why it was always so easy to walk right by four colossal statues and not be curious to find out where they came from. Indeed, someone must have created those statues for a reason, and I assumed it wasn't for them to sit in the sunlit lobby of the Louvre. "But for what reason were they born?" I started to wonder. "Why were they not residing where they were originally meant to be?" For the first time ever, I was curious to learn what story was hiding behind their bronze-colored eyes, contorted poses, and colossal sizes. The time had come for me to read their intriguing tale.

Upon reading the nearby plaque, I learned that the statues were called *The Four Captives*. The work was commissioned in 1679 by an ambitious courtier who had a rabid desire to show how great his king, Louis XIV was. This courtier, Francois d'Aubusson, contrived to have residential buildings removed and a great square created in the center of a densely populated area in Paris. In the center of the newly opened space, to be christened "the Place des Victoires," he intended to plop an oversized gilt bronze statue of Louis XIV being crowned by the allegory of Fame. His vision became a reality seven years later, but France, by that time, had lost its victorious sheen.

Under the oversized statue of Louis XIV were *The Four Captives,* representing the four nations France defeated when it signed the Treaties of Nijmegen seven years earlier. It was a rather flippant display of arrogance toward those defeated nations, and by the time the new square and statue were completed, the favor was not in Louis XIV's court. The king spent all of France's money waging wars he couldn't win, and erecting a statue of him stomping his enemies appeared to be out of some other place, some other time. He was not the same Louis XIV anymore, and he was embarrassed by the massive monument to glory. It represented the man he used to be, yet he failed to order the statue removed. Advisers to the king counseled that keeping the display could provoke war among those allegorically depicted nations, and over time, it essentially did. When the War of the Grand Alliance broke out, Louis XIV desired to be that king in that monument once again, but that king only existed in metal.

The statue of kingly glory was eventually melted down during the French Revolution, but the pedestal containing *The Four Captives* was respectfully spared. *The Four Captives* took on a new allegory, for the newly Enlightened populace saw them as victims of absolute power. The chains that shackled them were symbolically broken, and the statues were first moved to the Louvre, then to a retirement home for war veterans, and then to a pretty park located about six miles from the center of Paris. In 1992, the officials at the Louvre decided that *The Four Captives* needed to return so they could gussy up the space inside the lobby.

So, that was their story. I wouldn't have known any of that simply by looking at them. Yet, there seemed to be something "off" about those figures. They seemed to be missing something, a huge something, in fact. I got the sense that they were missing more than half of their former selves. Even the statues looked as though they were searching for that which was no longer there. The four figures flanked a square pedestal that held up nothing. Indeed, that empty space once held the likeness of Louis XIV.

Thus, I concluded that people likely believed it was better to fill that space with nothing than with the image of absolute power. Yet, saying that defies why Francois d'Aubusson had those figures created in the first place. The statues were there because Louis XIV lived, and had he not been king, no one today would even be gazing upon those bronze statues now.

Yet, uttering such thoughts echoes the sentiments of the Enlightenment; it doesn't allow the original voices of the generation that created these figures to be heard. Herein resides the creation's off-ness that I was referring to. Those statues were incomplete, for they were taken out of context and given new meanings. Those statues were not unique in this effect, for many museum pieces get displayed in improper elements. Time does not stop for museum pieces. Time, in fact, whittled away at the Louis XIV monument and chewed off the parts it felt were not worthy of gracing the eyes of the future populace. Thus, future humans gaze upon the monument's remains and declare the piece beautiful but lament its incompleteness. That was, of course, assuming that modern viewers even stopped long enough to look at the display.

Reading a wordy plaque takes too much precious time for many viewers, so they are perfectly content with not knowing what those sculptures mean. For many, it matters not what the figures mean because it'd be too much information anyway. Giant statues that used to be someplace, obviously not there now; they get it. The Louvre is full of such things. So is every museum in the world. It is, in fact, the very definition of what a museum is. No one really stops to ponder the philosophical ramifications of what museums mean to the objects themselves, for that would be absurd. Museums are merely time receptacles, a place where things go when their own time leaves them behind.

Perhaps it was poetic to read the expressions on those statues' faces as being the universal countenance of all museum pieces. Theirs was an expression of confusion. Their original purpose was obliterated when they became severed from their original location. "What are we doing here?" the statues possibly wondered. "Why did we not just die with the rest of them?" Was not the Louvre just one big open casket for modern people to lament the figures of ages past? Perhaps. Maybe the Louvre was nothing more than a giant tomb, a receptacle of unburied things. Perhaps museums should really be called mausoleums, and the Louvre should be synonymous with the Taj Mahal. Anyone who knows me knows that I love a good cemetery, so maybe that explains why I adore the Louvre as much as I do.

There are many rooms in the Louvre, and each one houses objects of some other age completely severed from our own. Each object has a voice that speaks from some other time, some other space, some other land. Without all the pottery shards, cuneiform tablets, or emerald-encrusted chalice cups, we would never be who we collectively are today. All historical objects had to have a beginning for us to see them at their end. Museum pieces are the only tangible links that connect modern humans to the humans we used to be. I dare say that there is something almost spiritual about that relationship that it blows my mind that museums don't come equipped with pulpits.

So, keeping in tune with ancient and noble things, I typically start my tour of the Louvre underground. The skeleton of the original twelfth-century castle lies buried in the secret world below the museum. If the modern Louvre can be considered a mausoleum, then this old Louvre is a tomb within a tomb.

The bottom half of the original Louvre castle looked as though someone buried it while it was still new. The warm earth tones of the 900-year-old stones were so clean that they appeared to have been set down only recently. It was strange to think those blocks were placed there by feudal hands at a time when men wore tights and pointy shoes. Yet, whoever set down those stones did not merely build a castle; they built an entire age.

This was where medieval France began, and it was here where it could be experienced, albeit in very shallow quarters, for there existed a ceiling above the castle where the sky used to be. "Where did the top three-quarters of the original Louvre go?" I wondered. Successive ages recycled the top portion and donated the bottom section to the ground. Just like the castle, the moat that once surrounded the original Louvre was also deemed obsolete and unceremoniously sent into the soil. A new Louvre replaced the old Louvre, and the old Louvre was buried.

Slowly, an underground visitor becomes one with the tomb. The stones gradually become familiar, as if one has seen this building before. Indeed, this is the same castle one has always seen in one's dreams. It is in the bowels of the Louvre where we all feel like we lived in the medieval era before. This, here, is home to us. It is the modern era that is now unfamiliar. Time and space blur whence standing beside a buried castle.

Only when a visitor reemerges above ground must they grapple with the fact that it is once again a different age. The visitor must mentally reenter the modern era, but, alas, the visitor is at a museum, so time matters not. The mind is now prepared to wander the rooms of the Louvre, for the concept of time and space is now malleable. It is best to get inside your museum head to get the most out of any museum visit. Your museum head is one where all the synapses are firing, and time and space become one giant helix. Generations' worth of creations are housed under one roof, and a visitor must string them together into one continuous train of thought.

There exists no better wing in the Louvre to allow one's synapses to fire than in the "Sully" wing, specifically in the section that was once the former palace apartments. The Louvre was once the home of France's kings and queens, and each generation felt it necessary to put their own stamp upon the palace. Louis XIV resided at the Louvre before relocating his entourage to Versailles, and the apartments he left behind are testaments to his radiant personality. Today's visitors can visit the Sun King's original apartments and revel in the glory of wood-paneled walls and gilded ceilings dripping with privilege and power. It was no irony that the relics of ancient Egypt's original Sun King, Akhenaten, were housed in Louis XIV's apartments, for those two men existed on opposite strands of the same double helix.

Ancient Egyptian art is insanely iconic. Ancient Egyptian sculpture, in particular, is instantly recognizable because nothing about their sculpture changed for nearly 3,000 years. All the portraits have the same idealized features – the same perfect smirk, the same perfect gaze, the same perfect jaw, the same perfect body, the same perfect everything. Ancient Egyptian sculpture was iconically *flawless*. Yet, there existed one moment in Egyptian history when it wasn't. There was nothing perfect about Akhenaten except how he perfectly embraced his imperfections.

Egypt gave the world religion. Egyptian gods became Greek gods, then Roman gods, and then, finally, Christian saints (or so I deduce). Christian prayers are closed with the word *Amen* which sounds oddly similar to the word ancient Egyptians associated with their highest deity Amun. Egypt gave the world polytheism, but for a brief moment, it also gave the world its first taste of monotheism, and its object of worship was the sun.

To be clear, Akhenaten did not worship the sun. Akhenaten worshiped God as personified by the sun. Akhenaten regarded the sun as a life bringer – if not for the sun, the world would not exist. All other gods had no meaning – the sun was all that mattered. Akhenaten deduced that God existed inside the sun and all life emanated from its powerful rays. Sculptures of Akhenaten show him and his family basking in the glory of the outstretched arms of the sun disk. These depictions are not of a typical Egyptian royal family – these are depictions of humanity at its most authentic. Akhenaten was depicted faithfully with his pudgy stomach, elongated face, and feminine hips. There was nothing regal about him save that he wore the pharaoh's double crown.

Louis XIV received the moniker "Sun King" for believing that France would not survive without him, just as the world would not survive without the sun. Only one person in the world could have been brave enough to tell Louis XIV that he didn't shine as bright as the sun, but that person didn't say anything because he had been dead for 3,000 years. Only Akhenaten was worthy of sleeping in Louis XIV's former chambers under a gilt coffered ceiling where bits of light caught glimmers of gold.

The world is abysmally bereft of statues of Akhenaten, for most of them were destroyed at the end of his reign. The fragmented statue displayed at the Louvre was about the most complete statue of him that I could ever hope to see, and he was shown at a kingly height well above my head. I had to look up to admire him, and doing so felt very appropriate, for he was a ruler who never looked down. All his energy came from above, and he felt the sun's power to be all-encompassing. He penned his thoughts in *The Great Hymn to the Aten* when he wrote:

> You are far, but your rays touch the Earth;
> Men see you, but know not your ways.

Indeed, Akhenaten knew that the sun was essential to life itself. In a world before science, there was only one word to describe the sun's power, and that word was synonymous with God. Akhenaten invented God when he worshiped the sun, and I had to admit that he wasn't too far off the mark. When the sun dies, everything will die with it.

CHAPTER SEVEN:
The Meeting, Nov 2006

New Job, New Life

My job at the travel agency wasn't the same after 9/11. The internet was already threatening to take our jobs away as it was, and the fallout of events after the attacks hammered the final nails into that gradually built coffin.

I remember the day when the layoffs occurred. Our company of over 300 agents dropped to less than 100 several months after 9/11. Those getting laid off were stopped on their way to the elevator and told flat-out they were fired. I remember walking into work that day and wondering why so many people were crying. I somehow made it past the gauntlet, rode to the fifth floor, and entered a semi-ghost town. I was one of the lucky ones who still had a job, and I stayed there for another five years. During that time, I watched the travel business entirely change.

Eventually, there was no point in keeping that job anymore when all the freebies went away. Gone were the free airline tickets, comped hotel stays, and catered lunches. Being a travel agent became just a regular job, and the workload only increased when I got assigned to work at the "Emergency Desk." All the phone calls that I fielded were nothing but problems. One problem after another, every minute, every hour, every day. The work just wasn't fun anymore. So, I decided to go back to school. I toyed around with every possible career and settled upon one that would allow me to take pictures all day. I learned how to be an x-ray tech and accepted a position at a hospital. (Little did I know a worldwide pandemic would happen 14 years later, and I would be stuck knee-deep in those trenches. Alas, that's a story for some other book I currently have no desire to write.)

Going to x-ray school was a long two years that left me little time to focus on myself. Once my new career was finally in place, I threw my gaze inward. I quickly decided that I didn't want to be alone anymore, so I placed a very specific ad in the Yahoo personals. And by "a very specific ad," I mean I laid it on thick. My ad was hilarious yet serious, and I knew that my chosen words would turn off more than half of the male population (I made it perfectly clear that I was a cat-loving, artistic, politically opinionated, granola-type agnostic). I didn't want to waste anyone's time, especially my own. Thus, I knew that whoever responded would be 110% my type of companion. This, dear readers, was how I met my current husband, Ryan.

Being the cheap wad that I was (and forever will be), I mentioned in the ad that I would only be running it for the free 30-day trial period, after which I vowed to be single forever if no one responded. Ryan felt the fire under his butt when he came across my ad relatively late in the game. He quickly whipped up a profile and immediately replied on day 27 of my 30-day advertisement. Had he looked at Yahoo personals four days later, we never would have met.

To make a long story short, I'll simply say we clicked right away. I knew I was in love with him the very first moment I saw the back of his head. The day we met in person was almost a disaster, though, when I waited around forever for him, and he wasn't showing up. Apparently, he walked inside the sushi restaurant where we arranged to meet, and he failed to find me in the massive crowd. I had a strange feeling that he was probably waiting outside, so I went there looking for him and recognized him immediately from the pictures he shared. Granted, his back was facing the door when I exited, but there weren't too many men around with hair as long as his, so I knew it was him, and I found him *amazing*. It was love at first sight, indeed, and there hasn't been a day I haven't thought about him since. He's always on my brain, and his being in my life makes everything, including thinking, easier. Coffee helps too, but that's a different subject. So does wine. Wine helps me think. Alas, I digress.

Minor Detour

Ryan and I had only been dating for a month before I suggested that we hurry up and fly to Milwaukee so that he could meet my mom while she was still relatively lucid. I disclosed to him that my mom suffered from extreme depression and that her mental faculties were steadily declining. Her psychotic episodes that would materialize out of nowhere were sadly becoming more frequent, but she was recently going through a period of relative calm. I explained that it was in our best interest to seize the moment and meet her while she was feeling peppy instead of meeting her during one of her funks. Surprisingly, Ryan approached the idea of going to Wisconsin with a girl he had only recently met to meet her potentially depressed mother with an open mind. He gave the proposition a minute's worth of thought before saying, "Yes, I would love to go." Two weeks later, we were both on a plane heading to the one place I couldn't seem to avoid and the one place that Ryan had never thought of going to before.

Fares to Milwaukee are, for some reason, commonly

overpriced, and more often than not, it's cheaper to fly into Chicago than it is to fly into Milwaukee. Thus, we unsurprisingly flew into Chicago's Midway airport and rented a car. Ryan was excited that he basically scored two cities for the price of one and excitedly inquired if we had time to see at least one Chicago highlight. No doubt, he was thinking along the lines of taking in the view from the Sears Tower, a joy ride down the Magnificent Mile, or a couple of hours at The Art Institute. However, I completely hijacked all the possible scenarios when I suggested taking him to a place I had only recently read about. Indeed, there were probably a few moments when he quietly wondered what stars had to align to find himself looking at colossal objects that he knew absolutely nothing about at the not-so-famous-but-it-should-be Oriental Institute at the University of Chicago.

To be fair, I didn't 100% deprive Ryan of a proper Chicago experience. We took the scenic route down pot-hole-riddled streets and admired many fine buildings along the way while we wiped ketchup off our faces after every bump because eating hot dogs and joy-riding was not a winning combination. However, we didn't have a lot of time on our hands if we wanted to beat the living nightmare known as Chicago rush-hour traffic, so there was a reason why I selected going to a small museum. Besides, I figured a smaller museum – one that boasted nearly the best near Eastern and ancient Egyptian collections in America – would pack the biggest possible punch.

Once there, I occasionally caught Ryan in mid-thought while he stood in front of something very ancient. I figured that he must have been musing over the meaning of a venerated object, but more than likely, he was probably wondering whether or not the Suns would win the basketball game that evening. I think that I found that museum way more fascinating than he did, but it did hammer home that not everyone was as rabid about ancient history as me. I needed to learn that not everyone was as inclined to revere a ginormous stone head of a bull that used to guard the entrance of the Hundred Column Hall in ancient Persepolis as I was. He, on the other hand, found the museum to be the perfect venue to reveal his ardent passion for *Star Trek* to me. For a brief moment, it looked as though our relationship had a zero chance of surviving. It was evident that if I made Ryan stay in that museum any longer, we'd have to have a conversation about how great *Star Trek* was, and I was having a difficult time seeing the connection.

"No, seriously," Ryan said, "these objects are making me think of the period in Vulcan history referred to as *The Time of Awakening*."

"The time of what?" I asked.

"*The Time of Awakening*," he reiterated. "It was a time when a group of Vulcans wanted to return to savage ways, so they instigated a nuclear attack upon Surak and his enlightened society."

I looked him dead in the eye and said, "I have absolutely no idea what you're talking about."

"Ya, so, these Vulcans abandoned their home planet, colonized the planets Romulus and Remus, and created a warlike society. Spock eventually succeeded Surak and became one of the most respected figures in the United Federation of Planets."

"Is this your way of telling me that you're done with this museum?" I asked.

"Ya, pretty much," he said. "You have no idea what *Star Trek* is about, and I have absolutely no idea what any of these objects mean."

"Fair enough," I said. "So, are you ready to go to Milwaukee?"

"Let's do it!" he exclaimed.

So, off to Wisconsin we went.

Mom

On the drive up to Milwaukee, I have to admit that I was stalling when I suggested we visit the Bavarian-inspired *Cheese Castle* and do some unnecessary food shopping. I was kind of dreading taking him to meet my mom, so I thought eating some scrumptious cheese curds would alleviate my anxiety. A big part of me just wanted to say, "forget it," and I seriously toyed with sabotaging the whole endeavor by taking too long to get there. I wasn't 100% sure which version of my mother we'd be meeting that day, so all I could do was hope for the best but brace for the worst. I was really depending on her making a good impression because, and I'm being perfectly honest here, what she'd be like would directly reflect upon me. I was digging this Ryan guy, and I didn't want him to judge me if my mom decided she was too depressed to open the door. I knew I was feeling selfish, but this wasn't just about her; this was also about me. I had spent many hours, days, weeks, and years concerned about my mom's mental well-being, and I, for once, didn't want to worry about her. I just wanted her to be genuinely happy, not the temporarily-happy-because-someone-did-something-to-cheer-her-up happy. I wasn't in the mood for mental gymnastics that day. I just really needed her to be normal.

I rang the doorbell and was more than relieved when she opened it with a cheerful demeanor. I had barely introduced Ryan to her before she reached out and gave him a big hug. Neither of us had even stepped over the threshold before she blurted out, "Do you want to look at some photographs of Krista from when she was in high school? I spent all day putting them together!" I was still standing on the doorstep voicing my objections when a photo album was thrust into his hands. Yup. That woman was mental, alright. Certifiably insane. Two minutes after our arrival, my mom and Ryan were bonding over photographs of 1980s me decked out in neon t-shirts, stone-washed jeans, jelly shoes, braces, and puffy hair. I was left standing there completely aghast.

Not less than five minutes later, she started telling him a story I hadn't heard of before. "Did you know that Krista was born on a Friday?" she began. "I also was born on a Friday, and my mother was born on a Friday, too!" That was complete news to me. Boy, oh boy, she was sure divulging all the family secrets to this guy she had just met five minutes ago. Honestly, I was hoping for happiness, but whatever this was could have been toned down a notch. This was extreme happiness, and I suspected it would be followed by a crash, which, of course, it was. Yet, all was as good for the moment, and we rolled with it.

We took her to dinner at a German restaurant called Mader's and laughed as we drank beer out of glasses shaped like a boot. All in all, it was one of the better evenings I ever had with her, but it was going to be the only evening we'd get. I was glad we had a good time because it allowed Ryan to see my mom at her best, which molded a nice version of her inside his head. For years after, this was the only image he had of her because even though we spent two days in Milwaukee, we only really got to see her that one time because a massive blizzard kept us away most of the second day we were there.

The Quiet Blizzard

I was massively allergic to my mom's cat, so I could never stay overnight at her house. I got used to staying at the Motel 6 located a few miles away at the top of an incredibly long hill at the intersection of two major roadways. I always stayed there by myself, so I didn't think too much about it when I habitually booked it for our not-so-romantic getaway.

The view from the hotel's window was never very spectacular, but it always allowed for some decent traffic watching if there was a shortage of things to do. I also discovered that I could watch a proper blizzard from the comfort of that perch as well, not that Ryan initially believed me when I told him. He had no idea why I crawled back under the covers two seconds after I glanced out the window early in the morning. I declared there was no point in getting up because it was blizzarding outside. He, not being from a snowy state, asked me to define what "blizzarding" meant. I told him to look outside the window and see what that meant for himself.

So, to the window he went and tentatively opened the curtain. He couldn't believe his eyes when he saw millions of silent snowflakes falling from the sky, blanketing the landscape in a cozy sheet of white.

"I've never seen a blizzard before," he said with his face glued to the window. "I had no idea blizzards were so quiet."

Indeed, the world was totally silent. No background noise filled the space between our ears because the ordinarily busy roadways were entirely devoid of cars.

"Let's go outside!" he exclaimed, disregarding the fact that he lacked boots, gloves, hat, scarf, or warm jacket.

"Ya, have fun with that," I told him and proceeded to bury myself deeper under the covers.

"Poo-poo, you're no fun," he said. "I'm going out there!"

Unsurprisingly, he was back inside less than five minutes later.

"Did you enjoy it out there?" I asked him.

"Oh my God, I can't believe how much snow is falling!" he said. "It falls super fast, too, like lightning-speed snowflakes. Snow is everywhere, piles of it. Is this normal for here?"

"It's not normal-normal, just sometimes normal," I said. "Blizzards don't happen every year. As a kid, I wanted blizzards all the time because then the schools would close, but as an adult, blizzards suck because they only mean one thing, and that's all-around shitty driving."

By 9:00 a.m., it was apparent that the snow was not going to stop anytime soon, so we called my mom and told her that we had to wait and see how the day played out. There was no way in hell I was even going to attempt to drive down that steep hill in the middle of a blizzard, so we basically had no choice but to stay put. By 9:30 a.m., we were bored out of our gourds sitting in a motel room, so we decided to venture out on foot and see how the rest of the world was doing. We were glad we decided to go outside because what was happening on the roadways proved way more entertaining than anything playing on the five dull TV channels we weren't watching.

The plows hadn't come through yet, but that apparently wasn't reason enough to prevent some folks from taking a car out of their garage. The snow mound in front of our motel became a sizable receiving receptacle for vehicles that failed to complete the final stages of climbing up the monstrous hill. We took it upon ourselves to become everyone's benevolent heroes by being there at the right place at the right time, just when someone needed another set of hands to help dig their vehicle out of a giant fluffy pillow of failure. The first rescue was a complete circus because we knew nothing about pulling cars out of snowbanks, but we managed to perfect our method after the second recovery. It proved to be the perfect vacation for a couple of desert dwellers because it was the complete opposite of rescuing people from too much sunshine.

Unfortunately, our fun balloon popped immediately after the plow came through an hour into our self-declared rescue mission. Effectively, the plow put a complete kibosh on our entertainment because it meant that our services were no longer required. Thus, the roads being cleared meant that we could drive again, so I called my mom and told her that we were ready to take her out to lunch. We were having such a delightful morning getting cold and wet in inappropriate winter wear that I didn't think there could be anything in the world that would make the day any less delightful. At least, that was what I thought until I got on the phone with my manic-depressive mother.

"I'm not feeling well," she explained. "I don't think you should come over."

"Well, crap," I thought to myself, "I should have expected that." I knew I needed to brace myself for the moment when her depression would rear its ugly head. Yet, I was determined not to let her have it.

"Let us take you to the Art Museum," I offered, thinking that usually cheered her up.

"No, I don't want to. You two go," she countered.

"We came all this way to be with you," I tried to reason. "Just let us take you out to lunch then."

"I have no appetite," she said. "Really, Krista, I don't want to go anywhere right now."

"Then let us hang out with you at your place," I said. We don't have to do anything. I can deal with my allergies for a couple of hours."

"No, I don't want that," she stated. "I don't want anything. I'm not even dressed yet."

The conversation went on and on, but it was pointless. It was obvious that she had put all her effort into the day before, and the morning snowstorm put her mind into a different compartment. It was evident that she had made the dreaded cerebral switch, and she was going to stay in that alternate mode for quite a while. I had seen her like this oodles of times before, but I couldn't help being perturbed that she couldn't get a grip on herself just this once. I can't claim to understand depression, but I know what it feels like to be affected by a loved one that suffers from it. It's frustrating as hell to be on the outside looking in on someone who's paralyzed with inaction. No amount of shaking will release someone out of their stupor when they are in the throes of despair. I had learned long ago to simply lay off her and wait for her to turn herself around, which took more time than I often had to spare.

Unfortunately, Ryan and I did not have the luxury of time on our sides, so I had to tell him that we were on our own for the day.

"What do you mean she doesn't want to do anything with us?" he asked.

"It's that whole depression thing," I tried to explain. "It is what it is. I guess she can't help it."

I didn't have to explain the details of her condition to him because he was a licensed social worker intimately familiar with the whole gamut of mood disorders. Nevertheless, I could sense that he was just as baffled as I was that we came all this way for what amounted to one single evening.

"Welcome to my world," was all I could say about it.

We ended up doing a bunch of little sightseeing things that day. Most memorable was our little stroll around St. Josaphat Basilica, where the coldest blast of wind came around a corner and impressively cut clear through the center of our souls. It was a familiar cold to me, but that burst of wind caused Ryan to ask where the heck that absolute chill came from. I explained to him "the lake effect," which was Milwaukee lingo for cold as shit, or in other words, winter. His desert butt had never felt real cold before, and I was proud that my hometown was able to give him a dose of its best medicine. It also helped explain why I had no desire to move back to that frigid tundra of a place. To this day, we continue to measure cold against that spectacular blast of terror. If ever we complain that we are cold, we inquire if we are "St. Josaphat cold." As it stands, we still have not experienced anything colder than that bracing blow of

St. Josaphat's wind.

I called my mom again later that day to inquire if she was in the mood to hang out with us, and she complained that she was feeling even worse. I asked her to define what "worse" was, and she gave me a litany of hypochondriacal ailments. I asked if she needed us to take her to the doctor, and she said she just wanted to be alone. There was no one specific thing wrong with her; she was just in one of her funks. At that point, I threw in the towel and said, "forget it." I wasn't really angry at her; I was angry at the situation. Okay, maybe I was a little angry at her. I mean, really, what was her problem? That night, Ryan and I ended up in a divey bar at the bottom of the hill and had ourselves some drinks.

"See," I said and waved my arms at the general situation, "this is why I had to get away from here. She would've driven me to become an alcoholic."

Ryan did his best to console me. "No worries," he said, "I totally get it. Depression is hard to deal with."

"Hard doesn't even explain it!" I practically yelled before drowning my face in a glass of Miller Lite. "She's incorrigible! She does nothing to help herself! Agh! She makes it impossible to love her!"

"Now, now," Ryan tried to calm me, "I wouldn't go that far."

"Oh, you have no idea what it was like living with her," I defended. "She would constantly mope around and say over and over again that she wanted to kill herself. For years! I had to listen to that for years! Ever since I was a little kid! I mean, what the actual fuck? Agh, I hate depression! It's the worst! She would suck all the joy out of life first thing in the morning.

And then she would call me and my sister brats for trying to ignore her. It's like she wanted to fight with us because it somehow made her feel better. My God, would she ever yell at us about anything. Constantly! Always fighting! I hated living there so much. And I was allergic to the cat! Agh, today brought back all those bad memories."

"But I thought you loved cats," Ryan half-drunkenly stated.

"I do!" I said and slammed down my beer. "That was the suckiest part about the whole thing! I love cats, but I can't be around them. They cause my eyes to get all puffy. I grew up with a cat, and my allergies only kicked in when I got older. We all loved that cat, so we couldn't get rid of it. I just learned to suffer."

"Well, at least we had a good day with her yesterday," Ryan deflected.

"Yes," I agreed, "that we did. We can definitely say cheers to that!"

Ching-Ching! We clanked our beers, took our last sips, and moseyed back up the hill to our nondescript motel room.

All things considered, everything was and was not exactly how I imagined our trip to Milwaukee to be.

Do You Believe in Aliens?

I didn't give my mom a chance to say no to us the following day when we simply showed up on her doorstep to say a proper goodbye. I wanted to make sure that she was alright, which, of course, she kind of was; she was just in one of her downswings. I hated leaving her like that, but that's just who she was. I think that she preferred isolating herself. One day of company was more than enough for her; any additional days were too suffocating. I just had to hug her and let her go. To love her properly, I had to accept her condition and find my own place in her complicated world. It's not to say that she was an easy person to love, but luckily a child's love for a parent is automatic. But, damn, she sure managed to make things more difficult than they had to be. As much as I don't like to say it, I believe she inadvertently taught me how to hate someone as well.

I know for a fact that I cultivated a certain kind of hate toward my mother that I've never directed toward anyone else. I absolutely hated her clinically depressed condition; I absolutely couldn't stand her when she acted like life wasn't worth an ounce of effort. There were a gazillion times when I wanted to kick her, yell at her, or tear her completely apart. Her mood swings were as unpredictable as they were unbearable. Worst of all was when my dad had a stroke and ended up in a nursing home. That understandably pushed her over the edge. She would yell at my sister and me at five in the morning about how she wanted him to die. She effectively functioned as a morbid alarm clock, and we simply had to tolerate it. Antidepressant pills didn't work on her, and she tried them all. I basically grew up with a pill-popping drug addict as a role model, and I can't say it was a positive experience.

Simply put, our family was the very definition of dysfunctional, rife with all the convoluted innuendos of love-hate dynamics. I was always ready to leave and never return because unconditional love only went so far when my sanity was at stake. It hardly phased me at all that she welcomed us with open arms and then pushed us away the very next day. Seriously, whatever, screw it; who cared anymore? I knew that a small part of me still cared, but a huge part didn't. I just didn't have the energy to get worked up over the situation anymore.

"Well, that's over with," I said. "You officially met my mother. Everything you just witnessed was basically her in a nutshell. Evidently, she thought it prudent to leave you with no mysteries. I guess I should say that I'm sorry, but I don't know why."

"No, don't worry about it. I'm totally familiar with her type," Ryan assured me. "At least she had one good day, so it was worth it."

"Really?" I asked. "Was one good day seriously worth it? Why couldn't she have allowed us to have two good days? How hard would that have been?"

My feathers got all ruffled up, and it took all of my power to let the subject go. Once I regained my composure, I suggested we get the heck out of Wisconsin.

"I heard there's a decent King Tut exhibit on display at The Field Museum in Chicago," I said, hoping he'd be interested.

Ryan was not exactly thrilled with the proposition. "Are you seriously proposing we go to another ancient civilization museum?"

I sheepishly said, "Well, yes, but this one is special! It's all King Tuttie things! It'll be stuff you've probably seen before in pictures!"

Ryan contemplated for a moment. "Will his gold mask be there?" he inquired. "I'll agree to go if his mask is on display."

I actually knew the answer to that question. "I want to lie to you and say yes, but that mask is never allowed to leave Egypt. All kinds of other good stuff will be there, though. This tour is kind of a big deal, and you gotta trust me when I say that we really shouldn't miss it. Besides, I was going to surprise you because we already have tickets. Surprise!"

"Oh my God, does being with you mean I'll have to go to every history museum on the planet?" Ryan wanted to know.

I thought about the question for a millisecond before answering, "Ya, pretty much. It's not my fault that science fiction museums don't exist. You should make one! You could fill it with *Star Trek-y* things."

Ryan got all excited about the idea. "That would be so awesome! A science fiction museum would be the best museum in the world! I would totally go to that!"

"Ya, well, that only sounds okay to me, so I get your perspective," I said. "But, hey, some people think aliens built the pyramids, so that's something to consider. Maybe we're going to a sci-fi exhibit after all!"

"That's actually quite true," Ryan agreed.

"What's quite true?" I asked.

"About the pyramids," he said without elaborating.

"What about the pyramids?" I wanted to know. "Are you saying it's true that aliens built the pyramids? Or are you saying it's true that some people *think* aliens built the pyramids?"

"I'm saying it's true that some people *think* aliens built the pyramids," he clarified.

"Oh, whew," I gasped. "For a second there, I thought you were going to say that you believed that aliens built the pyramids."

"Au contraire," Ryan countered, "I didn't explicitly say that I *didn't* think that aliens built the pyramids. How do you know I'm not someone who thinks they did?"

"Oh my God, just come out and say it!" I exclaimed. "Just

break it to me now that you believe in alien technology. Come on; I'm ready to hear about the time you got probed by aliens in a spaceship."

"Oh, don't I wish!" Ryan declared. "I mean, not the getting probed part, but wouldn't it be cool to get abducted by aliens? That would at least prove they existed, so I wouldn't have to wonder anymore."

"So, does that mean you *don't* believe that aliens built the pyramids?" I asked.

"Correct," Ryan stated. "I'm not convinced that aliens built the pyramids."

"But you're saying that you could be convinced otherwise if given *inalienable* proof?" I asked.

"Oh my God, I'm not even sure that word can be used like that in a sentence! That has got to be the best-worst pun I've ever heard," Ryan said while laughing and crying simultaneously.

"I hope you like puns because I tend to *alienate* myself from crowds real quick with 'em, so you'll often be left standing alone with me," I explained through some giggles.

"If that's your worst social skill, I think we'll get along marvelously," Ryan declared.

"Well, I don't know if that's my *worst* social skill," I confessed, "as I think that's reserved for my total disdain for being around large groups of people. Get me in a large group, and, poof, I'll disappear. I'll either clam up, slip out, or fade into a wall. I'm not a big people person, so I think you should know that."

"Oh my gosh, how the heck did I find you?" Ryan wanted to know. "I'm the exact same way! Big crowds aren't my thing either!"

"Perfect!" I exclaimed. "We can be introverts together! Finally, we won't be all alone."

"No, that we will not," Ryan agreed. "And hopefully, we'll get abducted by aliens together, too! I'd hate to get alien probed all by myself. I mean, we're a team, right?"

"Right," I said. "No getting alien probed without each other. Deal?"

"Deal."

It Doesn't Get More Chicago Than This

The consummate cheap wad in me thought I was being clever when I came up with the bright idea to park the car and ride the elevated train downtown to the Field Museum. As always, I was all about saving money in addition to getting an early start. I showed off my winning combination when ours was the very first vehicle to arrive at an ice-covered suburban park-and-ride lot early in the morning. It had not gotten any warmer since the blizzard the day before, and an overnight freeze ensured job security for whoever was responsible for sprinkling a big bag of salt all over an insanely large swath of pavement. Being the first car there also meant that we didn't have to walk clear across an oversized parking lot; thus, we scored what I like to call "Rock Star Parking," which was my way of saying that we got the spot closest to the entrance. We noted the number hanging on a wire above where we parked and proceeded to pay our fee at the little rusty kiosk that accepted payments old-school style via cash inside an envelope. If there was anywhere in the world that needed to go electronic in the parking lot payment department, this place definitely did, for it might have installed some safety measures that could have prevented us from parking in a spot that someone apparently owned.

Naturally, we got to the Field Museum way too early and had to find a way to kill some time. We wandered around empty city streets searching for a coffee shop and quickly learned how Chicago earned its nickname, "The Windy City." Lordy be, did it get gusty walking around urban canyons lined with skyscrapers. Yet, as cold as the "downdraught effect" was, we both agreed it wasn't quite "St. Josaphat cold," and that's how we realized we had a new bar to measure temperature with.

We eventually found a coffee shop, took some seats by a window, and started to watch people for entertainment. Everyone who walked by the window must have been a tourist because no one seemed to know how to walk against a strong blast of wind. We saw more people lose their hats than we had ever seen during our combined lifetimes, and it got progressively funnier each time it happened. Right when we thought there was no way someone else could possibly lose their hat, the next person who walked by the window did. My god, that was stupid hilarious. We damn near spit coffee out of our noses from laughing so hard.

We got to the Field Museum right as it opened and spent the entire day there. The thought crossed my mind of describing every artifact we saw in detail, but there are museum guides for that, so I've decided against sounding like a pamphlet. However, I will say that seeing King Tut's funeral accouterments was a memorable experience that lived up to its expectations, for no art can hold a candle to anything that emerged out of that boy king's spectacular tomb.

There's something about ancient Egypt that speaks to our souls. There was a wisdom about them that has since been lost to the world. The more I see of ancient Egypt, the greater my desire becomes to see even more. There was a fearlessness about them that I admire, for they were not afraid to take life by the horns and run with it as far as it could go. I marvel at their attempts to push life into the beyond, for the realm here on Earth was never enough to satisfy them. Whenever I think I'm near them, they escape ever further away.

The exhibit was phenomenal and left us both at a loss for words. We left the museum thoroughly satisfied and thought it prudent to get to the airport a little early. We took the "L" back to where we parked and discovered a minivan parked in the spot where our rented compact car that had all our stuff in it used to be.

"Am I crazy, or did our car grow while we were gone?" Ryan genuinely inquired.

"This *is* where we parked, right?" I asked, knowing full well that we parked in the very first spot right outside the door.

"Oh, this is where we parked, alright," Ryan said while he pointed at the minivan with a giant *Chicago Bears* bumper sticker slapped on the back window.

"Did we seriously get *towed*?" I asked no one in particular. "I know that we paid the fee."

Right as I said that, I saw the writing on the ground on an empty parking spot nearby.

"*What* did that say?" Ryan immediately asked after I read out loud the words that a layer of tundra initially covered up when we arrived.

"It says not to park here unless you own this spot!" I practically yelled. "How the hell did it allow us to park here then?! Did we just pay for the privilege of getting our car towed?"

I then proceeded to stare at the minivan in disbelief.

"*Da Bears,*" I said.

Ryan gave me a quizzical look. "I'm sorry, but what did you just say?"

I pointed to the *Bears* bumper sticker and said with a hint of horror in my voice, "They parked here because they went to a Bears game! The owners of this parking spot are Bears fans! Of course, they would show up today! They ordered our asses towed!"

"No way did they tow us," Ryan said in disbelief.

"No?" I said. "You honestly don't think so? Then how do you explain *this*?" I asked and angrily pointed at the minivan that was definitely not our car.

"Okay, ya," Ryan admitted. "We definitely got towed."

I was so pissed that I went straight into war mode. *The Packers* and *The Bears* had always been rivals, but this was a new level of combat as far as I was concerned. Our flight was in two and a half hours, and we had no idea where our rental car had disappeared to. Damned if I was going to let Chicago steal a vehicle from a Milwaukeean. I was going to get that car back in time for our flight.

I figured it couldn't be that hard, considering how many "you will be towed" signs were posted all over the place. "Easy-peasy," I thought. "All we needed to do was call the tow company." The only problem was that no tow company phone numbers were listed on the signs.

"How can there be a million "you will be towed" signs, but not one with a phone number on it?" I asked no one in particular.

There were all kinds of signs posted all over the place, and a good number of them were for the Chicago Transit Authority, who, I presumed, operated the "L."

"Well, these signs have a phone number on them. I'm gonna call them," I said and started dialing.

"They're not going to know who towed the car!" Ryan bemoaned.

"They might!" I countered, then squished the phone close to my ear so I could better hear a long-winded recording. Precious minutes were passing, and I clicked through about 50 prompts only to get hung up by an agent when someone finally answered.

"She hung up on me!" I yelled and almost threw my phone. "That's it! We need to start moving!"

"Move?" Ryan wanted to know. "Move where?"

I was already 100 steps ahead of him. "Come on!" I yelled. "We need to talk to someone!"

I was hoping there would be someone inside the terminal that would have some insight into the situation. Indeed, there was someone there, but he claimed ignorance of knowing who the tow company was. Meanwhile, I kept redialing the Transit Authority phone number in the hopes of getting a hold of someone. I got hung up on three more times and only got through on the fourth attempt simply because I yelled at the person at the other end not to hang up on me. I begged her to just tell me who the company that towed park-and-ride vehicles was. I told her what station I was at, and she gave me the company's name, then *click*. Winner, winner, chicken dinner!

"It's Blah, Blah, Blah Tow Company!" I declared (or whatever it was, I don't remember). "Look up the number and start calling them!"

Ryan immediately called them but only got a recording. "Should I leave a message?" he asked.

"It's Sunday!" I lamented. "There's no way they're calling us back. I say we just go to them, locate our car, and take it. I already looked up their address. It's two metro stops away. I suggest we go."

I didn't even give Ryan a chance to offer an alternative. I was again 100 steps ahead of him and already waiting for the train before he caught up to me.

"Do you honestly think this is going to work?" Ryan asked.

"Well, I guess we're going to find out!" I said in the most optimistic voice I could muster.

So, we took the train the requisite two stops away and asked the train attendant to point us in the right direction. Once outside, I didn't want to waste any time, so I started running. On ice. The funniest part of this story was not our car getting towed; it was watching a guy who grew up nowhere near snow try to run on icy sidewalks. It was an element of distraction that we absurdly didn't have time for, but there it was, a full-blown unnecessary comedy sketch at the most inopportune moment. He eventually stopped running, well, because. I was glad that he didn't have a hat to lose, too, for that would have sent me over the edge. Ryan, for his part, didn't think that his antics were all that hilarious. (Oh, but they were my dear; they most certainly were. Don't worry; in the very near future, karma will be a bitch, and you will get to

216

laugh at me when a giant oversized noodle smacks me in the face.)

So, I got to the locked gate at Blah, Blah, Blah Tow Company, and it was evident that no one was there. In an instant, I realized that the whole adventure was over. We were going to miss our flight and be charged change fees, tow fees, and a night in a hotel. I had just gotten a new job and was still on my six-month probation period. I thought I might even lose my job over this because I was expected to be at work the following day. Additionally, neither of us had any of our bags, as we left them in the trunk of the rental car. Things were looking quite crap from where I was standing.

Ryan eventually caught up to me and saw me standing there looking dejected.

"They're not here, are they?" he asked.

"Nope," I said.

"So, you ran all the way up here for nothing," he said.

I gave him the "Ya, I know" look.

"Now what?" he asked.

"We break in?" I somewhat seriously suggested.

Right as I said that, a moment occurred that when it happens in movies, I get irritated at how impossibly convenient it seems. Materializing out of the golden hues of a grungy suburban Chicago sunset, a tow truck rolled up to the scene with some other poor sap's vehicle attached to its hitch. The mechanical gate opened to receive this vision of superbly timed perfection, and we took advantage of the situation by riding its coattails. The gates closed, and we were inside. I wasn't going to be polite and wait for the tow truck guy to casually notice our existence; I was going to approach him the moment he got out of his tow truck and ask him to release our vehicle.

"We don't keep the cars here," he dryly stated.

"Say what?" I immediately pegged him to be a lying jerk.

"We store all the cars at the lot down the street," he claimed.

"Okay, fine, whatever," I said. "Can we pay the fee and go get it? We have a flight to catch in an hour and what you impounded was a rental car that we needed to return an hour ago."

Well, that story just tickled him pink.

We forked over $175, and he gave us a ride to the impound lot, which was not just down the street; it was more like ten red lights and a two-mile ride away. The whole way there, he regaled us with tow truck stories glorifying how Chicago loves to tow cars for the slightest reason. Thanks to his insight, I will forever be paranoid about parking a car anywhere in Chicago.

To this day, neither of us has ever tasted a more delicious overpriced airport Corona beer than we did at Midway airport that evening. We were absolutely giddy that we had gone through all that and still had enough time left over to grab a drink. Hell, we flaunted how much time we had leftover and even ordered a plate of nachos.

"So," I asked Ryan, "did this trip satisfy your Chicago cravings?"

"Ya," Ryan said and took a big gulp of beer. "I do believe I'll be good for a while."

CHAPTER EIGHT:
Yucatan, Jan 2007 & Jan 2017

Return to Paradise

I will never forget the last morning Ryan and I had at our beach hotel in Tulum, Mexico, back in January 2007. We barely managed to get ourselves out of bed at 7:00 a.m. because we were still groggy from the previous evening's festivities of drinking wine, looking at stars, and listening to the wind whip through coconut trees. We woke up to another perfect morning in paradise, so we celebrated our existence by plopping our bodies into the ocean for one farewell swim. There was an absolute calm about being out there so early in the morning and allowing ourselves to be one with the waves as they glimmered under the first rays of sunlight. I remember bobbing with the ocean and feeling that life didn't get any more perfect than that. A sense of serenity washed over me and seeped into my pores.

When we left Tulum, we both immediately announced that we desperately wanted to return. We intended to make Tulum our own special place and vowed to go back the following year. Yet, one year turned into ten before we ever saw paradise again.

Life essentially got in the way of our best intentions for a speedy Tulum return. Ryan got wrapped up with his master's program while I kept scuttling back to Wisconsin to visit my ailing parents. When Ryan graduated, we celebrated with a European vacation instead of a Yucatan one, and doing so officially moved Tulum onto the back burner, where it simmered for the next handful of years.

Eventually, we bought a house and slowly created our private patch of paradise. While decorating our new home, we rekindled the idea of returning to Tulum because I had found a perfect spot to hang a gourd lamp we didn't own because we didn't buy one when we had the chance. We decided to remedy the situation by going back to Tulum so we could return with the object that would plug the hole that needed to be filled.

When I started the trip planning process, I naively assumed that nothing would have changed in the span of ten years. However, it quickly became apparent that our second trip to paradise would not be nearly as affordable as it was the first time around.

"Honey, that hotel we stayed at on the beach for $65 a night ten years ago goes for $375 now," I announced with a mix of surprise and disappointment.

"You've got to be freaking kidding me," Ryan said, equally confounded. "Who'd pay that much for a place that barely has electricity?"

Indeed, that was a good question. When we stayed there in 2007, all the Tulum beach hotels ran on loud generators that only operated at certain hours of the day. Either that, or they didn't use any electricity at all. All the hotels without power were also hotels without any beds, for those off-grid properties were nothing more than glorified huts equipped with hammocks that went for a paltry $19 a night.

"We'll just rent one of those hammock rooms then," I deftly counter-maneuvered.

It was a good idea, but, unfortunately, those hammock hotels didn't seem to exist anymore. I was gradually getting the impression that our little patch of paradise had significantly changed when I figured out that our former generator hotel now boasted full-time electricity. Other people had apparently discovered how amazing Tulum was, so they decided to make it expensive. In short, I couldn't find a single hotel on the beach that went for anything less than $250 a night.

"Looks like we won't be staying on the beach this time around," I said and frugally booked us at an inner-city hotel that was nowhere near the beach for the "paltry" price of $125 a night.

"Well, hopefully, that trampoline is still there," I blurted out as I fondly recalled how we randomly discovered a large trampoline on the beach next to one of those $19 hammock properties. We absolutely adored jumping on that thing even though we both knew we probably weren't technically supposed to. Unfortunately, we'd soon discover that the trampoline no longer existed, but its disappearance won't even phase us because change would soon prove to be our only constant.

Two Trips to Paradise

Our original trip to Tulum was our first real trip together as a way for us to celebrate surviving Chicago. We were on the plane ride back when I suggested performing a "redo" trip, and I proposed a romantic getaway to the Caribbean. I had been to Tulum once before, way back in high school, and I always recalled my visit there fondly. Granted, I went with my Spanish class, and my most vivid memory was of a gruesome bullfight where the bull had to be stabbed multiple times by a matador-in-training, but I also remembered doing other (nicer) things as well. What always stuck with me the most, though, was the color of the water. The Caribbean was a shade of turquoise that was magical to behold, and I wanted us to experience that mystical color together.

Our first trip to Tulum was a resounding success, and it forever set the bar for what a perfect trip needed to look like. Of course, that trip was not without its snafus – no trip to Mexico ever is – but we viewed our mishaps as part of its charm. Okay, well, maybe I should say that *I* saw our mishaps as part of its charm, for I doubt that Ryan holds the same opinion. Indeed, Ryan likely has a different view when he looks back on his original Tulum memories, for he probably sees them through splashes of water that I kept throwing on his face when we went kayaking in circles in a lagoon.

So, back to Tulum we went, ten years since we last visited it. Relationship-wise, ten years was a record for us, for neither had been with anyone as long before. Ten years – I didn't think it was even possible. I couldn't believe how incredibly fast the time went. For the first time in my life, I was beginning to understand how people became old. Time flies by when you find contentment.

Just like our first trip to the area, our second trip started in Cancun, but only because we needed to utilize the services of their airport. We immediately transferred to a bus and made the two-hour journey down the coast to our ultimate destination. Once we arrived, we immediately checked into our hotel that was nowhere near the beach, and did the requisite walk around the city. We kept repeating the phrase, "That wasn't here ten years ago," ad nauseam until we grew tired of being nowhere near the water. We saved the best for last and finally hired a taxi to take us to the place of our fondest recollections.

We started walking the length of the beach, and doing so felt like we were walking through bombed-out memories. We saw that our old Tulum was there, but it existed as a shell of its former self. All the old off-grid palapa hotels were shredded into bits and obscured by wild vegetation. Sand dunes were piled up in massive clumps in front of the abandoned properties and gave off the appearance of oversized tumbleweeds. Each unused hotel was roped off in its own special way, whether by physical ropes, large posted "warning" signs, or the unsettling presence of machete-wielding guards. Everything else in between was luxury hotels with lounge chairs that visitors had to pay an exorbitant fee to sit on. The juxtaposition was so surreal that it was beyond comprehension. We thought this was no longer the Tulum of our dreams but rather the very stuff of nightmares.

It had only been ten years, but the Tulum we used to know and love had evidently disappeared. We walked up and down the crowded beach a few times over in search of that trampoline and realized that it wouldn't even matter if we found it because there would've been no way we'd get anywhere near it if we weren't paying guests. Looking around, it was obvious that the "hippie" days were over. Tulum was in the midst of transforming itself into a fast-paced, money-grabbing, Instagram-porn destination, and we wanted to tell it that it didn't have to go there. Tulum was perfectly fine the way it was in 2007, but that Tulum didn't make enough cash. Tulum gave into the temptation to go the greedy kind of green rather than stick to the environmental shade of color that struggled to cover all the bills.

We visited our former hotel and saw that it was in the process of being revamped into a higher-end property. It was now charging $30 just for the privilege to loiter on their particular plot of sand, and we, of course, learned of this fee the hard way when we were accosted just for being there when they caught us nostalgically walking around the manicured grounds. We immediately sounded like old fogies when we tried telling the staff that we were reminiscing about the good 'ol days when the hotel was a tiny six-room property with barely any electricity. Of course, they didn't care to hear any of our tales. They told us we needed to fork over $30 each or leave the premises. We chose not to pay, so they unceremoniously swept us off the grounds as if we were annoying bits of rubbish.

Overall, there was a weird feeling in the air, as if something terrible was happening, but we couldn't figure out what. It was obvious that all the properties that we recalled as being more eco-like were the ones that were no longer operating. We were getting the sense that Tulum was in the process of being redesigned for the rich, and what we were witnessing was the transition phase. The presence of machete-wielding guards was an indication that the free-wheeling days were unmistakably over. No doubt, someone somewhere harbored a burning desire to make lots and lots of money, and transforming Tulum was the way they were going to do it. I had bet that in ten more years, all those abandoned hotels would reopen to the tune of $500 a night. (I was wrong. They reopened to the tune of $750 plus a night.) Something greedily sinister was amiss. We decided it best to enjoy our free stroll on the beach while we could because there was no guarantee that someone would pop up out of nowhere and charge us a fee for doing so. There were only a few affordable paradises left in the world, and soon Tulum wouldn't be among them.

Bikes and Kayaks, 2007

Back in 2007, riding bikes was definitely not a thing people did in Tulum, so I don't know where I got the idea that it would be fun to ride bikes all over the place. We rented bikes from the only bicycle shop that existed, and they rode as if they spent their entire lives getting wet from being parked outside during monsoon season. Neither of us had the better bike, as each bike was equally rusty and impossible to ride. We were stuck with whatever height the seats were at – his too high, and mine practically on the ground. Both our bikes had chain problems, which is a generic way of saying that the chains constantly fell off. The bikes were hard to peddle and butt-killing rides without any shocks. Tulum had no such thing as bike lanes, so we rode our crappy bikes that would randomly fall apart on streets in a town that never expected to see bicycles on the road. There was never anywhere safe to stop to fix a bike chain, and there were many times when we'd look behind and notice the other person wasn't there. It was hard to know whether one of us disappeared because we had to stop to fix a chain or if we weren't there because a car had run one of us over, for either scenario was always plausible.

On our second morning in Tulum, we rode our crappy bikes down a blissfully uncongested road to a site called Sian Ka'an Biosphere Reserve. I was enticed to travel there when I learned about it on the UNESCO World Heritage website, which described it as one of Mexico's largest protected areas. The reserve contained various habitats ranging from coastline to tropics and included a particularly extensive grove of mangrove trees. I had read that visitors could rent kayaks and tootle around the wonderfully pristine wetlands, so I thought that was reason enough to justify a visit.

Once at Sian Ka'an, we had the choice of renting either a single kayak or a tandem one, and we opted to go for the one that put us in a kayak together. Ten minutes into paddling out, I was sure that Ryan was regretting that he didn't opt for his own kayak because I instantly developed a rowing method that splashed water into his face with every stroke. It was a tad bit on the windy side, so I was putting some elbow grease into my paddles, but Ryan was not appreciating my efforts and told me to slow down. Slowing down made paddling even harder, though, because doing so made us a plaything for the wind. For every two strokes we went forward, the wind pushed us back one. We had only a single goal in mind, and that was to reach a far-off mangrove island where we thought we would be able to take a break and have a picnic. It took us nearly an hour to reach what we thought was an island, but we soon learned a thing or two about mangrove forests that we didn't know before. We learned that a patch of mangrove trees does not make an island; it just makes for a lot of trees growing in water.

Nevertheless, we both decided to take a much-needed rest. We laid back in the kayak, looked at the sky, and munched on some snacks. We heard a lot of birds rummaging around the mangroves, but the foliage was so dense that neither of us saw a single bird in a place that was famous for harboring over 300 species. More than anything, though, we both felt immersed in the color blue. The Caribbean was its own flavor, and we could practically taste its powdered hue. The pastel paleness made us believe that life itself was a special treat.

Our reverie ended when we started to overheat. Our kayak had drifted a ways from where we had initially stopped, so we now had that much further to paddle. If we thought we had it hard when we paddled out, we had no idea what we were in for on our paddle back. The wind was a muscle that worked against us on our return journey, and Ryan got soaking wet from all my relentless backsplashes. At some point during our return, neither of us cared what it would take to get us back; we just had to push through the wind no matter how miserable and overheated we became. All 300-plus species of birds might have flown over us during our return journey, but neither of us would have noticed because life was reduced to just paddling and nothing else. I thought I remembered us having fun kayaking that day, but Ryan harbored different memories of that excursion. When I asked him if he wanted to go kayaking at Sian Ka'an again in 2017, he gave me a definitive "nope" on the proposition.

After we spent an entire morning kayaking against the wind, the least ideal thing we wanted to do was peddle our impossibly ornery bicycles back to the hotel. However, that was precisely what we did next, and we did so on extremely parched bodies because we both ran out of bottled water hours ago. To say that there was a mild skirmish inside the hotel room when we raced for the single jug of water that sat prettily on the kitchen counter only barely describes the chaos that occurred inside our private domain.

Once we were adequately hydrated, we immediately jumped into the ocean and then quickly rinsed off under a freezing cold shower. After that, we ate a speedy lunch and then jumped back onto our bike-mobiles for another exciting excursion into the heart of Tulum.

Cenote, 2007

I had read ahead of time that there were a couple of cenotes we could swim around in, but I didn't know precisely where they were. Tulum wasn't all that big of a city, and there seemed to be only one main road in and out of town. The map I copied from a guidebook showed two cenotes as being only a handful of miles up the major street, and even though we were both completely tuckered out from kayaking, I figured we both had it in us to push ourselves another six miles. I assured Ryan that the journey would be worth it and that we'd be able to jump into some mystical water as our reward.

Well, it turned out that I figured fairly wrong. We quickly discovered that we barely had it in ourselves to make it a few miles from our hotel before we both got so overheated that we wanted to die. The ride from the beach to the city center was brutal, not only because there was no safe shoulder to ride on but also because there was absolutely no shade anywhere along the way. The only place to catch our breath was under a sliver of shade provided by a skinny light pole that barely shielded one person. Ryan complained that he didn't know what we were biking for, so he said he wanted to turn around.

"We can't!" I said. "We have to make it to the cenote."

Ryan was tuckered out, but willing to negotiate. "Tell me again, what's a cenote?"

"It's like what I said it was when you asked me last time," I explained, somewhat exasperated. "It's a sinkhole."

"Hmmm," Ryan mused. "I already forgot...why do we

want to swim in a sinkhole?"

"Because it will be like swimming inside a cave," I told him.

Ryan paused to consider the idea for a moment.

"Honestly, that doesn't sound very safe," he said.

"It's probably not," I agreed, "but I think it's worth checking out."

I barely managed to convince him to press onward, but once we got going, even I started regretting being out there on those corroded bicycles. I genuinely began to believe that if there was indeed a highway to hell, I could officially say that I knew exactly where the first six miles were and what mode of transportation to use while on it. Riding those bikes wasn't fun, and we were ultimately rewarded with the scariest-looking hole in the ground filled with the foulest water our eyes had ever seen when we finally encountered our first cenote.

"There's absolutely no way I'm getting into that murder hole," Ryan declared as if he actually needed to say something to that effect.

Of the two cenotes on my crudely drawn map, this first one didn't look like something that anyone would jump into unless they were suicidal or being sacrificed to the gods.

"That's one freaky-looking abyss right there," I wryly observed.

"Why the heck was this place even on your map?" Ryan genuinely wanted to know. "Do people actually swim in this thing?"

I honestly didn't know the answer to that question.

"I don't know," I said. "Maybe with a wetsuit and scuba gear, they do?" I answered as if it was a question.

"Do you still want to check the other one out? Ryan asked.

In all honesty, I really wanted to see how much worse another cenote could get, so I said, "Well, ya, I do. Aren't *you* curious about seeing another big gaping hole in the ground filled with water and possibly the dead?"

"Well," Ryan mused, "when you put it like that, how could I *not* want to see another cavernous pit that presumably leads to the underworld? These cenotes are so much fun!"

"There's the spirit!" I said, knowing full well that he was being sarcastic. "Let's get back on those metal things that dare to call themselves transportation and get moving!"

"Oh, yippie," Ryan said and slowly crawled back onto his metal contraption.

We rode our "things" (they didn't deserve to be called bicycles) another mile up the road to the second hole in the ground and got rewarded with a grand cavernous prize. The place was called "Great Cenote," and great it was indeed. The cenote's appeal was instantaneous, for neither of us had ever seen anything more beautiful. We both stared in awe at the clear blue water tucked inside a stalagmite-filled cavern and wasted not a single minute before jumping into the watery dream.

The water was refreshing and felt like liquid gold. We swam through a small tunnel and emerged in a patch of sunlight at a spot that was open to the sky. This here was a magical realm seemingly not of this planet. The Mayans were right to think their gods resided in places such as this, for this watery paradise was too perfect to be from this Earth. I was tempted to convert to the ancient Mayan religion right then and there and start worshiping a slew of unpronounceable gods that, in all likelihood, had the letter x tucked somewhere in their names.

Yet, I was beginning to understand that words and names had no meanings in places such as this. Faith in this watery realm was purely a state of mind. I got the sense that one could believe in the cenote because the cenote believed in humankind. Indeed, the world wouldn't offer up such gorgeousness if it didn't believe in those who inhabited it. The cenote served as a benevolent gift, a liquid anointment to pour over our bodies and enrich our inner souls. It didn't take much proselytizing to convert me to the ancient Mayan religion.

We could have easily stayed in that enchanting world forever, but we had to leave at 5:00 p.m. when they literally swept all of us who were in there out with a broom. (I'm not kidding. Come closing time, no one wanted to leave, so out came the brooms!)

We had such a wonderful time swimming that we completely forgot that our ornery bicycles were outside waiting for us.

"Agh, those things again," we sighed in unison at the sight of them.

"Back to the bike-mobiles, we go!" I said and made little vroom-vroom noises in a futile attempt to make the idea of riding them fun.

"Ah, don't kid yourself," Ryan said, "riding these things is *work*!"

"Ya," I said, "and they don't pay very well, either!"

"Hey, I don't know about you, but I'm *starving*," Ryan declared.

"What do you mean? Don't nuts and crackers sustain you all day?" I joked. "But, ya, you're probably right. We should really get something to eat."

So off to the sunset we went, searching for something delectable to eat. We successfully followed our noses into town and landed at one of the many chicken joints that lined the principal street. Tulum circa 2007 had a certain smell wafting through the air, and it was the scent of delicious fire-roasted chicken. I still, to this day, think about the chicken we ate there because I will forever remember it as being the best-tasting chicken that ever crossed my taste buds. Dang, that chicken was good! However, that chicken was pretty much gone circa 2017. The prominent smell we'd both reminisced about for an entire decade was thoroughly scrubbed out of the atmosphere when we returned for a second serving of chicken amazingness. We walked the entire length of the main street twice in our desperate search for delicious chicken, yet we somehow overlooked the one place that apparently still served it. I know this because I searched the internet when we returned and saw that there was a restaurant called Pollo Bronco that we blatantly missed. Writing this right now is making me want to go back and correct our unfortunate mistake.

I don't know why, but it took me a while to learn that time only happens once. The Tulum chicken we had in 2007 will forever stay in 2007, along with all our other 2007 memories. One can never return to a location and expect to recreate the same life as one formerly experienced it. Thus, it was unfortunate that we couldn't regurgitate our memories upon the landscape and relive our past in the present moment, but, in certain scenarios, that ultimately proved to be a good thing. Namely, the monsoon bicycles were gone by 2017, and in their place were normal-functioning bicycles with seat-altering capabilities and chains that actually stayed on. Ten bike shops now existed where there used to be one, and they all operated to put tourists comfortably on the road to hell, which now wasn't so bad since it was paved and lined with shade structures. I was almost disappointed that we weren't going to have to risk our lives the second time around and was admittedly slightly perturbed that none of the new tourists were subjected to the suffering such as we once endured.

Speaking of suffering, I can't even begin to imagine the toil that went into building all the ancient pyramids *by hand* in a humid Yucatan jungle as the Mayans did all over the godforsaken place. Equally unfathomable was the suffering the Victorian explorers must have endured when they almost killed themselves in their efforts to clear the pyramids of hundreds of years worth of unchecked vegetation. I willingly conclude that Indiana Jones' fear of snakes was justifiably well-founded, but if I were him, I'd also be terrified of mosquitoes. Spending months under the sun to clear an ancient crumbling structure while the whole body ached from malaria does not sound like the epitome of fun to me, but that describes how many explorers functioned. How the Mayans concocted an entire civilization despite the constant threat of snakes, jungle fevers, and oppressive heat is an absolute wonder. I wouldn't think any society would have been motivated enough to invent numbers or build anything beyond a simple thatched hut under such impossible conditions. Yet, the Mayans didn't seem too bothered that they lived in a challenging environment, for they fully embraced their landscape and all that was thrown at them. Indeed, what they managed to achieve in the Yucatan was nothing short of extraordinary.

There is so much about the ancient Mayans that will never

be known, which makes it all the more tantalizing to visit their ancient cities. This lack of knowledge allows one's imagination to roam as one wanders around the ruins of someone else's former reality. Every ancient city offers a small piece of itself to place inside the puzzle that slowly builds inside one's head. Yet, I can only wonder what kind of puzzle the Spanish explorers created inside their heads when they first saw the Mayan world from the bow of their ships.

Tulum was only one of a handful of cities the Mayans built along the coast, and a group of Spanish explorers gawked in awe when they sailed past its brightly painted temples in 1518. The city was still inhabited at the time, but the explorers decided against making any physical contact. I genuinely wonder if the Mayans aimed at the explorers with their weapons as the curious ship sailed past them and whether or not they had a sinking feeling that this ship was the harbinger of bad things to come. Indeed, by the end of that century, European diseases would wipe out the population, and the gloriously painted city would morph into a faded ghost town.

Tulum Ruins, 2007

Nowadays, one does not first see the ruins of Tulum from the water but instead sees them from the behind. Visitors today approach Tulum from the back of its gates and enter the site through an opening in a wall. *"Tulum "* was the word for *wall* in the Yucatec language, and even though the city was encircled by one, that's not what the native inhabitants called this domain. To them, this city was *"Zama, "* which was their word for *dawn,* and that name suited it perfectly, for its temples proudly greeted the sun every morning when it rose over the horizon.

The city sat beautifully atop an elevated limestone cliff, and its strategic position ensured its importance as a trading hub. To say that the site was dramatic back in its day probably doesn't describe it enough, for it must have been beyond spectacular when it was at its painted apogee. I suspect those Spanish explorers must have felt intimidated when they first encountered Tulum and likely deemed themselves unworthy of stepping upon its soil. I generally don't imagine an incident where any Spanish explorer would ever feel humbled, but I genuinely imagine them feeling small when they laid their eyes upon Tulum. Indeed, many visitors today can relate to their sentiments, for there are few ruins in the world more romantic than this one.

Archaeologists speculate that the Mayan Empire was in a state of decline by the time Tulum was constructed, but that doesn't imply that Tulum itself wasn't a resounding success. Tulum was one of the last cities ever founded by the Mayans, and the fact that it thrived for several hundred years implies that they were doing *something* right for a very long while. It was here where the Mayan Empire retreated when the rest of their world fell apart. Maybe it was symbolic that they chose to found their city in such a beautiful location, for they probably figured they might as well have a good view if they had to face an inevitable demise. Yet, the real reason why they founded their city where they did had more to do with maritime trade. Tulum was where the sea, land, and rivers converged into an economic crescendo.

As successful as Tulum must have been, it struck me incongruous that its buildings appeared haphazardly constructed. Straight lines didn't seem to be much of a concern, nor did it apparently matter if roof lines were slanted. Some buildings looked as though they were whipped up in a matter of days, yet they were built so well that they lasted for centuries. There was a naivety about Tulum's constructions, and one could only smile when seeing a plaster-cast image of an upside-down figure. Here was a place that was easy to relate to, even though it was impossible to comprehend.

The chasm between our world and theirs is unimaginably deep, and one lands at the bottom of a pit when one attempts to cross it. I've spent many hours at the bottom of that well, and I always seem to enjoy spending some quality time down there. It's only when I look up from the lower levels of civilization that I gain a greater perspective on how we all fit in. Life moves forward in very small increments, and each generation only looks back to the one that preceded it. It's only when one falls into a big gaping pit that one actually sees all the layers of earth holding up the soil on every side. Time is interconnected, for the present cannot exist without the past.

Overall, I admire what the inhabitants of Tulum did with their lives, for they left behind a breathtaking legacy. Tulum existed on the razor edge of paradise, and the view from their perch was all-encompassing. There is no doubt in my mind that they saw the Spanish explorers when they sailed below their cliffs, and the fact that they didn't kill them implies that their curiosity was aroused. Maybe they were hoping that the explorers would come back and attempt to communicate, for I'm certain the Mayans would have wanted to know what they had to offer. The inhabitants of Tulum knew the importance of exchange, whether it be goods or ideas, but no matter how the stars may have aligned, the Mayans' remarkable run was destined to come to an end.

Chichen Itza Ruins, 2017

Chichen Itza rose to power several hundred years earlier than Tulum, and it, too, owed its existence to the presence of water. However, unlike Tulum, Chichen Itza sat nowhere near a beach but instead resided inland between two large cenotes. We currently live in a time when the answer to everything is *money* but the answer to everything used to be (and will likely again be in the very near future) *water*, and Chichen Itza had plenty of that until a severe drought took most of it away. No amount of sacrifice brought the water back, yet it remains unclear whether or not Chichen Itza was wholly abandoned by the time the Spanish arrived. What does remain clear, however, was that the Spanish were impressed with what they saw at Chichen Itza, so much so that they desired to make it their capital, but the natives living in the area thwarted their plans.

Evidence that the Mayans were desperate for rain was revealed when underwater archaeologists retrieved precious objects and human remains from the lowest reaches of their sacred well. I found it an eerie experience to stand at the edge of that watery grave, knowing that people were tossed into that liquid pit. Despite all their best efforts, the rain refused to bestow its presence. I could only imagine what a crushing feeling it must have been to believe the rain god scorned your very existence after all you had given it. The rain god did not want their jades, textiles, or human bodies; no, the rain god wanted them gone. How many sacrifices did it finally take before the Mayans realized there was no point in feeding their deities anymore? It's easy to be amazed at everything the

Mayans achieved, but it's even more amazing to think about what it took for them to walk away from a city like Chichen Itza.

The Sacred Cenote existed in an area all on its own, so it was easy to compartmentalize my thoughts when there wasn't a pyramid looming overhead to distract me. However, my thoughts got all jumbled up the moment I walked away from the sacred well because it was hard to look at all the ruins and think it was all for nothing in the end.

"I want to know what happened here," I said to Ryan while a million thoughts raced inside my brain.

"What do you mean?" Ryan replied. "Because that's a pretty broad statement."

"I mean, I want to know *everything*," I answered. "I want to know the beginning, middle, and end. I want to know who originally strolled up to this place and said, *here – this is where we'll build a new city*."

Ryan contemplated the idea for a moment and said, "I mean, ya, how crazy is it to think that this place used to be empty? Like, can you imagine the pyramid *not* being here? Or the large ballcourt? "

"Or the observatory, or the Temple of a Thousand Pillars?" I added.

"Right?" Ryan exclaimed. "I mean, there's just *so* much, and didn't you say there was even more of it still buried?"

"Oh, there's *always* more of it still buried no matter what Mayan site you go to," I said, "and that only enhances their mystery."

"If there's one thing you can accuse the Mayans of being, it's mysterious, that's for sure," Ryan declared.

"Oh, my gosh, right?" I agreed. "But, wouldn't it be cool if they *weren't* so mysterious anymore? Like, wouldn't it be awesome to know the minutiae of everyday Chichen Itza life? I say we pretend that we live here now."

"Okay," Ryan said, "but it doesn't look like it's gonna rain any time soon, so maybe we should start with sacrificing you to the rain god."

"Darling," I demurely stated, "did you already forget that I'm not a virgin anymore? You know the rain god wouldn't be pleased."

"Oh, ya, I forgot about that part," Ryan admitted. "Say, maybe we should start with watching one of those ball games!"

"Yes!" I agreed. "That will be so cool to see! I always wanted to know how they played without their hands."

Thus, we explored Chichen Itza with our imaginations and pretended to know what everything was. Nothing was mysterious anymore when we gave everything our own meanings. That platform over there with all the skulls carved on its sides? Ya, that was where we did our moon dances in the middle of the night to keep all the evil at bay. See that crumbled ruin off in the distance that no one bothered to excavate yet? That was where we used to live. With our imaginations, every building that we encountered was something we were familiar with, and we had to beat each other to the punch to say what something was.

"That's the courthouse where we got married!" I said to Ryan as I pointed to an intricately carved building with traces of stucco. "Do you remember how we tried to squeeze like 100 people in there to witness the ceremony?"

"Oh, how could I forget!" Ryan quickly exclaimed. "And

do you recall how we had our wedding reception in that building with all those pillars? Remember when my crazy uncle got so drunk that he almost knocked them all over like dominos?"

"Oh, my gosh, I almost forgot about that!" I said. "I was so embarrassed that I tried erasing it from my memory! And then, later that night, do you remember when the priest ran all the way over from the observatory and told us that a huge comet was barrelling our way?"

"Yes!" Ryan said, "he told us we were all going to die that night!"

"So everyone just got smashed!" I said. "I've never been more drunk in all my life."

"Me either," Ryan said. "It forever set the bar for the drunkest I've ever been."

"Oh, my," I sighed. "weren't *those* the days?"

"Man, they sure were." Ryan sighed back.

"Say," I quipped, "what do you think that priest actually saw that night when he thought the world was going to end?"

"Hmm," Ryan mused, "that's a good question. Weren't the Mayans super good at astronomy? I can't imagine that he saw anything mistakenly. Maybe it was a near miss, and the Earth got incredibly lucky that night."

"I bet that's *exactly* what happened," I said.

We both stood quietly for a moment and contemplated how the Earth dodged a disastrous bullet.

"Say," I started, "do you think the observatory at Chichen Itza was the only one the Mayans ever made?"

"Oh, man," Ryan exclaimed, "you would know that answer better than I would. I know nothing about Mayan history."

"Ya," I said, "I think it was. I've read that it was unique in Mayan architecture. The fact that all the windows lined up to various celestial events makes me wonder how many generations needed to observe the skies before they knew how to create that culminating structure."

"Wow," Ryan mused, "that's a pretty intense thought when you contemplate it."

"Right?" I agreed. "It's really something to realize that the Chichen Itza observatory was likely the culmination of all ancient astronomical knowledge. Without a doubt, that structure epitomized the farthest they got with knowing about their place in the universe. I mean, seriously, wow, right?"

"Kablooey!" Ryan said and made an explosion gesture with his hands beside his head. "It blows my mind to think about what they must have known."

"The whole concept reminds me of that opening character in *The Hitchhiker's Guide to the Galaxy* novel where she figures out the meaning of life right before the world explodes."

"Hmm, that's not how that story starts," Ryan said.

"Are you sure?" I asked. "Didn't she discover that the meaning of life was the number 42?"

"Oh, wow," Ryan sighed, "that's not even remotely how the story goes."

"Oh, well, good," I said, "because none of that ever made any sense to me. I think that's why I never finished reading it."

"Well," Ryan said, "the way you're describing it tells me that you never *started* to read it."

"Ya, I didn't get very far with it," I admitted. "I generally don't read a whole lot of fiction."

"But, yes," Ryan said, "I get what you're saying about the Mayans being right on the cusp of figuring it all out right before they disappeared."

"Well, they didn't entirely disappear," I explained. "Sure, they got decimated, conquered, and absorbed. But they still exist as a people."

"That's just semantics," Ryan defended. "Sure, the Mayans are still here, but most of their *knowledge* disappeared."

"Yes," I agreed, "and a lot of what they wrote was systematically destroyed. The world will never know what it lost now that all the ancient knowledge is gone."

"Then again, what you don't know can't hurt you," Ryan said.

"So true," I agreed. "It's much better not to know when the alien overlords will finally return."

"See!" Ryan exclaimed. "There's the spirit! Sneak attacks are so much better."

"Ya," I declared, "who needs the Mayans to tell us when the end of the world will happen? I'd rather it be a surprise!"

"To the end!" Ryan cheered.

"To the end!" I cheered back.

And with that, we concluded our visit to Chichen Itza, our former stomping ground that never was.

Coba Ruins, 2007

Ancient Mayan cities are curious places, and no two are exactly alike despite sharing common features. Usually, each major Mayan city boasted at least one distinctive component or structure that deviated from the expected norm that gave each city a unique appearance. In the city known as Coba, their stand-out feature was its collection of long white roads that emanated from its central core. As all roads led to Rome in Europe, all roads in the Mayan world flowed into Coba. Okay, maybe it's a little hyperbolic to say it like that, but it does imply that Coba was pretty darn important.

I found its roads to be a tantalizing feature that warranted some serious exploring. I was curious to follow a road or two to see where they went, but to my surprise, Ryan didn't share the same curiosity. Our legs were aching from riding those stupid bicycles, and walking for miles down some unknown path to God only knew where didn't appeal to Ryan's sensibilities. Additionally, Ryan was not appreciating how the mosquitoes were slowly eating him alive while he choked on the air because he forgot to bring his inhaler. Despite his protestations, I dragged him along a long white causeway through a densely wooded forest, after which I was immediately banned from following any more routes since the path I chose didn't have an end anywhere in sight. Of all the roads I could have chosen to follow, I happened to choose the longest one, which ran for 62 miles to the ancient site of Yaxuná. I was willing to follow the route until it ended, but Ryan didn't think that was such a brilliant idea.

Before we jaunted into the jungle, we had spent a good amount of time exploring the remains of Coba itself. We focused most of our attention on the insanely tall Nohoch Mul Pyramid since it was the largest thing there, and tourists were allowed to climb it. It used to be that all visitors were allowed to climb any pyramid they happened to come across anywhere in the Yucatan peninsula, but climbing pyramids is now generally prohibited. Yet, for whatever unknown reason, no one was barred from climbing the pyramid at Coba, which, incidentally, was one of the tallest ones the Mayans ever created. Not only was this stone edifice fabulously towering, but it was also preposterously steep and scary to ascend.

Ryan and I and every person on that pyramid climbed all 120 steps on hands and knees because walking upright was darn near impossible. The whole time I climbed, I wondered why the Mayans needed their pyramids to be so freaking treacherous. My best conclusion was that the primary goal of a pyramid was to raise it as far into the sky as humanly possible; thus, the steeper the pyramid, the faster it reached into the atmosphere. Did the Mayans think they were closer to their gods if they performed their rituals in the clouds? The Mayan landscape was generally flat, so if they wanted to rise above the treetops, they had to create that height themselves. I naturally concluded that pyramids essentially became their sacred mountains.

People have an insatiable desire to always see more, so the view from mountaintops is likely what motivates people to climb. There is something spiritual about drinking in the world's vastness through a humble pair of eyes while standing on top of a peak. One finds internal peace when one rises above the cacophony that humans create. Mountains are where people go when they need to hear themselves think. There must be a reason why so many cultures put their gods on top of mountains, for where else would knowledge ultimately reside? It is on top of the world where answers are usually found when they can't be discovered anywhere at the bottom.

When we reached the top of the Nohoch Mul Pyramid, we came upon a little temple once sacred to the Mayan priests.

Hundreds of years' worth of rituals were oozing from the temple walls and spilling ghostlike into the surrounding space. I thought perhaps this was where all the Mayan gods ultimately resided, so I looked inside and discovered all the Mayan spirits inhabiting one sleeping dog. Incredibly, some pooch had climbed up all those steps and found himself a thousand-year-old dog house. We considered the possibility that this mangy creature was a reincarnated Mayan deity, so we toyed with the idea of consulting this canine about our futures. Yet, we wisely refrained from doing so only because everyone knows to let sleeping dogs lie. If we were still up there when the dog awoke, we would undoubtedly bow to the animal and seek its wisdom. Until then, we simply admired the view from our lofty perch.

Even though the scenery was breathtaking, I was thoroughly distracted by thoughts of being physically tossed from the top of the pyramid. The Mayans were famously keen on removing a victim's beating heart and throwing the corpse down the pyramid's staircase. As much as I admire the Mayans, I will forever struggle to understand why they practiced human sacrifice. I mean, I get it; they were afraid *not* to perform that ritual. They convinced themselves that their gods demanded it. They truly believed their entire existence depended on whether or not they adequately placated their deities. I don't know how the Mayans (or the Aztecs, for that matter) could have remained true to themselves had they been allowed to continue their culture minus the human sacrifice bit. So much of how they identified with the universe involved maintaining what they perceived to be the status quo, and that maintenance involved a steady flow of human blood. When the Spanish took away their ability to feed their hungry gods, it was equivalent to them taking away their very existence. There was nothing left for them to believe in once they were told they could no longer murder people on top of their pyramids. Thus, the Mesoamericans had to give up their life in the clouds.

Speaking of standing, we did nothing of the sort when we descended that scary staircase almost entirely on our butts. The whole reason why most pyramids are roped off for climbing is that they are actually quite dangerous. (Which does nothing to explain why climbing the pyramid at Coba was allowed. However, I'm also aware that most pyramids are off-limits to prevent further erosion.) Yet, no matter how anyone makes it down, it's always better to get to the bottom alive rather than deceased.

Aside from the whole sacrificing component, the Mayan world, in general, was filled with intense beauty. The Mayans must have known that the rest of the world was nowhere near as beautiful as where they happened to live. The Mayans must have known that they were not alone, for theirs was a culture that studied the stars. I suspect they believed in a grander purpose for themselves; they just lacked the means to express themselves fully. Perhaps their existence was a case of being born too soon or being born on the wrong planet. The Mayans would have been fantastic interstellar neighbors had they existed in a solar system with multiple inhabited realms in contact with one another.

Part of me is of the opinion that the ancient Mayans got stuck in a psychological rut. Perhaps they got too wrapped up in pleasing their gods that they lost track of who they needed to be. I personally think they were left to their own devices for too long. What they really needed was a heavy dose of outside influence to pull them out of their quagmire. What Europe should have done was send over their scholars, not their missionaries and murderers. Imagine what could have been gleaned from the wealth of Mayan knowledge had it not been destroyed before it was given a chance to disseminate. The Mayans could have been so much more than they were, but instead, they went down as one of history's greatest "what ifs."

Xcaret Park, 2017

If I had to say where my favorite place in Mexico was, I'd have a difficult time selecting an answer. The place is chock-full of a dazzling variety of sites and locations, and it's almost impossible to narrow the decision down to one. However, if I absolutely had to choose, I think my answer would surprise me, as I'm leaning toward crowning a theme park with the official title of "favorite."

There's no one reason why I'd choose Xcaret Park as my favorite place to visit in Mexico. All I can say is there was just *something* about that park that got burned into my brain as being incredibly special. Yet, if someone twisted my arm and insisted that I give a reason, I suppose I would say it fulfilled my desire to release my inner Indiana Jones.

Without getting into too much detail about the park's history, I will say that it was essential for us to know that the park resided upon the ruins of an ancient Mayan village. The town's original name was *P'ole'*, which arose from the Mayan root word meaning "merchandise." That name indicated that the city was an important location for trade, and indeed, it most certainly was, being strategically located next to a small inlet. Thus, the ruins of this once-prosperous village were nestled inside the confines of the modern-day ecological park; however, it was a little too easy to stumble upon the crumbling buildings and not know whether the ruins were actual or imagined. Fake and real meshed with the past, present, and future into a cohesive dreamy haze. We eventually got to the point where we didn't *want* to know what era we were residing in anymore. As far as we knew, we had entered the ancient world of the Maya, and everything about Xcaret Park convinced us that the modern age had no interest in visiting.

The experience at Xcaret Park was immersive and focused on reality rather than fantasy. The jungle setting was the epitome of romance, and seeing the morning sunlight filtering through a canopy of trees was the very thing of memories. It became a theme to pinch ourselves every so often to ensure we weren't dreaming. We damn near drowned a hundred times when we went swimming through an underground river replete with dark tunnels, narrow passages, and vaulted ceilings because we kept gasping at how fantastic everything was. We didn't even care that it was January and the water was freezing us to death, for we were exactly where we wanted to be: here, on this watery highway of amazingness. If I could ever go back in time and repeat one single experience, I'd repeat that underground swim.

Of course, not everything at Xcaret tempted us, for they offered a whole slew of attractions that we didn't consider doing. Neither of us was keen to pay hard-earned cash to "Sea Trek" (walk underwater with a scuba helmet on), swim with stingrays (we'll pass on that, thank you), or swim with dolphins in an unnatural environment ("Dolphinaris" – don't even get me started). However, we enjoyed just about everything else the park had to offer. The lush jungle setting housed incredible plant and animal pavilions, and the nearby beautiful beach was practically worth dying for. We watched every pre-Hispanic dance show their replicated Mayan village offered up and witnessed all the local craftspeople create their wonderful wares. Xcaret did a lot of things right, and we both agreed that they outdid themselves with the last performance of the evening. *The Xcaret México Espectacular* was two hours long and featured hundreds of performers. It was nothing short of the entire history of Mexico through interpretative dance, and we've never seen anything like it before or since. In short, there was no one thing about Xcaret Park that caused it to earn its spot as my favorite place in Mexico, for there were too many things to like about that alluring destination.

Cozumel, 2017

We took a ferry from Playa del Carmen to Cozumel as one of the last things we did on our 2017 trip. I very much wanted to go there not to lounge on the beach or go trinket shopping but rather to pay my respects to the aged jaguar goddess of midwifery and medicine, Ixchel. Historically, the Mayans made an annual journey from either Xcaret or Playa del Carmen to the island of Cozumel on a trip they called "The Sacred Crossing." It was especially important for Mayan women to make that pilgrimage at least once in their lives to consult a celebrated oracle. I, being female, desired to connect with my ancient sisters and told Ryan about my intent to ask the oracle about our futures.

"Oh, cool!" Ryan said. "I love a good oracle. Will it be like the famous one at Delphi?"

"Funny you should ask," I said, "as I wondered the same thing. I kinda fell into a deep rabbit hole reading about this place before our trip, and it struck me as really strange how similar the two oracles were."

"Oh, hey, wait a minute," Ryan declared. "I didn't think you were being serious. Are you saying that we're *really* going to visit an oracle?"

"Well, it won't be working anymore!" I exclaimed. "The hollow statue no longer exists for a priest to crawl inside and give out prophecies."

"I'm not following," Ryan said. "Are you saying the Mayans used oracles?"

"Are you kidding?" I asked. "What ancient civilization *didn't* use oracles? Those things were like so necessary! No major decision was ever made without consulting some higher power."

"Humpf, I guess I never thought about that," Ryan said. "So, I take it we're going to visit the place where the Mayan oracle used to be?"

"Yup!" I exclaimed. "However, we'll have to pretend it's still there. I'm not even sure which building the statue was in, so we'll just have to pick one."

"You do realize that has been the theme of almost every trip we've ever been on together, right?" Ryan stated.

"Of course! We never go anywhere without our imaginations," I said. "However, before we go, I want to stress that mostly *females* consulted this oracle. Oddly, only male priests would inhabit the female statue, though, so you'll have to play the role of oracle when we get there. It's the total opposite of the one at Delphi. Only females inhabited that one."

"Well, that doesn't sound like a bad gig to me," Ryan declared.

"Ya, well, it won't be so great when I ask you when we're going to have a baby," I said.

"Bah, that's easy!" Ryan proclaimed. "I'll tell you the answer is never!"

"What a relief," I said. "I guess we don't need to visit the oracle now."

"Well, that was a fun trip!" Ryan beamed.

"Ya," I said, "I'm so glad we went!"

In all seriousness, though, we did visit the San Gervasio ruins (*"Tantun Cuzamil"* to the ancient Mayans) and explored every nook and cranny until there was no stone left to unturn. Naturally, that statement is not true, though, as three-quarters of the site remained unexcavated; however, we thoroughly inspected all that was revealed. The spirit of Ixchel hung heavy over the site, and it was impossible not to think of her whenever we entered a ruined structure. Any of those buildings could have been her ancient domain, so we felt her presence inside every room. Here the Mayan goddess always lived, and here she would always remain.

The ancient Mayans may have left this planet, but who was to say their deities went with them?

Conclusion

Tulum will always hold a special place in our hearts, but it is not somewhere we'll be returning anytime soon. The Mayan ruins remain, but the Tulum we used to know and love is essentially gone. The EDM and Instagram crowd has taken over the beach, and what they haven't claimed, investors and cartels have. Prices have risen along with the crime, but apparently not enough to keep visitors away. A non-native seaweed now seasonally saturates the beach and makes getting in the water less enjoyable. Armed police openly roam the streets and knowingly extort tourists when given a chance. Tulum never expected to grow as much as it did, and its infrastructure strains under such impossible weight.

I understand the only constant is change, but the changes occurring in Tulum are rather alarming. Many websites exist to answer the question, "is Tulum safe?" and many conclude the answer is "sort of" rather than delivering a flat-out "no."

When I first visited the Yucatan with my Spanish class in high school, we were allowed to climb any pyramid we stumbled upon. My most vivid memory was when I climbed *inside* The Castillo pyramid at Chichen Itza and saw the red jaguar throne and reclining Chac Mool statue residing inside. To obtain such a view is practically impossible today unless one pulls out an archaeologist card. I guess the point I'm trying to make is that every experience is unique and can never be replicated. I saw those statues once with my very own eyes, and they will never be something I'll ever see again. Do I lament that Ryan and I were unable to share such an experience together? Yes, indeed, of course I do. Those statues were amazing. They were the tangible remnants of an *older* time, a past event that existed *below* a more recent age. The current pyramid we see today was superimposed upon a previous one. I mean, how incredible is that? And how phenomenal was it to be able to climb the stairs of an older pyramid nestled inside a newer one? It was enough to blow my mind into a thousand little pieces and make me want to become an archaeologist. Indeed, it was enough to set my passion for history into cerebral stone.

Everyone wants to believe that the Mayans were insanely special, or dare I say, an anomaly. Yet, I wonder if they were either of those things, for I believe they were simply human beings. Left to our own devices, humans are capable of doing incredible things. Indeed, the Mayans were a determined people, and even though they left plenty behind, we will never fully know what they were thinking. Sure, we can *see* the image of their Serpent God wriggling down Chichen Itza's pyramid at certain times of the year, but we will never know if the Mayans put it there or if *we* accidentally did so during reconstruction. Yet, one doesn't need an equinox-induced light show to prove the Mayans were familiar with the skies because the fact that they survived for over 2,000 years proves they knew what they were doing. The Mayans were sedentary people who knew how to farm, and their survival depended upon being able to read the seasons.

We rarely stop to think about what we're missing by losing sight of the night sky, but the Mayans would have died had they lost access to the sun, moon, and stars. Theirs was a world that extended into outer space, and they didn't need NASA to tell them they weren't alone. The Mayans kept a watchful eye on Venus, Mars, Saturn, and Jupiter and believed their alignments were signals from their gods. To them, the universe was an integrated whole, and their place in the world fit within a much larger picture. We today never look at Venus and think it has any influence over our lives, but by doing so, we have lost our sense of place in the world. For all the technology we have today to see deep into outer space, we find it impossible to look beyond our little domain.

CHAPTER NINE:
Louisiana, Jun 2000 & Apr 2008
Remembering Katrina

When Hurricane Katrina hit New Orleans in August 2005, I watched the horrible scene unfold live on TV from the comfort of my couch. The grip that Katrina exerted to strangle the life out of what I believed to be one of America's most unique cities was so utterly surreal that it was impossible to stop staring at it without my jaw agape. Katrina looked like a glutton as she tore through New Orleans as if it was a buffet. It was obvious that Katrina arrived with an appetite, and she wasn't going to depart until her belly was full. Her tummy required a hearty meal of broken levees, flooded highways, damaged houses, destroyed vehicles, looted stores, and a leaky Superdome. Katrina was a ravenous beast who swallowed New Orleans whole.

For days, the whole nation watched not only Louisiana, but large portions of Mississippi, suffer all the ill consequences that a devastating hurricane could cause. Disaster relief wasn't coming quickly enough, and seeing hoards of people sitting on their roofs for x amount of days showed me that I didn't live in the country I thought I did. The whole Katrina thing shined a spotlight on who we were as a nation, and it proved to me that America was a country of haves and have-nots. Preference was given to those predetermined worthy, and poor blacks living in low-lying areas could never expect to make the cut.

Those who lived in the swampy areas were destined for failure, but they didn't know it. Sadly, officials were aware of the levee's flaws but chose against doing anything about them. The focus of New Orleans has always been the French Quarter and the Garden District, not The Lower Ninth Ward, where many of its creative citizens sprang. Adversity brings about creativity, and creativity was the adhesive that famously held New Orleans together. Unfortunately, wet glue never sticks, and allowing half the city to soak in water was the worst decision the city ever made. There were measures available to prevent the worst from happening; however, all those options were willfully ignored. One indeed reaps what one sows, and Katrina served New Orleans a bountiful harvest.

There has always been an allure about New Orleans that captures the imagination, and the unspoken fear after Katrina was that its special sparkle got washed out to sea. At least, that was my concern. I've always adored that city's decaying facades, its delicate wrought-iron balconies, its soundtrack of trumpets and trombones, and the general feeling that floats in the air and tickles my nose. Indeed, no other city feels quite like this one.

It's a shame I don't live there, but I could never afford the lifestyle of my desires. My dream life envisions me living in a perfectly appointed Second Empire-style French Quarter abode replete with gas lamps and chandeliers; however, reality would see me living in a post-Katrina catastrophe of a house loaded with mold and broken windows. Indeed, real life doesn't happen in the fantasy world of gilded mansions and mirrors but instead occurs at ground level, where people have to scrub all the layers of muck and grime off the walls.

The Lower Ninth Ward

I've traveled to New Orleans on two separate occasions, and

each trip was spurred out of anger. The first time I went, I was mad at Napoleon, and the second time, I was angry at us. My first trip was to visit Napoleon's death mask so I could yell at him in person, and the second trip was to see what America didn't do after Katrina. Since I started this chapter with thoughts about Katrina, I will revisit those memories first and order Napoleon to wait despite my fear of telling him what to do.

A huge part of me wanted to go to New Orleans sooner rather than later after Katrina hit, but I didn't feel comfortable being a disaster tourist. I did, however, immediately search if there was anything a tourist could offer in the way of a weekend's worth of volunteering, but I failed to come across anything specific. Looking back on it now, I should have just gone there when I initially wanted to. I could have helped clean up the mess, for I'm pretty sure that no one would have told me they didn't appreciate the extra assistance. Then again, I still don't know what the post-disaster protocols are. Does anyone know? Are there any? You'd think with all the many disasters later we'd all know by now how to rally at this point, but still, everyone seems to stay home after a catastrophe strikes. I don't know if I'm supposed to feel guilty or nonchalant about it anymore. I presume that everyone is saving themselves for when a disaster strikes them personally because we're all bracing for something at the rate things are going.

So, despite my better intentions, I decided to wait. For three years, I held back and watched the city "heal" from afar. I put heal in quotations because "healing" meant leaving the city for good for many residents. Help wasn't coming fast enough for those who needed assistance, so the best solution for many was to pick up and leave. I was mad at us for how we treated nature and mad at everyone for how we treated each other. I was tired of how everything was disposable. We throw away everything, even entire families, as one afternoon of driving around the Lower Ninth Ward unabashedly revealed.

When I drove around The Lower Ninth Ward three years post-major disaster, the neighborhood still appeared grossly disjointed. I couldn't tell which houses were inhabited versus which ones were not, as either scenario just as plausibly had a couch rotting on the front lawn or broken steps leading up to a missing porch. People were there, but they also weren't. It was as though I was driving around a living ghost town where the ghosts were actual people that I occasionally saw crossing the street. It was evident the city resigned itself to its fate, albeit it wasn't necessarily embracing it. The neighborhood was just there, simply limping along. Debris was piled up on street corners, houses were spray-painted with cryptic red "X's," roofs were missing shingles, windows were covered with plywood, cars were melting on weedy lawns, houses were missing doors, and facades had scars where porches used to be. Not a single house there denied that it stood as a testament that something terrible had recently happened. And by "recent," I had to remind myself that the cause of all this destruction occurred three long years ago.

I had never before seen something look so devastatingly real, and I had to question whether or not this set a precedent for what would eventually become the new normal. The thought crossed my mind of tossing in a polar bear floating on an iceberg and a fracking drill or two on someone's front lawn to ensure its status of becoming the future's most quintessential American city. I barely flinched at the thought that there was something wrong with that scenario because, standing in the middle of The Lower Ninth Ward, it was hard to deny that none of this was okay. I didn't feel the need to ask any of the living ghosts how they were doing because I could see for myself how they were faring. I didn't need to ask myself if I wanted to trade places with anyone I saw because I knew I was better off than these unfortunate souls.

It was hard not to get out of the car and shake hands with every person who crossed my way, for I interpreted every Lower Ninth Warder as being a much stronger person than I could ever be. It takes an insurmountable amount of strength to muster through a tragedy the scale of Katrina. A moment of weakness could cause one's soul to sink into the abyss, and I couldn't say that I wouldn't have fallen headfirst into that bottomless pit. Sometimes it takes a disaster to discover who you really are as a person, and I perceived every individual fighting for The Lower Ninth Ward to be an unsung hero.

Between the chaos and destruction, I saw slivers of beauty. I saw the people picking up their scattered remains as walking Rembrandts. The entire post-Katrina world was a real-life Dutch painting in all its chiaroscuro. The broken Lower Ninth Ward presented itself as America's Louvre, and the verdict was still out on whether to regard the artists as prodigies, failures, or misunderstood geniuses. The general consensus was to allow posterity to decide. For the moment, no judgments were being made on the merit of leaving a half-ruined shotgun house to sit tilted on its foundation, for it was going to sit like that whether someone preferred to frame the scene and hang it on a wall or not. All of The Lower Ninth Ward was on display just as it was: America's fucking mess. If ever a city personified what people stare at when they're unable to turn their heads away from a train wreck, The Lower Ninth Ward nailed that look perfectly. It was almost a shame that models couldn't drape the city on their shoulders and walk it down a runway because it would have been a hit with upper-class socialites. The Lower Ninth Ward was oddly attractive in its swampy post-apocalyptic way.

People are like gardens, so becoming someone requires cultivation. It's much easier to grow a healthier and happier person when conditions are clean and favorable rather than poor and disadvantaged. One would never eat a tomato produced inside a nuclear reactor because that tomato would be toxic; yet, metaphorically speaking, we grow people in those similar conditions all the time. So, the question remained as to how to avoid growing the next generation of nuclear tomatoes. The slate was wiped clean, but, probably to no one's surprise, New Orleans was failing to seize the opportunity to sow a better garden.

Today, urban blight remains, albeit the only difference now is that it's interspersed with the occasional colorful Brad Pitt Foundation-designed home. Fewer people live in the Lower Ninth Ward now than before Katrina paid them a visit, which some may argue might not be such a bad thing, but I disagree. If there was a way to embrace the water that's naturally a part of the environment rather than keep it unnaturally at bay, then I think the Lower Ninth Ward ought to return and flourish. Plenty of cities have been built in swamps before, and there are correct ways to create those cities with the proper use of canals, dikes, and stilted houses. In truth, it wasn't nature's fault that it took out a low-lying neighborhood as it did. As always, it came down to the haves and have-nots: the French Quarter had natural protection, whereas the Lower Ninth Ward sat on vulnerable ground.

Yet, there is no reason not to allow the Lower Ninth Ward to have its Renaissance, save that others just don't want them to have it. By denying them a future, we are only shooting ourselves in the foot, for soon, many will suffer a similar fate. Water is rising everywhere, and a version of Katrina happens somewhere every year. Indeed, learning how to embrace nature sooner rather than later would be to our benefit. We need to learn how to live on this planet, not only with nature but also with each other. Only when we realize that we are all in this together will we start to see any semblance of improvement. Although deep down, I know nothing will change. If anything changes at all, it will most likely be too little, too late. We need to save ourselves now while our heads are (mostly) above the water. If not, well, there is no better place to practice being dead than in New Orleans.

Mad at Napoleon

New Orleans is a place for the weird and the wonderful. It's a place where life and death collide. The city serves up beignets and po'boys with as much finesse as it serves up cemeteries and vampires. The city is a kaleidoscope of all that makes us human. There are many reasons to go there, be it food, drink, or music, but the main reason is to simply *feel*. People go to New Orleans because they want to feel their humanity in all its many facets. However, people also go there to get a head start on what it will feel like not to be alive anymore, for New

Orleans exists to show people what they will miss when they are no longer living on this planet.

In New Orleans, it's possible to ask Napoleon what it is like to be dead, and I took the opportunity to do so when I interrogated his bronze death mask inside The Cabildo Museum. True, talking to a death mask was not necessarily the most normal thing in the world to do, but it sure beat trying to converse with him through six layers of coffins placed high on a massive marble pedestal parked inside an elaborate domed building in the heart of Paris thronging with tourists, such as I once attempted to do. I discovered that I much preferred to meet France's former leader inside New Orleans' historic city hall, where fewer people seemed to know he was even there.

Louisiana is the best place to go when one wants to commune with spirits, and, as it was, I had a bone to pick with Napoleon's ghost. I spent a greater portion of my early 20s writing a novel, and Napoleon was why I ran into a literary brick wall. I experienced my own private Waterloo when I encountered Napoleon with my pen, only in my case, it was Napoleon who emerged as the victor. He was too formidable a force for me to battle on paper, and I developed a love/hate relationship with him for all his complexities. For sure, many people dislike him for all sorts of reasons, but I now understand how the French fell under his spell. He was a complicated badass in a way that few men can ever manage to be. The Napoleon I met on paper was a fierce warrior full of grand ideas. I fought Napoleon on the page but lacked the tactical skills required to outmaneuver him. Thus, I admitted defeat, laid down my pen, and parked my unfinished novel in the closet where it will likely forever remain.

Napoleon staked a flag on my soul, and I needed to meet my captor in a Stockholm syndrome kind of way. I wanted to go to New Orleans specifically to face Napoleon so I could ask him why he had to be such a glorious prick. I had read that the death mask was modeled after the plaster cast done directly from his face the day after he died, so this would legitimately be as close to him as I was ever going to be. Also, I was morbidly curious to see what he really looked like in person, and I was intrigued to find out whether or not he matched the image I had of him inside my head.

Napoleon was only 51 years old when he died in exile on a remote island in the middle of the Atlantic, where the odds of him escaping (again) were minimal. The story of how the death mask ended up in The Cabildo was a convoluted tale, but not an entirely strange one once I learned that Napoleon almost ended up in Louisiana himself. (Local New Orleans legend claimed that Napoleon was to move there after his exile.)

So, I was admittedly surprised when I found him to be more handsome than I expected. I was fully anticipating a puffy and bloated head but instead saw that he resembled the classic image depicted in a Jacques-Louis David painting. In those pictures, Napoleon looked like a man that people wanted to believe in, for Napoleon became someone mythical when Jacques-Louis David held onto the brush. Thanks to his official portraitist, Napoleon consistently appeared as the ever-resplendent wind-blown-haired hero astride a horse with an air of confidence hanging over him like a halo. The artist David cultivated an image of what a man needed to look like to save France from itself, and that man looked exactly like what was lying in a glass box before me. I was looking at the barely discernible furrowed lines of a nation's former savior. Death apparently suited him, for it made him look 20 years younger and every bit the man he used to be.

When I looked at Napoleon's sleeping face, I could see in his features that he was used to winning. There was something about his aquiline nose combined with his chiseled cheeks that conspired to make him appear as someone not to trifle with. Nevertheless, I was there to yell at him; however, one look at him made me nearly forget what I was there to do. I was there to rail and to admire. Each generation has its hero, and for the generation that lived in France after the Revolution, Napoleon was theirs. I was looking at a nation's hero cast in bronze, and I couldn't help but feel that *meant* something. Even though Napoleon figuratively kicked my butt, I marveled at his essence floating in the room.

The planet evidently has an impossible time shaking Napoleon off its back, and we'll always be stuck with him in some way, shape, or form. Even if someone was to throw this bronze death mask away, there were three others just like it residing elsewhere. This man was a presence, and I rather enjoyed studying his face despite my desire to spit on it and kiss it simultaneously. Even in death, Napoleon looked ever-ready to conquer the world. He looked as though he could reanimate and continue right where he left off. Looking at him made me want to believe in him more. His face was preserved in frozen silence, yet I felt I could have sat beside him and listened to him speak for hours.

That face in front of me was *Napoleon*. I wanted to believe the good in him as well as the evil. That cranium once belonged to him. What nuggets were stored inside that chiseled head? I wanted to crack it open and allow its contents to spill out. Yet, I also desired to kick it like a football, for smashing his face might have provided me with some satisfaction. I spent four years writing a book I never finished. Four years, and I had absolutely nothing to show for it. Napoleon conquered me somewhere in Egypt. I was writing a story about the relationship between religion and architecture and wasn't remotely expecting to encounter so much as a skirmish at any point in the tale. Napoleon entrapped me somewhere between the Rosetta Stone and the Louvre, which was curious because neither had anything to do with religion or architecture (well, the Louvre did, but not extensively). I obviously allowed my story to grow well beyond my original intentions, and Napoleon caught me in the act red-handed. I had to either rewrite the whole thing or fight a pitched battle before moving on. Considering that I showed up relatively unarmed, it made sense that I got pulverized when I opted for war. Thus, I parked the unfinished story deep inside the closet and occasionally return to it to see if Napoleon's army is still there. Indeed, my shelves continue to serve as a garrison for two-hundred-year-old troops, so if anyone wants to interview a division of the Grande Armée, let me know because they live between my old tax returns and piles of magazines. I have no idea what they do there all day, but they must be doing something because they're apparently never bored enough to organize the contents of my closet.

When I fell into that literary pit nearly twenty years ago, I decided to make a home down there and wrote an entire screenplay about ghosts that also never made it past the closet.

However, I did submit the script to a professional reviewer once, and she replied that my story was "ambitious and outrageous but had too many moving parts." She assumed the screenplay had more than one author, and she gave "us" tips on how to rewrite it to make it marketable. Yet, I found the endeavor entirely too daunting and decided to park the whole thing next to the army. To say I have a massive "need to rewrite pile" doesn't quite describe the mountain of papers that taunts me in my nightmares.

Film Ideas

I've been to New Orleans twice now, and both journals I kept are nearly devoid of details describing what I did while there. Instead, both notebooks are filled with the outlines of movies I thought of while I sat inside various bars and cafes. New Orleans is a city meant for writers, and if there was such a thing as a magic screenwriting machine, I could quickly churn out many years' worth of films in a matter of days.

I once came across a particularly atmospheric cobblestone alley that glowed under a street lamp right after a rain, and the scenery conjured up the outlines of a story that begged to be written. The New Orleans muse inspired me to remedy the fact that Hollywood has yet to tackle a sweeping drama about America's greatest hero. However, I questioned whether or not George Washington was too sacred a topic to make a blockbuster movie about. I quietly deliberated with myself and ultimately concluded that he deserved to be immortalized on the big screen with an equally big budget, replete with mansions, parasols, and battle scenes. Alas, this idea came to me before the advent of mini-series programming, so I now

266

desire to revamp the concept and allow it to stretch on for days. With no end date in sight, I could genuinely explore his personality in the greatest possible detail and sort out myths from realities.

Sticking with the theme of historical movie ideas, I wondered why Hollywood hadn't made a legitimately decent film about one of Egypt's greatest pharaohs yet. Ramesses the Great is one of history's most fascinating figures, and I could think of no good reason why an epic film depicting the exciting life of Ramesses II shouldn't exist. It was while I was sipping a beer at Lafitte's Blacksmith Shop Bar that I conjured up the idea of ensconcing myself in a French Quarter hotel room to furiously write the Ramesses II script that the world so desperately needed. I privately declared that I wouldn't reemerge until I wrote a script that did the historical figure proper justice, but then I realized the hotel room would have the potential of becoming my tomb. Sifting through five thousand years' worth of Egyptian history to reach the core of one single man might prove too daunting a task for one measly mind to conquer. I would certainly need a team of writers holed up in that room with me to ensure our collective survival.

I knew I was pretend-pitching for some seriously costly movies to be made, but then again, the churning out of another CGI superhero film that absolutely nobody ever needs isn't always the cheapest thing to create, either. However, a sweeping historical drama might be too rich for some people's blood, so I thought the general public might prefer something baser – something along the lines of a *Heavy Metal Western*. I came up with this idea when I stared at a piano sitting in the back of a bar, and the tagline, *If the Wild West could have listened to any music, they would have listened to Slayer*, came to me. The movie would, of course, be about absolutely nothing, but it would look good and have a killer soundtrack. People would watch it just to see Jesse James kick everyone's ass in a mosh pit.

In short, I don't know why New Orleans makes me think of screenplays I'll never write, but it does. There's just something about that city that makes me think creatively. Indeed, I could go on and on with movie pitches, so if any studio is interested in hiring me, I wouldn't say "no," so long as I get an office in the French Quarter with a stipend for enough po'boys and jambalaya to keep me sustained.

Yet, as much as I love writing, my number one hobby has always been traveling. My "places to go" list has always been long, and I check off an item whenever an opportunity presents itself. Such an opportunity presented itself when I was too close to an unpronounceably named swamp deep in Cajun country to skip out on taking a swamp tour. Thus, I drove a couple of hours from New Orleans to the Atchafalaya river and got on the water. The ride was on a glorified canoe, and I learned about water snakes, alligators, cypress trees, and nutrias. My apologies, do you need me to say that last word again? Nutrias. They are river rats, and they are freakishly huge.

Swamp Tour

I didn't know what I was seeing when I saw oversized rodents swimming around like figments of my imagination, so I spoke up and asked, "Excuse me, but am I seeing rats on steroids, or am I just imagining it?"

"Yes," the tour guide confirmed, "you're seeing nutrias."

"Come again?" I replied, as his answer clarified nothing for me. Was this "nutria" thing the name of an animal, or was it the brand name of a high-fiber granola bar? I was not privy to a creature I had never heard of before.

"Well," the tour guide started, "back in the fur trapping days, the hunters ran out of beavers, so they brought in the river rat as a source of fur. They called these animals "nutria," which was the Spanish word for otter. However, nowadays, no one wants nutria pelts, only nutria tails. The nutria breeds quickly and destroys the environment, and the state will pay five dollars for each nutria tail brought to them."

That story got my creative juices flowing. I immediately thought of inventing a show called *Nutria Bounty Hunters*. I instantly figured out how the first episode would play out, for I was fairly convinced that I was already starring in the pilot episode at the start of this conversation.

When the tour guide said, "The state will pay five dollars for each nutria tail brought to them," I interpreted it as the cue to bring in the nutria bounty hunter. Suddenly, I could hear the TV show's theme music playing in the background. I quickly turned my head and saw a mysterious man emerge from the cattails in camouflage attire. "Who was this mysterious figure?" I wondered. "Why, it was none other than the man who hunted rats. Large rats, bigger than your biggest rat nightmare. This man does not fear rats; the rats fear him. This man knows how to eat those rats for dinner. This man knows how to make nutria granola bars, and in this first episode, he will share his secret recipe with us."

"They're really high in protein," the nutria bounty hunter

will say as he takes a bite out of his chewy snack before cutting to a commercial. Move over *Duck Dynasty* reruns; there's a new show in town. Everyone will want to know what kind of men hunt rats for a living. I know that I'm more than intrigued to find out. I hope at least one of them mounts their nutria kills on their walls like trophies because that would be so weird it would be awesome. The guy who did that would be hands down the star of the show and would probably know how to whip up a mean nutria jerky and inspire viewers to order batches of them off his website. The more I think about it, the more I believe this show needs to happen. I mean, c'mon, who doesn't want to know about the secret life of a nutria bounty hunter? The show practically writes itself.

Zydeco Queen

Since I was on a roll thinking up the best TV shows ever, I began to wonder where my TV crew was when a particular woman caught my attention in Lafayette, Louisiana. However, before I delve into too much detail about this mysterious lady, I must first provide a backdrop. I need to begin by painting a scene. For Cajun country, that scene is sound, specifically, the sound of Cajun music. The arsenal of instruments used to make the scene where this story takes place includes all the eclectic ones, such as accordions, fiddles, triangles, washboards, and harmonicas, along with the usual suspects, such as guitars and bass. Obviously, any ordinary person will have absolutely no idea how to dance to the music produced by such an unconventional array of instruments. Thus, the person envisioning this scene will not have to dance but will happily watch. The people on the dance floor will know how to move to this music, and one particular female will dazzlingly stand out. She'll have long brown hair, a denim outfit that can only be described as country zydeco, and feet that will move twice as fast as her hips. Every man will vie to be her partner, and in between sets, she will invite a lucky male to enjoy a cigarette with her in her powdered blue convertible parked in front of the venue. This woman will live the life that every Cajun girl only dreams about, but alas, not every girl gets to grow up to become the Zydeco Queen.

From all appearances, this denim lady with her sexy blue car did not look like she would be giving up her crown any time soon. As an observer, I wanted to know more about her and what she did with her life when the music stopped playing. Alas, I resisted the temptation to become a Zydeco Queen stalker, as I assumed she probably had enough of those types lurking around already. I did have to admit that she intrigued me, though, as I had never seen anyone bred into such a specific role before. She was born to own the Cajun dance floor, for no other life could have possibly suited her. I was instantly envious of her and wished I had an identity like hers. I wished I knew *exactly* what I was born for. I thought of all the hobbies I wasted my time on searching for who I was, only to realize that I wasn't the person I thought I was to be. As a kid, I was always pretty sporty and artistic, but I eventually realized I wasn't bred to be a gymnast, dancer, or artist. It's only now that I'm trying to figure out if I was born to be a writer. I was under the impression that the Zydeco Queen never questioned her identity. I ended up staring at her for way longer than was probably healthy, though, and I quickly figured out that she and I had equal stamina. We were both at the Blue Moon

Saloon And Guest House for the same reason: to listen to music – a whole weekend's worth. Every band nominated for a 2008 Grammy Award for the Best Zydeco or Cajun Music Album category was scheduled to play a set that weekend, and neither she nor I would leave until we listened to them all.

I had never heard live Cajun music before that weekend, and now I can say that I've heard too much. No, I'm lying because who could ever say that their ears have been assaulted with too much accordion? Man, I'm not gonna lie, though – that was a lot of accordions. Indeed, what I heard was wholly unexpected yet immensely appreciated by all who were there.

Before I traveled to Lafayette, I researched what venues offered Cajun-slash-Zydeco music because I desperately wanted to hear some live bands while being in that part of the country. The only place I found that guaranteed live music every night was a local institution called Prejean's Restaurant, so I more or less planned on being there every evening. I booked a stay at Blue Moon Saloon And Guest House because it was cheap; however, I noticed that their website mentioned something about them being a live music venue as well.

By the time I arrived, I had completely forgotten that the hotel also doubled as a music venue, so I was caught slightly off guard when the guy at the front desk asked me if I was there for the live show they were having that weekend.

I was in that neck of the woods for the specific purpose of hearing live Cajun music, so I told a white lie and said, "Yes, I was here for that," not knowing what I just said "yes" to.

"Great!" he said. "You do know who's playing this weekend, right?"

"No idea," I confessed.

The hotel guy let out a bellowing laugh. "Why, it's everyone nominated for a Grammy in the Cajun or Zydeco category! They're all locals here. The event will last all weekend!"

"Holy crap," I thought to myself. "I hit a gold mine. And I don't even have to leave my hotel."

"Oh, and no charge for you because you're a guest," he told me.

This guy had to be kidding me. I had never been this lucky before.

That event went down in my personal history as the best musical weekend of my life. Unfortunately, it was an occasion that can never be repeated, though, since the Best Zydeco or Cajun Music Album is a Grammy Award category that no longer exists. What I experienced was one of those magical moments that occur in travel when all the stars happen to align just right.

I'll never know what happened to the Zydeco Queen, but she sometimes dances in my sleep. I don't dream about Zydeco music, though, as that would be too obnoxious. No, in my dreams, the Zydeco Queen is a ballerina, but she occasionally headbangs to Metallica. What can I say? Dreams don't have to make sense.

Stream of Thoughts

Louisiana is a fascinating place whose history is fraught with complications. Indeed, a lot of what makes Louisiana a photographer's dream is deeply intertwined with its checkered past. The plantations that made Louisiana fabulously wealthy also made Louisiana fabulously beautiful. It's definitely a challenge to enjoy the sites without feeling a measure of guilt, though, and I felt guilty for admiring the stately row of centuries-old oak trees as I stood under their majestic branches at the infamous Oak Alley Plantation.

The avenue of trees was an incredible sight to behold as they made a canopied path from the Mississippi River to the front doors of a mansion. Oddly, no one was exactly sure who planted those 28 trees, nor was anyone sure whether they were planted as seedlings in the 1700s or as transplants in the 1800s. The only thing that was certain was that whoever planted those trees definitely had a vision. Someone took a long hard look deep into the future and envisioned a sight they would never behold. The double row of southern live oak trees took three hundred years to reach their current state of maturity; however, it will take a million lifetimes or more to erase the plantation's past.

The memory of slavery hangs over the American South like an invisible shroud. The corpse of slavery remains covered up, but the outline of its shape is easy to discern. The ancient oak trees at Oak Alley Plantation were knowing, and they would never forget that they grew up on the breath exhaled by those involved with slavery.

Indeed, the breath of ghosts was an essential element in the oxygen I breathed while I explored the haunted state of Louisiana. At one point, I found myself walking among the ghosts of slavery's past at The LSU Rural Life Museum. The museum possessed an extensive collection of 18th and 19th-century material culture, and the artifacts allowed for seamless communication with a host of archaic spirits. The museum sprawled over 25 acres and included 32 historic buildings, and I made it a point to go inside every one. According to its website, the museum's purpose was "to increase the appreciation of our heritage and the way of life of our ancestors, their hardships, toils, vision, inspiration, and determination by preserving some of the architecture and artifacts from our rural past." I felt the museum accomplished its stated goals, for I spent an entire day looking at every little detail. It was a very immersive experience, and I walked away with a fuller understanding of Louisiana and Lower Mississippi River Valley culture.

Slavery was an inseparable part of the story, and the museum did not shy away from presenting its unfortunate tale. The museum offered a "Working Plantation Section," and it was impossible not to feel sadness when going inside an authentic slave cabin. The way the enslaved people were dehumanized was nothing short of shocking, and it felt both necessary and uncomfortable to stand inside that wretched space. I tried imagining an entire family eking out their pitiful existence inside such a tiny room, and the whole thing struck me as wrong. Everything about slavery was wrong, and it wasn't something that could ever be righted. The past is the past, but the future sometimes never moves forward. Indeed, the slave cabin never disappeared, for I was standing right in the middle of it. That struck me as rather symbolic in a metaphorical kind of way. "Was it *this* cabin's shadow casting an ever-long darkness over the land?" I wondered. Racism wasn't just a problem in the American South, though, for this cabin's shadow was the size of an entire continent, which was much larger than the space it contained.

It's safe to say that every plantation house is tainted by its history, and it's important to acknowledge the past whenever one visits those historic estates. Yet, history is never static, for it's full of complicated layers and varying stories. The fate of many plantation homes was to fall into disrepair after the Reconstruction, and several estates deteriorated beyond recognition. However, that doesn't describe the fate of The Oakley Plantation House, where John James Audubon once famously stayed.

In 1821, cotton fields covered the Oakley Plantation, and the woods it was carved out of still existed in extensive tracts for the 36-year-old John James Audubon to roam around. He declared his intention to "paint every bird in North America" the previous year, and it was at The Oakley Plantation where he began that ambitious task. The plantation owners brought him there to give drawing lessons to their daughter, yet he had enough free time to create the first 32 pages of what would become his 435-page magnum opus of illustrated books.

Audubon's book *The Birds of America* was a sight to behold in its breadth and beauty. There had never been an illustrated book like it before, and there will never be another one like it again. For one, an artist like Audubon only comes around once, and for two, some of the birds he painted no longer exist. The picture he painted of the now-extinct Carolina parakeet (*Conuropsis carolinensis*), for example, perfectly illustrated what the world will now never see. His hand-colored, life-size print of green birds with bright yellow heads was painted so animatedly that the viewer can practically hear them. I was so enamored when I saw this print online while writing this chapter that it inspired me to learn more about these charming little creatures. The birds apparently lived in huge, noisy flocks that stretched as far north as Wisconsin and as far west as eastern Colorado. Curiously, cats usually died when they swallowed those birds because the parakeets enjoyed snacking toxic cocklebur seeds. The birds went extinct due to habitat loss, and the last captive Carolina parakeet died at the Cincinnati Zoo in the same cage that housed the last passenger pigeon. I barely had it in me to look up what Audubon's drawing of the passenger pigeon looked like after reading that tragic tale, but I mustered the energy to do so and was happy that I did. One look at his drawings is all it takes to get a sense of a bird's natural behavior. I now know what passenger pigeons and Carolina parakeets each looked like, even though I will never see a live one in person.

Fortunately, Louisiana's storied past stretches far beyond its plantation history. It extends deep into the recesses of time as the domain of an ancient mound-building civilization that stretched from the Mississippi to the Ohio valleys. Remnants of that culture remain scattered throughout the breadth of the state, yet, no one is exactly sure why so many mounds were constructed. Research ultimately determined not every mound was destined to be a tomb; however, I don't find that revelation all that surprising. I believe people realized they needed to live *on* elevated platforms after they experienced one too many floods. If Katrina taught me anything, it's that form follows function, and the best way to survive a disaster is to escape it. I believe the mound-building culture lasted as long as it did (5,000 years) because they found a way to thrive in an inundated landscape.

The Mound Builders lived in North America for thousands (not hundreds, *thousands*) of years, and seeing one sight does not equate to seeing them all. No two sites are ever the same, and I've seen quite a few of them, but not the granddaddy of them all. (Okay, I've seen Cahokia, which could arguably be the granddaddy of them all, so pretend I rephrased what I just said to something less grandiose.) I will always say there's a reason to go back to Louisiana, and the next time I go there will be to see the Late Archaic site known as Poverty Point.

It's unfortunate that one of North America's most fascinating ruins goes by a name that conjures up images of destitution. From what I've read, Poverty Point was anything but poor. The site was named after a local plantation, which naturally makes me wonder how successful that plantation could have possibly been. Part of me wants to go down a rabbit hole and see where researching Poverty Point Plantation will take me, but I've had my fill with enough plantations for a while and recognize that I'm suffering from the familiar Louisiana tourist ailment known as plantation fatigue. Yet, before I move on, I want to say that I'm not usually a conspiracy theorist, but I suspect these ruins were given that deplorable name to deflect attention away from one of North America's most resounding success stories.

Like I said earlier, I've never been there, but it's a place I want to visit. I just now looked at a map and noticed that it's located 15 miles from the current flow of the Mississippi River. For some reason, I thought it was *on* the Mississippi River itself, but then it dawned on me how long ago 3,700 years was. The flow of *any* big river eventually changes, so now I wonder where the Mississippi River was when Poverty Point was inhabited. I just now tried looking up the answer but couldn't find the solution. See, this is why traveling is so important. It's always easier to find answers to questions by going straight to a source.

I am fascinated with ancient history, yet so much of North America's oldest history remains relatively unknown. No one knows why the Mound Builders created this massive site of six concentric, C-shaped ridges so enormous that it took aerial photography to finally reveal its geometric design. When I read about Poverty Point, it sounds a lot like Chaco when archaeologists describe it as having served more a ceremonial purpose than a domestic one. I personally have my doubts that either site was purely ceremonial, though, for there's too much about either culture that we don't know enough about to make that determination. A lack of evidence of domestic structures doesn't necessarily mean those structures were never there. It might simply suggest that the *kind* of structures archeologists typically look for might not have existed. Archaeology is a science; however, it leaves too much room for subjective interpretation. I'm, of course, no archaeologist, but I would still like to go to Poverty Point and develop my own theories. It always takes seeing somewhere in person to gain a greater sense of knowledge, and I would like to someday stand on top of one of those mounds and ponder what it would have been like to reside in a a landscape potentially surrounded by floods.

Speaking of gaining a greater sense of something, I, for some reason, decided that I was going to grow my own chicory plants and brew some New Orleans-style coffee at home. Their coffee is famous for having a unique Cajun flavor, and to make a long story short, the chicory coffee I made at home tasted nothing like the real thing. I didn't know I was supposed to mix my roasted and ground chicory roots with some actual coffee grounds to impart a blended flavor, so I combined my chicory roots with nothing, and the result was that it tasted like dirt.

"But it tastes "earthy," right?" I said to Ryan as he winced after taking his first (and only) sip.

"Ya, that's one way to describe it, I suppose," he kindly replied.

"At least it tastes better than that wine I tried making last year," I said as I forced myself to take another swig.

"Oh, you mean that wine that tasted like a musty attic?" he said. "Ya, I agree this tastes better than that."

"Well," I said, "I guess this coffee will join that wine in the compost bin, then. At least the garden will appreciate my efforts."

"If it's any consolation," Ryan started, "I think you're a pretty good gardener and do a fantastic job growing lettuce greens."

"Hey, thanks," I said. "Maybe next, I will learn how to can."

"What?" Ryan asked, almost spitting out the coffee that wasn't in his mouth. "You're going to can *salad*? Why the heck would you do that?"

"No, silly," I said. "I mean, I want to learn how to can food in general. How are we going to be doomsday preppers if I don't know how to can?"

"Well, if your wine or coffee are any indications, we're going to starve before the nuclear blast gets us," Ryan said ever so kindly.

"I guess we're destined to be eternal city slickers, then, aren't we?"

"Honestly, if it's hinging on whether or not you get good at canning, then I think we both know what that answer is."

"True dat!" I declared.

We both paused and stared at our full cups of chicory coffee.

"Do you want any more coffee?" I asked.

"Sure," Ryan said. "Am I driving to Starbucks, or are you?"

CHAPTER TEN:
Florida and The Caribbean, Dec 2009 & Oct 2010

Chilhood Memories

Growing up, my family only took one trip every couple of years, and it was the same trip every time. My parents weren't the most creative travelers in the world, but they sure knew how to keep their kids happy because that one unvarying vacation always took us to Florida. Granted, caravanning there in a station wagon took a dreadfully boring 18 long hours to accomplish, but the drive was always worth it once we arrived. Everyone on my dad's side of the family permanently high-tailed it to the sunshine state years before I was born, and I never understood why my dad opted to stay behind in Wisconsin. Life always looked better in Florida, especially in late February and early March when the sky was much bluer than the gray sky we perpetually drove away from. I only had one real low point during my childhood, and it revisited me like a recurring nightmare every time we pulled back into our driveway after having just spent two weeks in the one place I would have rather stayed. There were few things in life worse than returning to the dead of winter after tasting the sweet, sweet flavor of eternal spring. I think my disdain for the cold festered inside me like an ulcer after experiencing one too many trips to the happy place.

My mom was the picture taker in our family, and from the evidence that she left behind, she only pulled out the camera during Christmas and while on vacation in Florida. Most of my childhood photos show me standing next to a Christmas tree or playing on a beach. There was no in-between, so it's safe to assume those two events summed up the entirety of my upbringing. In her mind, she was probably documenting birthdays, for I was born near Christmas, and my sister's birthday always coincided with our trip to Florida at the end of February. My parents would get away with cheating on gifts because they would call the trip to Disney my sister's birthday gift and the entire Christmas holiday mine. I remember my mom feeling bad one year when the only thing my sister got for her birthday was an ice cream cone, and she dropped it. It's not that my parents were malicious or anything; they were just frugal to a fault.

I remember the year that EPCOT opened because my dad was excited that there would be something other than Disney World to visit. I remember not understanding what EPCOT (aka Experimental Prototype Community of Tomorrow) was supposed to be about after my dad tried explaining it, but that's probably because he had no idea what it was supposed to be about either. The place sounded strangely intriguing, yet my main concern was whether or not there would be any rides. My dad was vague on the answer, cryptically saying that "it was Disney, so there had to be rides." That wasn't a definitive yes, but the word "Disney" was enough of a sell that I wasn't too worried about what to expect.

It was good that we didn't know what to expect the day we were there on March 8, 1983, because officials told us not to expect to see at least half of the park until sometime after four o'clock due to a large swath of it being closed for a special event. I have no idea if my dad intentionally planned to take his family to EPCOT the same day President Reagan was there to give some park-related speech to a preselected audience or if it was simply a coincidence. It's possible that my dad might have thought that we'd all get a chance to hear the president speak, but if that was the case, then his hopes were dashed when we were told that visitors needed to be corralled around the EPCOT Dome like human sheep until the pivotal hour when we'd be allowed to roam free. It was almost a year to the day when someone shot Reagan, so the park was taking extreme precautions to ensure that history wouldn't repeat itself on their newly consecrated grounds.

Looking back on it now, I have two memories that prominently stand out when I think about that day. One was how my dad moped around the corral fuming because he was unimpressed that he got charged full price to see a limited version of the park, and two was how really, really, *really* familiar we got with the inside of EPCOT's Dome. There was really only one ride in there to speak of, and we rode it three times, maybe even four. We never did see much of the rest of the park, but for whatever reason, I remember thinking the place was fun. However, my dad never suggested visiting there ever again, so we continued with our Disney World tradition the following years. Considering that my dad was never too keen on Reagan (even though he looked just like him), I believe he forever held EPCOT against him.

Splendid China

I had pretty much forgotten about EPCOT until it came up in a conversation with Ryan when he revealed that he had never been there. I asked him what he thought EPCOT was about, and he confessed that he wasn't sure. I told him that reply was completely normal, for I was there once a long time ago, and I still wasn't sure what it was about either. Thus, I immediately proposed we go there together and solve the elusive mystery. He thought about it for a nanosecond and said he was game. Excited, I quickly launched into trip-planning mode and pulled out a ten-year-old Florida guidebook that languished on a shelf.

I had picked up that guidebook for twenty-five cents at a library book sale forever ago and was happy to finally have an excuse to read it. Normally, I would turn to the internet to properly plan a trip, but Florida was a personal classic, so I thought it fitting to go old-school-style and physically flip through a guidebook for itinerary ideas. It had been so long since I visited Orlando that I really wasn't sure what parks were there anymore. I didn't necessarily want to go to Disney World because I had been there too many times already, and Ryan thankfully claimed to have been to Disney*land* enough times that he, too, was plenty good on the Disney front. Thus, we resolved to find other things to do in Orlando that didn't involve people running around with a pair of mouse ears on their heads, and that's when the park called "Splendid China" piqued our interest.

Splendid China was not a park I was familiar with. However, the fact that I had never heard of it before didn't necessarily surprise me. It apparently opened in 1993, and anything regarding Florida fell off my personal radar sometime in the mid-'80s. My 1997 Eyewitness guidebook described Splendid China as "Orlando's most cultural, adult-oriented theme park; wonderfully peaceful; almost too sedate." Reading on, I surmised that even if the park had been open in the early 1980s, there would have been no way that my parents would have dragged two bored kids around a 76-acre park full of miniature replicas of China's most famous landmarks. No doubt, my mom would've enjoyed the park because she genuinely appreciated Asian art and culture, but she likely would've had to go there by herself if she wanted to relish it properly. I thought the park sounded appealing now that I was an adult myself, so I proposed putting it on our list of must-see attractions. Ryan's father immigrated to America from China by way of Taiwan in the 1970s, so a Chinese-related theme park was not a hard sell for him. Ryan had wanted to visit China for as long as he could remember, so a Floridian version of China was something he was interested in experiencing.

It wasn't until I jumped online to look up Splendid China's current operating hours and pricing that I sensed something was amiss. It took me a while to put two and two together before I realized that consulting an out-of-date guidebook wasn't the most practical thing to do. All the information on the internet pointedly told me that the park, which cost China $100 million to build only to remain open for a handful of years, was permanently closed. Further sleuthing revealed the park struggled to function properly the entire ten years it was in business. It had attracted more protesters than visitors, and they perpetually lost their Chinese employees when they claimed political asylum. The bottom line was that the park didn't appeal to the average, run-of-the-mill Florida tourist, so the attraction hemorrhaged oodles of cash. Of course, reading all that made me want to go there even more, but I was having a difficult time figuring out where the park once sat on a current map.

"It's gotta still be there," I said.

"Why does it matter?" Ryan asked. "It's closed."

Indeed it was, but that fact only made the place more intriguing.

"Aren't you curious?" I asked.

"Curious about what?"

"Curious about what an abandoned Splendid China theme park looks like?"

"Sure, I don't know, maybe, I guess?"

I gave him a knowing look.

"You're going to make us go there, aren't you?"

He saw that I was feverishly studying a Google map.

"You know that could get us arrested, right?" Ryan said. "I mean it. Didn't you say the park was owned by the *Chinese*?"

"Oh, phooey, who cares?" I said. "It's not like anyone will be there. The place has been closed for five years now. The question now is whether or not it's still there because I can't seem to find it on a map."

"Good," Ryan declared. "Maybe that means the place is officially gone. You should give up. It sounds like a bad idea to go there anyway."

"Bingo!" I announced. "I just found it!"

"Darn it," Ryan sighed. "Really?"

"Ya," I beamed, "but you'll be happy to know there appears to be a huge wall encircling its perimeter."

"Okay, then," Ryan reasoned, "that probably means security guards are monitoring the place."

"I doubt it," I said. "I bet there's a break in the wall that's not showing on the satellite map. We'll have to channel our inner Genghis Khans and storm the walls when we get there."

Ryan looked at me. I looked at him.

"Aw, crap!" Ryan exclaimed. "Why do you make us do these things?"

"Because it will be fun!" I announced. "It's not every day that we get to break into an abandoned Chinese theme park in America!"

"You do realize that everything you just said sounds massively wrong?"

"Ya, I heard myself," I stated, "but there's no guarantee we'll even get in. I say we go there and give it a shot."

"That's not the word I would have used," Ryan remarked.

"Ha!" I laughed, "That's a good point! Hopefully, those won't become our famous last words!"

The day eventually arrived when we found ourselves in front of a splendid wall. It turned out that there was a residential neighborhood nearby, so there was already a breach in the barrier that allowed people in. Thus, we left Florida and landed somewhere between Guangdong Province and Tibet in an instant. Evidence that the neighborhood kids were having the best childhoods of their lives abounded, for it was obvious that the fallow theme park was now one gigantic skateboard park extravaganza. We quickly concluded there'd be no one around to give us a hard time, so we let our guards down once we saw that teenagers were clearly not afraid. Broken debris was scattered on what we assumed were former manicured paths, and the overall appearance was that Splendid China was truly abandoned. We were definitely going to be on our own here, and there'd be no miniature terra-cotta army to save us if something were to happen. Alas, our adventure had officially begun.

Once we stepped over the threshold, we were no longer

mere mortals, for crossing the barrier transformed us into super-sized giants. Other visitors had apparently alighted in the same form long before our arrival and took it upon themselves to stomp their feet over the entirety of the place. Here was China after a King Kong-style Apocalypse, for there wasn't a single miniature replica that wasn't smashed into tiny bits. The ruined park was sensory overload, so we left our brains at the crumbled-down entrance and walked around without any thoughts. The place was simply too weird that it defied comprehension. We let ourselves loose and relished having a ruined country all to ourselves.

The only miniature building still intact was the one-tenth-scale replica of the Potala Palace. We guessed the only reason the building was still there was because it was perched on too steep of an incline for the local kids to scamper. In a surreal way, it was ironic that it was one of the last structures remaining, for its depiction was one of the primary sources of contention with the protesters. Many people disagreed with China's overtaking of Tibet and interpreted the display of the Dalai Lama's winter palace as a source of Chinese propaganda. I wanted to perceive its preservation as a local version of respect for the plight of all Tibetans, but to do so would have required thought, and I couldn't do any thinking because I left my brain behind at the breach in the wall.

After the Tibet section, there really wasn't a single small building left standing in a solitary piece. Tiny bits of structures littered the overgrown walkways like hardened snowflakes that crunched whenever we unavoidably stepped on them. As we strolled around, we kept finding remnants of figurines, but oddly, not a single one boasted a head. We found whole torsos with arms and legs still attached, but all were mysteriously headless. It was almost creepy that our running game became "find a head, any head, even if it's not on a body." We never did find one the whole time we were there, although we did find part of a face. I suspected plenty of teenagers' bedrooms nearby were decorated with impressive collections of miniature heads, yet I wondered why so many miniature torsos were decidedly left behind.

"This place is so weird," Ryan and I both said, I don't know how many times.

"And you thought coming here would be a bad idea!" I reminded him, with a hint of gloating in my voice.

"No, no," Ryan defended, "you were right to suggest it. This place is amazing!"

I always love it when he says I was right about something.

"I'm sorry," I said, "I didn't hear you. Can you say whatever you just said again?"

Ryan knew what I wanted to hear him say again. "I said, oh, look over there! Is that the Forbidden City?"

I turned my head and saw the fabulous miniature ruins of what must have been Splendid China's former centerpiece.

"Holy crap, even crumbled, it still looks impressive!" I proclaimed. "Let's go check it out!"

This, here, was the heart of Splendid China and where most of the current skateboarding was evidently taking place. The miniature city was full of little ramps that skateboarders were apparently using to crash land through the roofs of miniature palaces. Broken tiles abounded, and fragmented figurines were scattered everywhere.

"Hey, what do you say we piece this place back together?" I

suggested.

Ryan looked around at what could only be described as the fall-out of a miniature nuclear bomb and said, "Sure, I think we can do that!"

"Okay!" I proclaimed. "How 'bout I start at the bottom of the stairs, and you can start on one of the palaces?"

"Sure! That works!" Ryan exclaimed.

So, we split up momentarily and got hard at work on our respective projects. After about fifteen minutes, I found part of a staircase ornament that seemed to fit on the spot where I replaced it and then moseyed over to check on Ryan's progress of replacing an entire roof.

"See!" Ryan declared and pointed to something wildly insignificant. "I found a roof tile! It fits back on perfectly!"

"That's fantastic!" I said. "I replaced a staircase ornament! It's like this whole place is repaired now!"

We took stock of our accomplishments and deemed our achievements worthy. In our estimation, all of China was glued back together, even though it was completely shattered all around us.

"Shall we move on to the next project?" I asked. "Repairing this place is so easy."

For whatever reason, Ryan was feeling in a benevolent mood, so he took it upon himself to be the park's sole performing artist when we came across the ginormous stage that Chinese acrobats used for performances. I showed no one my ticket, took a center seat, and watched Ryan show off his prowess on the rope swing that precariously hung off some questionable rafters. I gave him a standing ovation and asked for an encore, but he explained that since he was the park's last employee, he needed to attend to all the other tasks necessary to keep the park functioning. Under that premise, we then moseyed over to what we assumed was the former administration building. There, Ryan found a half-torn time slip lying on the dirty carpet, so he pretended to punch in on a time clock machine that wasn't working. Once inside, he saw that he had oodles of offices to choose from where he could toil away a day's worth of number crunching. He ultimately settled on the only room that still had an office desk positioned upright. The fact that his chosen office had a ladder that came from who-knew-where laying across the floor, serving no purpose other than a tripping hazard, failed to distract him. If he decided he was thirsty at any point, he always had the option of taking a swig off the empty beer can that was lying crumpled up in the center of the room. Under these conditions, he completed his entire work day in less than five minutes, after which we both decided it was time to venture to the front and finally pretend-pay for our admission at the ticket booth.

Thus, we pretended to start from the beginning. We pulled up in our imaginary rental car and scored a parking spot right in the front while pretending not to notice that the parking lot was nothing but weeds and randomly scattered tires. We approached the ticket booth and pretended to see the attendant through all the paintball splotches that thoroughly coated the glass. We each received a map of the park, which we both valued as prize processions after we discovered a pristine stack of Splendid China brochures somewhere deep in the bowels of the administration building. We consulted our difficult-to-read-map-because-it-was-printed-with-minuscule-letters and deduced that we had missed a massive swath of the park. I don't think two people were ever happier to actually be at Splendid China than we were when we realized that we still had a lot more exploring left to do.

The day continued with Ryan providing the necessary function of an impromptu tour guide whenever we came across something that required a little bit of make-believe insight. I took loads of photographs of him posing like a statue and had him star in my random under-one-minute films. We had so much fun there despite how overall depressing the place was.

If down the road was "The Happiest Place On Earth," this here was definitely the saddest. There really was no joy in looking at defaced objects and buildings, even if everything was designed to be kitsch. Real people were behind every item left behind for someone to ruin or steal. Walking around Splendid China was akin to walking around someone else's dreams because everything struck us as figments of imagination. Not a darn thing meant anything to anyone anymore, which made the whole place rather depressing. Splendid China belonged to no one, not even itself, and the sense of detachment was pervasive. It was easy to let ourselves go there because not a darn thing was tethered, not even us. We could have uprooted what remained of Splendid China and taken it all home with us, and no one would have cared. The whole park was going to be bulldozed soon anyway. It eventually got transformed into a Jimmy Buffet-themed condominium monstrosity, and darned if any Floridian would protest that. Today, Parrotheads lay their bird brains on pillows and dream of nothing regarding China.

EPCOT, Revisited

It was going to be hard for us to top our Splendid China experience, but, then again, EPCOT wasn't exactly the world's most normal place either. Now that I've returned from my second time around, I have to say that I'm still not entirely sure what EPCOT is trying to be aside from a little bit of everything. There's one thing I'm sure of, though, and that is its ride inside the dome hasn't changed since its inception. Oh. My. God. That ride put us both into tears because it was the most hilarious thing ever. The ride was a blast into my past, which was ironic because the attraction was designed to depict the future. However, the "future," according to the *Spaceship Earth* ride, ended sometime in 1983. The people currently running EPCOT must know how ridiculous the ride appears today. They also must collectively possess a wonderful sense of humor because they did something to make the attraction even more entertaining than it rightfully had a reason to be.

When visitors take their seats at the beginning of the ride, a little video screen instructs riders to pose for a picture. Thus, Ryan and I posed for our respective photos, unaware that we both stuck out our tongues for the photographs that would be immortalized for the next 15 minutes of our hilarious lives.

Throughout the duration of the ride, our supremely stupid faces were plastered onto cartoon figurines on the screens embedded in the seats before us. Every 30 seconds or so, we'd glance at the screens and see cartoon versions of ourselves running around doing something ridiculous. We were torn between deciding which was sillier: the archaic ride itself or the cartoon versions of us. When the ride neared its conclusion, it presented a vintage 1980s crappy compact car as the final installment depicting the future, and we completely lost it. This single ride alone made us forget an entire day's worth of hilarity spent at Splendid China just 24 hours earlier. We knew this last scene was a homage to those who invented the personal computer from the confines of a residential garage, but the car parked in the driveway got us rolling in tears. I totally remember seeing that same car when the attraction was new, and I distinctly remember thinking that car was the epitome of cool. Seeing that same car in the current setting made me nostalgic, but then I looked at the screen and saw the cartoon versions of us running around with our tongues sticking out. The whole thing added up to being entirely too hilarious that our stomachs ached from laughing so much. Thank you, EPCOT. We absolutely adored you.

There's a lot more that I *want* to say about EPCOT, but it's the kind of place that's hard to find words for. Now that I've been there both as an adult and as a kid, I have to say that going there as an adult was preferable. I feel I got *more* out of the experience seeing it through an older pair of eyes, especially while walking around the "worldly" neighborhoods. The entire park was divided into four themed areas, and we spent most of our time in the section called "World Showcase." Each district (Canada, UK, France, Morocco, Japan, USA, Italy, Germany, China, Norway, and Mexico) included architecture, landscapes, shops, restaurants, and attractions indicative of the location, and we happily spent our money on a German buffet. Live polka music roared as if we were in a bonafide Biergarten during Oktoberfest, and it felt so authentic that we checked it off our real-life bucket list. Overall, we both decided that if we ever moved to Orlando, we'd get season passes to EPCOT so we could eat at all the ethnic restaurants and save loads of cash by never traveling again. Why would we spend money going to Morocco if Morocco was right down the street?

Tampa

Orlando lies 54 miles from the nearest beach, so we missed out on experiencing a "proper" Florida vacation. Additionally, we returned home regretting that we didn't go out of our way to see the infamous manatees at Blue Spring State Park north of Orlando when we later learned that we were there at the height of manatee season. It would have been nice to see those curious creatures in their natural habitat, but fate determined that our eventual manatee sighting would occur somewhere a lot less beautiful. We returned to Florida the following year to attend a friend's wedding and doing so allowed us to see manatees swim in the warm discharge water around a coal-fired power plant. If anyone were to say that a power plant was a natural setting, I would suggest that someone go get their head examined, but then again, the word "natural" leaves a lot to be desired in Florida these days.

However, before we headed to the Big Bend Power Station, we popped inside the Salvador Dalí Museum. Naturally, we were baffled as to why St. Petersburg was home to such an extensive collection of Salvador Dalí's, considering that Dalí had absolutely nothing to do with Florida while he was alive. It turned out that the Dalí museum ended up being where it was simply because the location was more appealing than Ohio, where the collection was originally displayed. Thus, Surrealism was in full force right out of the gates merely because Dalí was somewhere we didn't expect him to be.

Surrealism was an artistic movement created in the fallout of World War I. Life after that war would never seem normal again, yet everyone was expected to act as if everything was okay. Unfortunately, *nothing* was okay after everyone saw what pain humans were capable of inflicting. There was no going back to "business as usual" once society got a taste of poisonous gasses. The world was now illogical and unnerving. No one expected anything to be as it was anymore, and artists believed traditional art was an unnatural way to express everyone's feelings. Artists saw how distorted the new reality was, so they invented a new way to convey those visions. I think André Breton, one of Surrealism's principal theorists, said it best when he described the new movement as "a way to resolve the previously contradictory conditions of dream and reality into an absolute reality, a super-reality, or *surreality.*" Thus, abnormal was the new normal, and the world gave birth to Salvador Dalí.

I highly doubt anyone can say they have a favorite Dalí painting, for how can anyone decide between melting clocks, distorted violins, or fragmented landscapes? Or choose between the body of Venus in the image of a face, a disappearing bust in the shape of Voltaire, the emergence of a man from an egg, or the self-portrait Dalí himself referred to as the *Great Masturbator?* There's simply too much to choose from that it's impossible to decide. His art was *too* good, and everything he created will surely stand the test of time. People will always be able to look at any of his paintings and know precisely what he was saying. Dalí's art speaks to that pit that sits in the bottom of our stomachs and eats us up inside. He painted who we know ourselves to be, whether we like ourselves or not. Dalí never hid from himself, and his art showed us that we should never hide from ourselves either. It was only by painting unrealities that he was able to show us what was truly real.

After the museum, we moved on to view the manatees. Nothing could have been more surreal than seeing endangered creatures swimming in heated water provided by a massive industrial power plant. Honestly, the word *surreal* didn't even describe it, for the imagery superseded even the oddest Dalí creation. I mean, manatees are weird enough, for they look like giant rocks and are closely related to elephants, and here they were swimming around with an enormous power plant spewing clouds of steam or smoke or whatever in the background. It was just too *strange*.

"Hum," Ryan started, "do you think it's okay for them to be swimming in that water?"

"I wouldn't think so," I said. "I mean, would *you* jump in if the manatees weren't there?"

"I doubt it," Ryan said. "We have all of Florida at our feet, so I don't believe I'd choose to swim around Power Plant Beach."

"So, why do the manatees do it?" I asked. "I know they like the warm water and all, but why do they choose to swim around *here*? It just seems so wrong."

Of course, a nearby plaque explained how the industrial wastewater was "clean." However, I had my suspicions with the words "industrial," "waste," "water," and "clean" strung together in the same sentence. The information went on to say that the manatees die if they get too cold, so they need warm water to get them through the winter. They used to stay mostly in the south during the coldest months, but extensive habitat loss forced them to broaden their range. They quickly discovered where the warmest water was; thus, the marriage of manatees and power plants was officiated in hell.

"That plaque doesn't actually say that, does it?" Ryan asked.

"I might have embellished it a little bit," I admitted, "but that's pretty much what it says."

The plaque went on to say that the Clean Power Plan aimed to close most, if not all, coal-fired plants, so the future of manatees remained undetermined.

"That it really *does* say," I wanted Ryan to know.

"*That* I believe," Ryan said. "So, does that mean we're rooting for the coal-fired power plant to stay open?"

I didn't know what that answer was.

"Crap," I sighed. "I say we file that answer in the surreal folder we started in our heads."

"Sounds good to me," Ryan agreed. "I'll file it right next to that murder hole we saw in Mexico."

"Murder holes and manatees," I said. "Sounds like a perfect title for a surreal painting Dalí never created."

"Ya, well, at least we both know what it would have looked like!" Ryan laughed.

"Gosh, what an image," I said, "An industrial plant in the middle of the jungle with manatees swimming in a gaping abyss."

"Yup," Ryan mused, "that about describes it."

"You know what?" I asked.

"What?" Ryan answered.

"We're two people who should never have gone to the Dalí museum."

Florida Thoughts

My parents would always say that "the Gulf side of Florida was better than the Atlantic side," and they maintained that bias for the duration of their vacationing lives. I have no memories of staying in hotels anywhere in or around Miami simply because that's not where we ever stayed. Indeed, most of my Florida memories were formulated on soft, white sandy beaches loaded with unmangled shells. The water was always warm, and the hotels were one-story mom-and-pop affairs that needed to be booked a year in advance. Our Florida vacations were invariably predictable throughout the 1970s but morphed into something less recognizable throughout the early '80s. One by one, the low-slung mom-and-pop motels were converted into high-rise contraptions. The water became crowded, and the beaches quickly abounded with the remnants of shattered shells. The Florida of my youth died while I was still young, and it was the first time in my life I saw the dramatic effects of change. I knew the world wasn't stagnant by the time I was 13. My memories of Florida are never far from my mind whenever I hear the word "progress" spoken in the context of cities. Progress often means there'll be more room in dystopia for everyone.

It had been nearly 20 years since I last vacationed anywhere near St. Petersburg, and the wedding we attended put us a stone's throw away from my family's former stomping grounds. Thus, I couldn't resist booking us a room at one of the last remaining vintage-style motels when an internet search revealed there were a handful remaining. I confess that I allowed the thoughts of our upcoming stay to preoccupy my mind throughout the lulls of the formal ceremony, and there were probably a few toasts to the couple that I missed because I was daydreaming about walking on the beach and scouring for seashells.

The day after the wedding, we drove our rental car to St. Petersburg and made our way to the spit of land affectionately known as *Treasure Island*. Hotels and condos lined both sides of the street, with all the beach views blocked by highrises. We passed a property called *The Thunderbird Resort* that sported an incredible neon sign that seemingly came straight out of the 1950s. I turned into a parking lot and saw the utter surprise on Ryan's face as he watched me park our car in front of a very non-descript-looking property that looked nothing like any of the larger hotels we passed along the way.

"We're here!" I announced.

Ryan looked at the diminutive hotel sandwiched between two much larger properties and said, "Here?" How did you even *find* this place?"

"Isn't it awesome?" I beamed. "Come on, let's check in and get onto that fabulous beach!"

To make a long story short, we arrived at that motel starving. However, I was too excited to eat, so I made us walk the length of the beach on empty stomachs. It was an hour or so before we wandered into a chicken shack and bought some overpriced chicken nuggets to share. We took the meal to the beach and started our saunter back to the motel.

I had never seen Ryan happier to have a chicken nugget in his hand when a seagull swept down and plucked it right out of his fingers.

"Swoop!" I laughed. "How quickly that nugget was *gone*!"

The seagull's maneuver was one of the most hilarious things I'd ever seen. I couldn't stop laughing.

"Damn it, that nugget was *mine*!" Ryan argued as he tried prying the nugget out of the seagull's beak.

The scene was simply too ridiculous.

"Oh my God!" I laughed. "You gotta let that nugget *go*. That nugget doesn't belong to you anymore!"

"But I'm *starving*!" Ryan yelled as if he was going to eat the darn thing if he wrestled it back.

In the end, the seagull won, and we had to buy another round of nuggets because losing that one apparently meant that whatever was left wasn't enough. I have since learned never to underestimate the power of a man's stomach. I will forever allow ourselves to eat sooner rather than later for fear of seeing what wrath a hungry man can unleash.

We spent three lovely days in one of the last mom-and-pop style motels that afforded us the same views that other people were paying top dollar for up and down the coast. We could sense that the days of affordable beach vacations were numbered, so we made sure to get our money's worth of shuffleboard, beachcombing, and fabulous sunsets. Unfortunately, there was one thing that no amount of money could possibly buy, though, and that was the privilege of actually going in the water.

Videos of pelicans coated in oil were still fresh on our minds, for the *Deepwater Horizon* explosion happened only months earlier. Signs were posted everywhere with bright red letters warning people against swimming in oil-slicked waves. It was a cruel twist of fate to stand on that beach and not be allowed a dip. A polluted Gulf of Mexico was to be my new memory now, and it was symbolic of how much things had really changed. I had to make space in my mind to file oil spills, and to make that room, I had to move my memories of swimming in the Gulf to the archival portion of my brain. It's hard to say if I'll ever consider swimming in the Gulf of Mexico again when current internet searches warn me of flesh-eating bacteria, marine life deaths, and splotches of oil still coating the bottom. Sure, the clean-up effort has been commendable, but as long as agricultural runoff and oil drilling continues, a healthy Gulf of Mexico will never prevail.

Puerto Rico

Before we returned home from our Orlando vacation in 2009, we flew to Puerto Rico and snuck in a quickie cruise. However, we were sad to bid our rental car goodbye and contemplated a way of taking it with us because it was hard to part with a brand-new Ford Mustang that wasn't our own. It wasn't the car we intentionally rented, though, for we only paid to drive around a compact-sized vehicle; however, they inadvertently doled out all the compact cars by the time we arrived. We, of course, didn't complain when they told us to choose between a Mustang and a Charger for the same affordable price. We instantly felt like uber-Americans driving a muscle car around the Happiest Place On Earth. Driving that car reminded me of when I had a friend from England visit me in Arizona. I rarely saw him because he rented a Mustang and seldom left its seat.

Neither of us had been on a Caribbean cruise before, and

we both wondered why they were so notoriously cheap. Granted, we paid a rock-bottom price because we opted for the most poorly situated room next to the ship's boilers or something, but we didn't care because it wasn't like we were going on this cruise to catch up on our sleep. No, we wanted to go on a Caribbean cruise so we could say that we did. We're all about experiencing the world, and a quickie cruise was an item we wanted to check off our lists. Also, neither of us had been to Puerto Rico before, so we killed two birds with one stone by flying into San Juan and spending a few days there before heading out to sea.

I'm admittedly not well-versed in Caribbean legends and lore. I know there must be a million stories about explorers, natives, and pirates to be told, but I'm unfortunately not the one to tell them. We went to San Juan knowing not a whole lot about it, and we left knowing not a whole lot more. San Juan was a place we "just wanted to see," and what we saw was very photogenic. We spent the majority of our time in Old San Juan, where the colors were vibrant and the buildings were old. The combination of sea salt and time wore Old San Juan down like an antique coin rubbed of its details, and it was curious to see people moving in and out of buildings with trees growing out of their roofs. The city was a feast for the eyes and a challenge for the legs. We spent the greater part of a day walking the perimeter of the formerly walled town and the rest of our time exploring the remains of a fort. The Castillo San Felipe del Morro was the largest Caribbean fortification built by the Spanish, and it was intriguing to see peeling plaster revealing stones set in place hundreds of years before. History happened here, and I couldn't help but wonder how many pirates gazed upon those walls and bribed their way through.

We only spent two days in Puerto Rico, yet we managed to see quite a bit. We spent the first day in San Juan proper and the second at El Yunque Rainforest and Luquillo Beach. Unsurprisingly, it rained while we visited the rainforest, and I honestly don't remember much about that hike other than getting pretty darn wet. We were on a tour with a bunch of other people, but it didn't take long before everyone voted unanimously to cut the trip short and head down to the beach.

So, on to Luquillo Beach we went, touted as one of Puerto Rico's most beautiful. The month was December, and the water was cold. However, the sun was shining, and the palm trees were swaying. The sand was pale and soft, and it was the kind of beach where you could lay down and sleep for hours. Sleeping wasn't necessarily an option, though, nor was swimming either. Ryan and I walked the length of the beach twice and then wondered what we were supposed to do with ourselves.

"We're not really beach people when it comes down to it, are we?" I asked Ryan, more or less rhetorically.

"Nope, we're not," Ryan agreed. "I'd rather be walking around San Juan right now. How much longer are we stuck here?"

I looked around for the members of our group and saw they were scattered everywhere.

"It looks like everyone else is enjoying themselves," I said. "So I bet we're stuck here for a while."

"It'd be better if we could go swimming," Ryan remarked.

I gazed longingly at the sea. The water was freezing, but it wasn't stopping others from going in.

"I say we do it."

Ryan looked at me like I was crazy.

Neither of us moved.

"Fuck it," Ryan said. "I didn't come all this way to not go into the Caribbean."

He stripped down to his bathing suit and got up to his waist. Two seconds later, I watched him go under, so I had to go in. I wasn't going to allow him to drown in freezing cold water without me.

Thus, our baptism was complete. We were officially in the Caribbean.

Quickie Cruise

We set out on our 4-day Royal Caribbean cruise a week before the Christmas holiday, so the atmosphere was definitely festive. We typically avoid traveling at such a busy time of year, but this trip served as my birthday-slash-Christmas present, so we made an exception. Ryan and I were still a relatively new couple, so we went out of our way to make our birthdays lavish affairs; however, there's little reason to suspect that we'll ever travel again during a holiday season. Alas, once upon a time, we allowed for exceptions; however, all it took was this one trip to the Caribbean to remind me why I usually stay home on my birthday. Not only were there hoards of people everywhere we went, but there apparently wasn't a body of water warm enough to dip our feet into anywhere north of the equator.

I don't know, maybe it was an anomaly that the water was as cold as it was when we were there in mid-December, but we both decided that if we ever went back, we certainly wouldn't go in the last month of the year. That jump in the water we did in San Juan was just a prelude of what to expect for our immediate futures because the water didn't get any warmer the further south we ventured. Granted, we only traveled 203 nautical miles from where we started, and most of that distance went sideways rather than south, so we shouldn't have expected the water to be all that much different. Anyhow, unseasonably cold (or maybe seasonably cold, we weren't exactly sure) water was something we got used to. Now, whenever we see pictures of the Caribbean, we perceive the images as looking rather chilly.

The voyage was only four days long, and we spent half of that time floating on the water. A big part of any cruising experience involves being on the ship, and in all honesty, I was okay with it but not enamored. For me, travel is all about the destination and not so much about the means of getting somewhere. I know that cruising is bad for the environment, and with it comes a whole slew of problems, but that's a Pandora's box I'm choosing to leave closed.

The thing about cruising is that it doesn't leave a whole lot of time to visit a destination. Our cruise allowed for two nine-hour visits: one at St. Maarten and the other at St. Kitts, and nine hours wasn't truly enough time for either, but we had to make do. Of course, we were given a long list of shore excursions to choose from, and it was hard not to think that we could zip-line, jeep ride, parasail, scuba dive, snorkel, and go on a cultural tour all in one day. Alas, the shore excursions were expensive, and the time provided was limited, so it was necessary to choose our shore excursions wisely. We were going on this cruise to have fun, but we also wanted to learn a thing or two. Thus, we opted for one snorkeling tour and one historical expedition to balance our experiences.

St. Kitts

I forget now which island we stopped at first, but if I had to guess, I would say it was St. Kittsten. Or was it St. Maaritts? Of course, I'm jokingly suggesting the islands were essentially the same. Admittedly, that was my initial fear, but reality proved that the islands were wildly different.

In all seriousness, though, I forgot which island we started with, but St. Kitts was the further of the two, so I'll presume we sailed to that one first. Now, before I begin talking about this island, I'm going to make a blanket statement and say that Caribbean history is wildly complicated. Colonialism wreaked havoc on this little patch of paradise, and rare is the island that doesn't wear some colonial scars.

St. Kitts was colonized by both the English and the French in the mid-1620s. Together they massacred 2,000 local inhabitants, partitioned the island, and either enslaved or deported the remaining natives. The Europeans discovered that the island was very fertile (the Carib people called this island *"Liamuiga, "* meaning "fertile island"), so they covered the island in tobacco before market conditions caused them to shift to labor-intensive sugarcane. Enslaved Africans were forced to do all the back-breaking work, and it's probably safe to assume that everyone knows where this story goes. Yet, Ryan and I wanted to be sure we had our stories straight, so we chose to go on a sugar plantation tour and get to the heart of the tales.

We took a tour of Wingfield Estate and hung onto every word that spilled off our tour guide's most eloquent tongue. My brain must have been in vacation mode while I listened, though, because I sadly can't regurgitate anything he said. I do, however, recall him being a walking encyclopedia of everything sugarcane related, and he gave such a thorough tour that he left nothing up to imagination. Strangely, it wasn't too difficult to envision what the plantation once looked like because overgrown sugarcane fields were melting under the sun. For what it was worth, it looked like the fallow fields still had potential, so I asked our tour guide why the sugarcane was growing unnoticed. His answer was the only specific thing I remember him saying, for his words struck me as poignant when he said, "We're watching those fields rot."

St. Maarten

Before I move on to reminiscing about St. Maarten, I want to look up how many Caribbean islands are declared independent. Yet, before I do that, I should figure out how many Caribbean islands there are to begin with. Okay, that answer is over 7,000. Crap. That's way more than I thought there would be. Luckily, I read that only 26 of them are recognized as countries. Okay, that helps to break things down. Of those, five belong to the British Overseas Territories, four belong to the Netherlands, four to France, and two are territories of the United States. So, how many is that? 15. Okay, so that leaves me with my answer. There are 11 independent Caribbean countries, and St. Maarten was not one of them (but St. Kitts was – they officially gained their independence in 1983). From what I read, independence can be a double-edged sword, but as I alluded to before, everything about the Caribbean is complicated. I know nothing about the status of the other 6,000-plus islands, and I'm not about to find anything more about them anytime soon.

St. Maarten's colonial history exists in its name, for it answers to Sint Maarten in Dutch or Saint Martin in French, depending on what side of the island one's on. Yet, St. Maarten (or St. Martin) wasn't the name that Christopher Columbus gave to this island, for he bestowed that name on a different location, but poorly drawn maps led to confusion, so this island was accidentally christened as such. Of course, the natives had their own name for their island, which translated to "Land of Salt" (*"Soualiga"*), and it was this commodity that ultimately led to its division between the two colonial powers.

So, there's always something in a name, right? Granted, not *every* name has a specific meaning, for some places are named arbitrarily, but a lot of places get bestowed a certain name for a reason. I mean, Greenland, notwithstanding, of course. That place was misnamed on purpose. But, how about somewhere named, say, "Mullet Bay?"

"Are you kidding me?" Ryan asked. "*That's* where you want to go snorkeling?"

"Ya! It'll be fun!" I exclaimed. "Can't you already imagine all the swimming hair-dos?"

"Oh my God," Ryan gasped. "You've made me imagine a lot of weird things before, but at least I was spared imagining swimming mullets until now."

"Ha!" I laughed. "It's certainly a weird one! I wonder if they wear swimsuits."

"A mullet in a swimsuit," Ryan mused. "Not a *guy* with a mullet in a swimsuit, just the mullet itself in a swimsuit."

"Yup!" I beamed. "It's where all the mullets are born with a beer can in their hair while driving a Trans Am."

"But then they wouldn't be swimming," Ryan noted.

"Hey," I said, "mullets can swim and drive cars simultaneously. Don't ever underestimate the power of a mullet, or as my friend Jenny used to say, *mulé.*"

"*Mulé?*"

"Ya, she claimed it was French for mullet. She called her car *bulé,* which she said was French for bullet. That car was butt ugly, but it drove really fast. She used to call it "the bullet car" but shortened it to *bulé* because it sounded fancier. Man, she had that car forever because it was so darn reliable. But it was brown and shaped like it could fit inside a gun barrel. Oh, how I miss the *bulé.* I bet it's still alive somewhere, making a teenager happy. I hope that kid sports a mullet."

Ryan looked at me weirdly.

"I forgot how this conversation started," he said.

"Mullet Bay," I explained. "I think we should go snorkeling there."

"Yes!" Ryan cheered. "Even if we don't see any swimming mullets."

"Hey, don't jinx it!" I admonished. "Besides, you'll only see them if you believe in them. You have to be worthy of the mullet to see them in their native environment."

"To be honest," Ryan started, "I thought their native environment was the 1980s."

'Yes," I agreed, "but these are modern mullets."

"So, you mean man buns."

"No, silly," I said. "It wouldn't be called Mullet Bay if it was full of man buns."

Ryan looked at me quizzically.

"You do know that a mullet is a fish, right?" Ryan inquired.

I genuinely didn't know that.

"Why would you say that?" I barked. "Now the *real* mullets won't show up because the faith in them is gone."

"Hey, maybe we'll be lucky, and...."

"Nope!" I bemoaned. "The only mullets we'll see will be the *fish* kind that you speak of."

"So, you mean the *normal* kind," Ryan confirmed.

"Hey, are you implying that mullets aren't normal?" I asked.

"Well, I guess they are if you're stuck in the past."

"True," I agreed. "Every mulleteer I've ever met sure likes to play 80s rock music at full blast."

"That, and bench press weights that are too heavy for them!" Ryan added.

"Hey," I said, "that reminds me. Do you know what I don't see anymore?"

"I don't know," Ryan answered. "High-top shoes? Neon accessories? Spandex shorts?"

"Ray-bans!" I blurted.

"Oh my gosh, yes!" Ryan agreed. "Who didn't have a pair of those?"

"Well, I never did," I said, "not the real kind. Mine were cheap knock-offs."

"So were mine!" Ryan cheered.

"So were everyone's!" I cheered back.

"Ah, the good 'ol '80s," Ryan sighed. "Do you think they'll ever come back?"

"I hear they do," I said, "but only for those who sport a mullet."

"Whelp, it looks like I'll be stuck in the here and now

forever then," Ryan lamented.

"So, are you saying that you're not willing to time travel when all you gotta do is get a haircut?"

"Correctomundo," Ryan declared. "That's one haircut not worth going back in time for!"

"Ya," I said, "I kinda have to agree with that. But, now, won't we be jealous whenever we see a time-traveling mulleteer walking down the street?"

"Nah," Ryan scoffed. "If I were to time travel, it certainly wouldn't be to the 1980s! The mulleteers can have that decade! I'd rather time travel forward to space."

"That sounds like something you'd say," I replied.

"Why? You wouldn't want to time travel to the future?"

"Nope," I said, "because what if the future is worse?"

"Worse than the past?" Ryan exclaimed. "The past is rife with diseases and all kinds of terrible things! I'd want to go nowhere near it! No, I'd say beam me forward 5,000 years!"

"5,000 years!" I gasped. "Do you really think that humans will last that long?"

"Sure!" Ryan exclaimed. "Why not? I mean, we might be mutants by then, but I'm willing to travel to the future and find out!"

"Ya, well, what if your non-mutant lungs can't handle breathing the poisonous air?"

"Ya, well, what will you do when you catch tuberculosis the same minute you exit the time machine?"

"Dude, why is time traveling not fun all of a sudden?" I asked.

"It's because we're only acclimated to our current environment," Ryan explained.

"Man, I never knew how wimpy we were."

"Ya," Ryan mused, "I guess there's a reason why humans aren't built for time traveling."

"Notwithstanding the fact that time traveling doesn't exist," I added.

"Or, maybe *because* time traveling doesn't exist," Ryan clarified.

"Are you suggesting that we invent time traveling to cure diseases?" I wondered.

"Hey, it's worth a shot," Ryan said. "It might be the cancer cure we've been looking for."

"What an insurance nightmare that would be," I lamented. "How could anyone pay their bills if they didn't live in the current era anymore? I could just see the insurers time traveling after you with a bill collector in tow."

"That's one detail the movies never show!"

"I've got the perfect tagline for a movie," I said. *"You can escape your cancer, but you can't escape your debts."*

"Coming to a theater near you in the future."

Cold Snorkeling and Cool Beaches

It was still early December, and the water hadn't gotten any warmer since we left Puerto Rico, but goddammit, we were going snorkeling. So, snorkeling, we did, even though it was a shock to our systems to put our heads underwater. It was so incongruous how warm the Caribbean Sea looked when we admired it from the beach and how cold it actually was once we got in. Surreal would be a good word to describe it, but I don't believe that was one of the words we chose to use at the time.

"Holy crap, this water is fucking freezing!"

"Damn it all! I came here to see mullets! Screw it. I'm going under!"

Ya, that sounds more like what I remember us saying.

So, we didn't see any mullets, fish or otherwise, but we did see a slew of other little fishies through a thick layer of swirling dirt. I don't know why the water was so cloudy, but considering we were the only ones out there, we both deduced that it wasn't the height of snorkeling season. It didn't matter to us, though, because snorkeling was what we wanted to do, so snorkeling was what we did. We rather enjoyed it. Sort of. Okay, so it wasn't the best snorkeling experience ever, but so what? At least we weren't at work. We were in *the Caribbean*. That meant something to us. Travel, any kind of travel, means that you're not sitting around at home. We both agreed that a cold and cloudy snorkeling excursion was better than any day spent at work. So, ya, we'd definitely do that again. And, hey, maybe we'd even see a genuine mullet next time!

There was something we saw that's worth mentioning, and that something was airplanes. I had heard of a beach where airplanes flew in super low, and from what we could tell, it looked like that beach was very nearby. Oddly, low-flying planes didn't look all that weird to us because there's a freeway in Phoenix where the same phenomenon occurs because Sky Harbor airport is almost *too* conveniently located. I sometimes forget that planes fly super low whenever I'm on that particular stretch of road, and there's been more than once when I thought a plane was going to crash land right on top of me. Nevertheless, it was a spectacle we deemed worthy of experiencing, so after we finished snorkeling, we headed to Maho beach and stood in the path of landing airplanes.

I'm not gonna lie – it was pretty thrilling to stand under the belly of a plane and feel it whiz by without the security of a vehicle to protect me. It was one thing to *see* the aircraft but something entirely else to practically *touch* it. The experience made me feel very small and fragile. One false move and everyone on that beach would've died instantly.

Sailing Back

Being newbie cruisers to the Dutch Caribbean, we were not privy to the tradition of buying a wheel of gouda cheese. Heck, even if we *were* privy to the tradition of buying a wheel of gouda cheese, I doubt that we would've bought one because never in our lives had we *ever* bought a wheel of cheese for ourselves before. Yet, everyone on our ship was walking around with one, and we started to feel weird for being empty-handed.

"Were we supposed to buy a giant wheel of cheese?" I asked Ryan.

"By the looks of it, yes, I think we were," Ryan replied.

"Hum. Do you think they'll let us back in America without one?" I wondered.

"I'm not sure," Ryan said. "We might have to explain that we didn't get the memo."

I looked around and saw too many people walking around with a giant red wheel of cheese that I wasn't sure what alternate universe we were living in.

"Have you ever felt weird for not buying a giant wheel of cheese before?" I asked.

"No. Never. You?"

"Absolutely not."

"Do you think we missed out on something?" Ryan

questioned.

"Well, it sure looks like we missed out on loads of cheese," I answered. "Overall, I think we'll survive, though."

Watching people parade around their cheeses got a little much for us, so we decided to escape the alter-reality and took refuge on one of the side decks. From there, we watched the sea glide under the very beginnings of a glorious sunset. The horizon turned a fiery red under a brilliant lavender sky. The day was tucking itself in for the night, and everything looked peaceful and calm.

I looked straight ahead and said to Ryan, "You know what?"

He, too, was staring at the sunset and didn't turn when he answered, "No, what?"

"I was thinking how the world doesn't look like it's going to crap when we see it from here."

We both gazed silently at the sunset that was turning into liquid gold.

"It's too bad the whole world doesn't look as it does when we see it from the middle of the Caribbean," Ryan mused.

"Indeed," I said, "then the world would be too perfect."

We watched the sun hang precariously on the horizon.

"Yes, but perfection is overrated," Ryan declared.

"I agree," I said. "I like life to be a little rough around the edges."

The sun let itself go, and the sky turned a deep shade of purple as it released the last bits of light.

"Shall we go drink some wine?" Ryan inquired.

"Yes," I said, "but only if it's served with an entire wheel of cheese."

Florida's Future?

Just as I was finishing this chapter, scenes of Hurricane Ian flashed across my screen. The bucolic Florida of many people's dreams came crashing through residential windows and yanked away roofs. Yet, I couldn't help but think that the images looked all too familiar, for it was impossible not to utter the word "Katrina" under my breath.

I used to want to live in New Orleans before Hurricane Katrina took that desire away, and now I have those same reservations toward the entire state of Florida. It used to be that the easy lifestyle of a Florida retirement appealed to me, but now that idea is wracked with concerns. The prospect of residing in a mobile home off a canal in Cape Coral might have appealed to my dad when he bought property there in the early 80s, but that would not be a purchase I'd consider making today. Catastrophic storms might ultimately be the new normal, so why would I live somewhere I'd always have to be ready to leave? I know it's an understatement to say that nowhere is perfect, but Florida is in a league of its own when it comes to precarious futures.

There is talk of the Doomsday Glacier possibly melting sooner rather than later, and if that happens, we could all kiss Florida goodbye. Thwaites Glacier holds enough water to raise sea levels by a couple of feet, so it wouldn't just affect Florida's coastline but the entire world's. We are all on this planet together, connected by this magical thing called "water." Life will end when that resource depletes to the point of being unattainable. Sadly, that point is already being reached by those who live in locations where their wells have run dry. The Water Wars haven't started yet, but the threat looms menacingly over the horizon.

Hurricane Ian was but a taste of what's likely to be expected for the near future and beyond. Violent storms like Hurricane Ian might have established the new bar with which to measure storms, and it's set at a level that's already well over our heads.

I hope to see that bar lowered during my lifetime, but I fear it will only rise higher with every passing year. To say that the climate is changing doesn't describe the situation enough, for it's more accurate to say it's accelerating. Humans need to run faster if they want to keep with the pace, but most of us have grown too lazy to get off our comfortable seats.

I'm not exactly sure who's qualified to live in Florida anymore, as cheaply produced buildings will no longer suffice. Hurricane-proof constructions need to become the norm, but they can't be sold to only house the rich. Poor people could barely afford the mobile homes that easily blew away, and it seems incredibly wrong to allow the same thing to happen again and again. At what point does society finally come together to blur the line between the haves and have nots? If that time isn't now, then I don't know when.

A new future can start now if we allow it to; otherwise, it will be just more of the same.

The End

Throughout my 20s, all my international trips were to Europe. I was obsessed with gothic architecture and Renaissance paintings. I desired to see as many Roman ruins as humanly possible and gladly went out of my way to see the littlest bits of marble. Those were the years I formulated most of my foundational views, so I thank Europe for being such an illuminating mentor. Credit also goes to my side of the world, for many of my core thoughts arose from North American experiences.

I reached my 30s thinking that my foundation was set in stone. There was nothing new for me to add and nothing to take away. I believed myself to be a well-rounded person who took everything I learned to heart. I had seen and done things that no one would ever think to ask me about, and I was perfectly okay with people never asking me about my trips. I tend to internalize my journeys by allowing them to change me on the inside while keeping my exterior always the same. No one would know by looking at me that I thought I had it all figured out after having traveled so extensively. Yet, deep down, I knew I hadn't traveled extensively enough. There was a whole other side of the world that I hadn't even seen.

Indeed, life was too short to travel the world in a single direction. The time had come to go the other way.

APPENDIX

Aldo Leopold Cabin

Redwoods, California

Welcome to my pretend-place infested with bees

Rhyolite Ghosts

Welcome to Anti-Paradise

Seats at "The Range"

The Colosseum

The Roman Forum

Venice

Moored Gondolas

Pompeii

Forever covered in ash

Temple of Debod

Dolmen of Menga

Trees, Tongeren

SWANS!

Dodecahedron

Carcassonne Castle

Author, circa 1989

Mom, in her younger years

Tulum Beach

Observatory in Chichen Itza

After Hurricane Katrina

Oak Alley Plantation

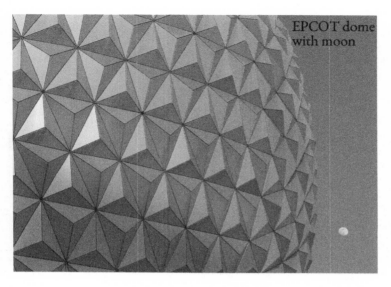

EPCOT dome
with moon

My dad looked a lot like Ronald Reagan

Dad

Fixing Splendid China

Splendid China's last employee

SELECT BIBLIOGRAPHY

Parks, destinations, and biography websites were utilized whenever applicable. The following is list of articles and websites that I accessed while writing this from Nov 2021 to Nov 2022:

CHAPTER ONE

A Sand County Almanac Summary. https://www.litcharts.com/lit/a-sand-county-almanac

Keeney, D. Leopold Speaks on Soil. *Leopold Center*. https://www.leopold.iastate.edu/content/leopold-speaks-soil

Muir, J. Chapter 9, Mormon Lilies. *Sierra Club*. https://vault.sierraclub.org/john_muir_exhibit/writings/steep_trails/chapter_9.aspx

Betuel, E. 73 Years Later, the "A-Bomb" Ginkgo Trees Still Grow in Hiroshima. *Inverse*. August 6, 2018. https://www.inverse.com/article/47833-hiroshima-gingko-trees-atomic-bomb

CHAPTER TWO

9 Circles of Hell (Dante's Inferno). https://historylists.org/art/9-circles-of-hell-dantes-inferno.html

Carter, G. Vulture Mine – History, Fact, and Fiction. *Westerm Mining History*. https://westernmininghistory.com/3747/vulture-mine-history-fact-and-fiction/

Albert Szukalski's Last Supper. *Atlas Obscura*. https://www.atlasobscura.com/places/albert-szukalskis-last-supper A

I'm Your Huckleberry. *Idioms Online*. https://www.idioms.online/im-your-huckleberry/

CHAPTER THREE

Where to see Caravaggio paintings in Rome. https://www.wantedinrome.com/news/where-to-see-caravaggio-paintings-in-rome.html

A Brief Introduction to Ostia. http://www.ostia-antica.org/intro.htm

Graham, E. The Quick and the Dead in the Extra-Urban Landscape: The Roman Cemetery at Ostia/Portus as a Lived Environment. Theoretical Roman Archaeology Journal. *Researchgate*. March, 2005. https://www.researchgate.net/publication/27649642_The_Quick%20_and_the_%20Dead_in_the_Extra-Urban_Landscape_%20The_Roman%20_Cemetery_at_OstiaPortus%20_as_a_%20Lived_Environment

Allum, F. Mafia in Naples is still going strong – and we must not forget how it affects everyday life in the city. *The Conversation*. July 17, 2019. https://theconversation.com/mafia-in-naples-is-still-going-strong-and-we-must-not-forget-how-it-affects-everyday-life-in-the-city-120177

Mingoia, J. Alexander Mosaic from the House of the Faun, Pompeii. *Smarthistory*. June 6, 2021. https://smarthistory.org/alexander-mosaic-from-the-house-of-the-faun-pompeii/

Portrait of Terentius Neo and his Wife. Frescos from Pompeii. https://joyofmuseums.com/museums/europe/italy-museums/naples-museums/national-archaeological-museum-naples/frescos-from-pompeii/

Albanese, C. The Long, Slow Death of Venice. *Bloomberg*. June 29, 2019. https://www.bloomberg.com/news/features/2019-06-30/venice-is-dying-a-long-slow-death

Murtinho, V. Leonardo's Vitruvian Man Drawing: A New Interpretation Looking at Leonardo's Geometric Constructions. *Springer*. April 9, 2015. https://link.springer.com/article/10.1007/s00004-015-0247-7

Attila's Throne. *Atlas Obscura*. https://www.atlasobscura.com/places/throne-of-attila

Pioneer plaque, photo. File:Pioneer plaque.svg. https://commons.wikimedia.org/wiki/File:Pioneer_plaque.svg

CHAPTER FOUR

Baynes, C. Spanish galleon laden with £13bn in gold found at bottom of Caribbean Sea, 300 years after sinking. *The Independent*. May 23, 2018. https://www.independent.co.uk/news/world/americas/spanish-galleon-found-caribbean-sea-gold-treasure-300-years-sinking-colombia-san-jose-a8363846.html

Kroll, B&R. Ten Surprising Discoveries on a Seville Cathedral Tour. *Kroll Travel*. http://www.krolltravel.com/stories/spain-seville-cathedral-tour-ten-surprising-discoveries.html

Minster, C. Where Are the Remains of Christopher Columbus? *ThoughtCo*. May 30, 2019. https://www.thoughtco.com/where-are-christopher-columbus-remains-2136433

History of Seville. Chapter 1. Hispalis, the Roman Seville. https://www.toursevilla.com/en/the-roman-seville-or-hispalis/

Leonard, N. "Always in all things changeable": The emperor and his tomb. *Following Hadrian*. September 19, 2018. https://followinghadrian.com/2018/09/19/guest-post-always-in-all-things-changeable-the-emperor-and-his-tomb/

Chaplaw, C. Antequera Dolmens. *Andalucia.com*. https://www.andalucia.com/antequera/dolmens-de-menga.htm

Burial of the Count Orgaz. *Khan Academy*. https://www.khanacademy.org/humanities/renaissance-reformation/xa6688040:spain-portugal-15th-16th-century/xa6688040:16th-century-spain/a/el-greco-burial-of-the-count-orgaz

CHAPTER FIVE

About Antique Flemish Tapestry. *Nejad*. https://www.nejad.com/antique-tapestry.html

Gruuthuse - Room 3. *Museabrugge*. https://www.museabrugge.be/en/virtual-tours/gruuthuse-zaal-3

Staff, NPR. Is This The World's Most Coveted Painting? *NPR*. December 23, 2010. https://www.npr.org/2010/12/25/132283848/is-this-the-worlds-most-coveted-painting

Gravensteen. *Atlas Obscura*. https://www.atlasobscura.com/places/gravensteen-2

Blyth, D. All Roads Lead to Tongeren. *The Low Countries.com*. October 23, 2019. https://www.the-low-countries.com/article/all-roads-lead-to-tongeren

Schoenmaekers, M. I Visit The Jekerhippodrome In Tongeren, Belgium, To See The Horse Races And Capture Its Strange Atmosphere. *Bored Panda*. https://www.boredpanda.com/jeker-hippodrome/?utm_source=google&utm_medium=organic&utm_campaign=orga

CHAPTER SIX

The Mellifulous, Magisterial Bernard of Clairvaux. https://alan-neale.com/the-mellifulous-magisterial-bernard-of-clairvaux/

Four Captives, photo. File: Four Captives. https://www.wikidata.org/wiki/Q26974941

Statue of Louis XIV, photo. File:Desjardins statue Louis XIV pl des Victoires.jpg. https://commons.wikimedia.org/wiki/File:Desjardins_statue_Louis_XIV_pl_des_Victoires.jpg

Room 638 of the Louvre, photo. File: Room 638. https://www.wikidata.org/wiki/Q24359688

Simpson, WK. The Literature of Ancient Egypt. New Edition. New Haven and London, Yale University Press. October 11, 2003. https://uh.edu/honors/human-situation/survival-kit/study-aids/Hymn%20to%20the%20Aten.pdf

Poem of Praise to the Sun. https://palmyria.co.uk/superstition/akhenaten.htm

CHAPTER SEVEN

Tulum: The Mayan Walled Beauty. *Aqvoyages*. August 14, 2019. https://www.aqvoyages.com/%20blog/tulum-the-mayan-walled-beauty/

Sandidge, S. The Descending God. *HistoricalMX*. August 14, 2019. http://www.historicalmx.org/items/show/10

Hoggarth, J. The political collapse of Chichén Itzá in climatic and cultural context. *Global and Planetary Change*, vol 138, March 16, pages 25-42.

Doyle, J. Into the Centipede's Jaws: Sumptuous Offerings from the Sacred Cenote at Chichén Itzá. *MetMuseum*. May 21, 2018. https://www.metmuseum.org/blogs/now-at-the-met/2018/golden-kingdoms-sacred-cenote-chichen-itza

Green, E. How Dangerous Is Tulum for Tourists Right Now? *Vice*. https://www.vice.com/en/article/4aw3x3/how-dangerous-is-tulum-for-tourists-right-now

Hirst, K. Ix Chel - Mayan Goddess(es) of the Moon, Fertility and Death. *ThoughtCo*. February 22, 2019. https://www.thoughtco.com/ix-chel-mayan-goddess-moon-fertility-death-171592

CHAPTER EIGHT

Broken Promises: Two Years After Katrina. *ACLU*. August 2007. https://www.aclu.org/report/report-broken-promises-two-years-after-katrina

Borger, J. Why did help take so long to arrive? *The Guardian*. September 2, 2005. https://www.theguardian.com/world/2005/sep/03/hurricanekatrina.usa1

Nobel, J. How Napoleon's "Death Mask" Got To New Orleans. *FuneralWise*. October 8, 2012. https://www.funeralwise.com/digital-dying/how-napoleons-death-mask-got-to-new-orleans/

John J. Audubon's Birds of America. *Audubon*. https://www.audubon.org/birds-of-america

Secrets Of Ancient Mound Builders In Louisiana Revealed. *AncientPages*. May 23, 2018. https://www.ancientpages.com/2018/05/23/secrets-of-ancient-mound-builders-in-louisiana-revealed/

Poverty Point. *Pyramids in America*. https://pyramidsinamerica.com/Pyramids_in_America_%20Home/Awulmeka_is_named_Poverty_Point.html

Clark, L. Controversy is a Theme of This Park. *Orlando Sentinel*. March 17, 1998. https://www.orlandosentinel.com/news/os-xpm-1998-03-18-9803180350-story.html

Modern Art – Surrealism. https://www.historyofcreativity.com/mid39/modern-art--surrealism

Associated Press. Is the Gulf of Mexico healthy 5 years after BP oil spill? *AL.com*. April 18, 2015. https://www.al.com/news/2015/04/is_gulf_of_mexico_healthy_5_ye.html

Barzey, U. How Many Independent Countries in the Caribbean? *Caribbean&Co*. November 20, 2021. https://www.caribbeanandco.com/independent-countries-in-the-caribbean/#:~:text=Of%20the%20sixteen%20independent%20countries,Suriname%2C%20and%20Trinidad%20%26%20Tobago.

Mack, E. 'Doomsday Glacier' The Size Of Florida Could Begin To Collapse This Decade, Remaking Coastlines Worldwide. *Forbes*. December 24, 2021. https://www.forbes.com/sites/eric-mack/2021/12/24/doomsday-glacier-the-size-of-florida-could-collapse-this-decade-remaking-coastlines-worldwide/?sh=74f7973f4537

Thank you for reading TIME TRAVELED!

Please consider posting a rating or review to your favorite book site. Reviews are the lifeblood of authors and help more readers like you find their new favorite books!

Krista has a blog! Please visit:
https://kmarson.com/blog/ for occasional musings.

Be the first to know when Krista Marson's next book is available! Follow her on her website: https://kmarson.com/ to get alerts whenever she has a new release, pre-order, or discounts!

Feel free to contact her at: memoryroadtrips@gmail.com

Please read this author's other books:

MEMORY ROAD TRIP: A RETROSPECTIVE TRAVEL JOURNEY

PAST POETRY

Made in United States
North Haven, CT
08 March 2023

33749444R00203